PSYCHOANALYSIS ONLINE

Library of Technology and Mental Health

Series editor: Jill Savege Scharff, MD

*Distance Psychoanalysis: The Theory and Practice of Using Communication Technology in the Clinic (2011)
by Ricardo Carlino, translated by James Nuss*

PSYCHOANALYSIS ONLINE
Mental Health, Teletherapy and Training

Editor

Jill Savege Scharff, MD

KARNAC

First published in 2013 by
Karnac Books Ltd
118 Finchley Road
London NW3 5HT

British Library Cataloguing in Publication Data

A C.I.P. for this book is available from the British Library

ISBN-13: 978-1-78049-154-7

Typeset by V Publishing Solutions Pvt Ltd., Chennai, India

www.karnacbooks.com

In memory of Joyce Aronson, PhD
who opened the door to teletherapy

CONTENTS

vii

ACKNOWLEDGEMENTS

Many thanks to my colleagues of the International Psychoanalytical Association and the International Institute for Psychoanalytic Training who participate in an international working group to study teleanalysis. Their commitment to innovation and thoughtful exploration of teletherapy—psychotherapy and psychoanalysis conducted on the telephone and over the internet—has been my support and inspiration. I also want to thank those who attended our panel and pre-congress workshop to immerse themselves in two days of intense study of the theory and process of teletherapy, and especially those who contributed chapters for this book. They have enabled me to collect views on the topic of technology, mental health, teletherapy, and teleanalysis from Kazakhstan, Germany, Argentina, Panama, Canada, and the eastern, mountain, and western US states. Many of the authors have had the privilege of discussing their ideas with colleagues at the International Psychotherapy Institute and the International Institute for Psychoanalytic Training, all of whom appreciate the value of technology in treatment and training.

My introduction includes ideas previously expressed in a letter to the editor, *International Journal of Psychoanalysis* (2012) 93(4): 1037–1039, and these are reused courtesy of Wiley.

Chapter Two is an unpublished paper translated from the German by A. M. Reid.

Chapter Six is slightly modified from "Clinical Issues in Analysis over the Telephone and the Internet" in the *International Journal of Psychoanalysis* (2012), *93*: 81–95, and is reproduced courtesy of Wiley.

Chapter Eleven is from an unpublished paper, "Cambios o transformaciones? Reconsideración del encuadre y de la transferencia-contratransferencia a la luz de las modificaciones tecnológicas" given at a workshop at the 43rd IPA Congress, New Orleans, translated from the Spanish by the author and rephrased and modified by the editor.

Chapter Fourteen is constructed from two chapters, "Presentación de material clínico del análisis telefónico" and "Reflexiones técnicas a partir de las sesiones de Irene", from *Tratamiento Psicoanalítico Telefónico* (Lima, Peru: Siklos, 2011), translated from the Spanish by the author, combined and condensed by the editor, and reproduced by permission of the copyright holder, Jaime Lutenberg.

Chapter Fifteen was translated from Spanish by James Nuss.

Chapter Sixteen is a slightly modified version of "Psychoanalysis in Cyberspace", from *The Candidate Journal*, 5: 1–12, by permission.

It was Oliver Rathbone of Karnac Books who suggested the Technology and Mental Health series to me and invited me to be its editor. I am grateful to him for giving me this opportunity and to James Darley for copy-editing, Leonard Rosenbaum for indexing, and Kate Pearce, Catherine Harwood, Constance Govindin, and Rod Tweedy for editorial and marketing assistance. I am grateful to them, to those who have contributed to this volume, and to Anna Innes, who untiringly does more to support innovative programmes and outreach than anyone can imagine.

CONTRIBUTORS

Jill Savege Scharff, MD: Co-founder and board member of the International Psychotherapy Institute; supervising analyst at the International Institute for Psychoanalytic Training; clinical professor of psychiatry at Georgetown University; and psychoanalyst and psychotherapist with individuals, couples, and families in Chevy Chase, Maryland. Author, editor, and series editor, her most recent book is *The Interpersonal Unconscious*, co-authored with David E. Scharff.

Geoffrey Anderson, PhD: Director of the International Psychotherapy Institute in Chevy Chase, Maryland; lecturer in psychiatry at Creighton University School of Medicine; teaching and personal analyst with the International Institute for Psychoanalytic Training.

Asbed Aryan, MD: Full member, Asociación Psicoanalítica de Buenos Aires (APdeBA), Argentina; full member, International Psychoanalytical Association; training analyst, IPA specialist in child and adolescent analysis; senior faculty member for specialization in psychoanalysis at the Institute of Mental Health of APdeBA; senior faculty member for child and adolescent psychoanalysis at the School of Medicine and School of Law at the University of Buenos Aires and the University of Matanza; former president of APdeBA; former coordinator of child and adolescent psychoanalysis for the Psychoanalytic Federation of Latin America (FEPAL); and author, *Clinica de Adolescentes* (Teseo, 2009).

Nancy L. Bakalar, MD: Faculty member, International Institute for Psychoanalytic Training, the Denver Institute for Psychoanalysis, and the University of Colorado School of Medicine; fellow, the American Psychiatric Association; psychoanalyst practising psychoanalysis and psychotherapy in Denver, Colorado, and Bethesda, Maryland.

Betty S. de Benaim, PhD: Member, International Psychoanalytical Association; faculty member, International Psychotherapy Institute (IPI), IPI-Panama, and International Institute for Psychoanalytic Training in Washington, DC; professor, Catholic University and Latin University in Panama; psychologist and psychoanalyst with individuals, couples, and families in Panama City, Panama.

Sharon Zalusky Blum, PhD: Senior faculty member at the New Center for Psychoanalysis in Los Angeles; recent board member, North American regional board of the International Psychoanalytical Association and North American editorial board of the International Journal of Psychoanalysis; author of numerous articles on telephone analysis and the impact of technology on the practice of psychoanalysis; in private practice of psychoanalysis and clinical psychology in Los Angeles, California.

Ricardo Carlino, MD: Full member, Asociación Psicoanalítica de Buenos Aires (APdeBA), Argentina. Full member, International Psychoanalytical Association; Author, *Distance Analysis* (Karnac, 2011).

Susan S. Cebulko, PhD: Faculty member, the Institute of Clinical Social Work, Chicago, and the International Psychotherapy Institute; author of *The Impact of Internet Pornography on Married Women: A Psychodynamic Perspective* (Cambria Press, 2007); private practice psychoanalytic psychotherapist in Indianapolis, Indiana with individuals and couples.

Irmgard Dettbarn, PhD: Psychologist and psychoanalyst in private practice in Berlin, Germany; IPA interim training analyst 2007–2010 in Beijing, China; special interest ethnopsychoanalytical studies; field stay in Africa: Kaokoland (Namibia) Himba tribe (2002).

Charles Hanly, PhD: Training analyst, Toronto Institute of Psychoanalysis; professor emeritus, University of Toronto; president, International Psychoanalytical Association (2009–2013) and formerly member of IPA executive council and board of representatives with leadership role in enabling the independent groups in the USA to become component societies, fostering the redevelopment of psychoanalysis in Eastern Europe and the formation of International New Groups; author of four books including *Existentialism and Psychoanalysis* (1979), *The Problem of Truth in Applied Psychoanalysis* (1991), and many clinical and scientific papers on psychoanalysis.

Anna Kudyarova, PhD: Director of Psychoanalytic Institute for Central Asia; former chair of education at Kazakh Institute of Education; president of the Kazakhstan Psychoanalytic Association; Fulbright Scholar to USA (2010–2011); author of many books, textbooks, and papers on education, psychology, and psychoanalysis; organiser of seminars on psychoanalysis and psychoanalytic treatment in Almaty, Kazakhstan.

Jaime Marcos Lutenberg, MD, MA: Training and supervising analyst in the Argentine Psychoanalytic Association and in private practice of psychoanalysis in Buenos Aires; teacher and trainer in the master's psychoanalysis course at Universidad de la Matanza, Provincia de Buenos Aires; seminar leader at various psychoanalytic institutions in America and Europe; author of seven books, five co-authored chapters, and more than seventy papers.

Debra A. Neumann, PhD: Psychologist and psychoanalyst in private practice in Bethesda, Maryland; advanced candidate, Psychoanalytic Training Institute of the Contemporary Freudian Society (formerly New York Freudian Society); former board member of the China American Psychoanalytic Alliance; faculty and steering committee member, Clinical Psychotherapy Practice Program at the Washington School of Psychiatry.

Angela Carter Martin, DNP, APRN: Instructor, Washington Center for Psychoanalysis (WCP) and supervisor, Modern Perspectives on Psychotherapy program at WCP; former director, family nurse practitioner training at Old Dominion University and the Uniformed Services University of the Health Sciences; psychoanalyst in private practice in Chevy Chase, Maryland.

Karen Sharer-Mohatt, PsyD: Fourth-year candidate, International Institute of Psychoanalytic Training; faculty member, International Psychotherapy Institute (IPI); chair, IPI-Nebraska; psychologist and psychoanalyst in private practice in Lincoln, Nebraska.

David E. Scharff, MD: Supervising analyst at the International Institute for Psychoanalytic Training; co-founder and board chair of the International Psychotherapy Institute; clinical professor of psychiatry at Georgetown University and the Uniformed Services University of the Health Sciences; psychoanalyst and psychotherapist with individuals, couples, and families in Chevy Chase, Maryland; author, editor, and series editor, currently co-editing with Sverre Varvin *Psychoanalysis in China* (Karnac, in preparation).

Caroline M. Sehon, MD: Chair, IPI Metro program, International Psychotherapy Institute; teaching and supervising faculty member, International Psychotherapy Institute; member, International Institute for Psychoanalytic Training, Chevy Chase, Maryland; member, American Psychoanalytic Association; clinical associate professor of psychiatry, Georgetown University; fellow, Royal College of Physicians and Surgeons of Canada; child and adult psychiatrist, psychoanalyst, and psychotherapist with individuals, couples, and families in Bethesda, Maryland.

Lea S. de Setton, PhD: Member, the International Psychoanalytical Association; Faculty member, International Psychotherapy Institute and International Institute for Psychoanalytic Training, Chevy Chase, Maryland; former Chair of IPI-Panama; Psychologist, psychoanalyst, and psychotherapist in private practice with individuals, couples, and families in Panama.

Michael Stadter, PhD: Clinical psychologist in private practice in Bethesda, Maryland; board member and faculty member, International Psychotherapy Institute; faculty member, Washington School of Psychiatry; author, *Presence and the Present: Relationship and Time in Contemporary Psychodynamic Therapy* (Jason Aronson, 2012).

Yolanda G. de P. de Varela, PhD: Member of the International Psychoanalytical Association; faculty member of the International Psychotherapy Institute and the International Institute for Psychoanalytic Training, Chevy Chase, Maryland; founding chair of IPI-Panama; psychologist, psychoanalyst, and psychotherapist with individuals, couples, and families in Panama.

Ernest Wallwork, PhD: Professor of ethics at Syracuse University, New York; psychoanalyst in private practice in Washington, DC and Syracuse, NY; teaching analyst, Washington Center for Psychoanalysis, and adjunct faculty member, International Institute for Psychoanalytic Training; author of many publications on ethical topics including *Psychoanalysis and Ethics* (Yale University Press, 1991), *Critical Issues in Modern Religion* (Prentice-Hall, 1990), and *Durkheim: Morality and Milieu* (Harvard University Press, 1972).

Janine Wanlass, PhD: Psychologist and psychoanalyst practising in Salt Lake City, Utah; director of the Masters in Professional Counseling program and professor of psychology at Westminster College; chair, Child, Couple, and Family program and national faculty member, International Psychotherapy Institute in Chevy Chase, Maryland.

INTRODUCTION

It is time for psychoanalytic therapists to adapt to the increased mobility of the global economy. As international trade increases, people have to travel and relocate for work. When these people develop mental health problems they find it difficult to find a therapist. If they are already in treatment, they lose continuity—unless they have a therapist willing to use communications technology. Teletherapy—psychotherapy by telephone, Voice over Internet Protocol (VoIP), or videoteleconference (VTC)—permits optimum frequency of sessions for established in-depth work, and enables outreach to patients in rural areas and repressed cultures where there is no specialised treatment.

Psychotherapists and psychoanalysts need to experience their own treatment in order to know themselves well enough to be sensitive and objective therapists. Like their patients, they need access to psychotherapy and psychoanalysis, intensely private treatments relying on trust and confidentiality. Those who have had their own treatment in a secure office in a clinic or private practice may find it hard to imagine treating any of their patients in teletherapy. But how else can we serve potential patients who cannot get to a therapist's office because they live and work in a remote area and cannot afford travel to the nearest qualified therapist? How can we respect our patients' right to continuity of care when they are required to relocate or are housebound by illness? Is it possible for such a patient to have an equally meaningful experience in teletherapy?

The authors in this volume speak to the need for teletherapy and to the extent of its effectiveness. We recognise that many psychotherapists are increasingly willing to offer teletherapy in response to more mobility in the population. Yet many other psychotherapists face resistances to practising teletherapy arising from individual concerns, ethical dilemmas, and institutional forces. Of course teletherapy is not for every patient, or indeed for every therapist. As the book continues we will look at the worries about teletherapy, its indications and contraindications, its technical problems, and the advantages and disadvantages of psychotherapy and psychoanalysis conducted over the phone and the internet. We will give some guidelines and many clinical examples so you can see inside the clinical situation and decide for yourself.

In Part I, we look at the impact of technology and social media on the person, the couple, and the society in which we live. Michael Stadter takes Thomas Ogden's psychoanalytic concept of *the third*, which refers to the unique extra dimension of each treatment that is more than the sum of the two participants and the relationship they construct together, and applies it to understanding the impact of technology on our minds and relationships. Irmgard Dettbarn, writing from experience in Germany and Asia, applies social theory to consider the impact of technology on our thinking and our clinical practice as psychoanalysts. Karen Sharer-Mohatt and I show how the computer may become a daily preoccupation, a substitute for relationships, and a metaphor for states of mind. Sue Cebulko presents her research into the cycles of despair, forgiveness, recovery, and relapse that couples engage in when one of the partners is a compulsive internet sex user. Sharon Zalusky, one of the pioneers of teletherapy and teleanalysis, and a major contributor to Joyce Aronson's groundbreaking book *The Use of the Telephone in Therapy*, shares her musings on therapy and technology.

In Part II, we focus on the practice of psychotherapy and psychoanalysis over the telephone and the internet. I introduce the various clinical issues that arise in teletherapy. Angela Martin presents the nuts and bolts of proper procedure, discusses the legal, clinical, and ethical concerns, and explains the rules and regulations governing teletherapy. Ernest Wallwork, a professor of ethics as well as a psychoanalyst, helps us to reflect on teletherapy: when we subject our decisions, our technique, and the effectiveness of our approach in each clinical instance to process and review, we are developing a truly ethical stance.

David Scharff gives an account of a single teleanalysis session that he agreed to for a woman who had to be away from in-person analysis for a long weekend. He might have viewed the woman's request as an avoidance of separation anxiety, but in acceding to it he discovered an aspect of the paternal transference and a side of his patient he had not imagined. Nancy Bakalar, an analyst who relocated, describes a treatment in which a telephone therapy usefully deepened to become a teleanalysis when the negative transference was evoked and analysed. She compares this treatment to that of another woman and man in treatment with her. Asbed Aryan from Argentina addresses the experience of providing continuity of care by agreeing to a patient's request for telephone treatment. He had to reconsider the frame of treatment, look at how transference and countertransference operate in this new setting, and allow himself to evolve along with this patient. Charles Hanly from Canada identifies with the traditional analyst who tries teleanalysis for the first time, and to his surprise finds it quite effective. In his role as president of the International Psychoanalytical Association, Hanly has tried to promote intensive study of teleanalysis. Caroline Sehon tells of arriving at the decision to treat a patient who was living his life through social media: would treatment simply collude with a defensive process, or could it provide an alternative, similar enough to appeal to him, but different enough to allow growth? Sehon shows us what developed in an unusual treatment. Writing from Argentina, Jaime Lutenberg presents his philosophy of teleanalysis and illustrates it with an extensive clinical example.

In Part III, we turn to distance education for mental health professionals. Also from Argentina, Ricardo Carlino, author of *Distance Psychoanalysis*, pairs up with Asbed Aryan applying

Foucault's ideas on power to confront the impact of the establishment in squashing or embracing an innovation such as teleanalysis. Debra Neumann examines the impact of technology on the frame of treatment in teleanalysis and looks at implications for the training of therapists. Anna Kudiyarova of Kazakhstan writes from her experience of Skype psychoanalysis as an effective treatment modality and a lifeline to psychoanalytic education. Four women analysts including Betty Benaim, Lea Setton, and Yolanda Varela from the republic of Panama, and a male analyst, Geoffrey Anderson, from Omaha, Nebraska reflect back on their time as candidates when they experienced teleanalysis as part of their training in psychoanalysis and now sometimes practise teletherapy as graduate analysts. Janine Wanlass explores the ethical practice of supervision conducted with supervisees who are doing psychotherapy or counselling in remote locations in other cultures. I close with a review of the application of technology in education for mental health professionals. I refer to seminars and case conferences on teleconference call, seminars on videoconference, and individual supervision on the telephone or Skype. Angela Martin returns with an appendix that lists mental health resources that might be useful for those who want to learn more about telemental health.

We do not recommend one resource over another. We have various opinions based on our experience with teletherapy to date. It is not our intention to present a single authoritative view. The field of teletherapy is so new that standards of practice and learning resources are still being developed. None of us has enough experience as yet to be definitive but we all feel the need to open up the topic for discussion.

Psychotherapists and psychoanalysts face many different opinions as to the effectiveness of teletherapy. We find that the naysayers are psychotherapists who have no experience of the method. Those of us who might want to try teletherapy face confusing information on the privacy, security, and ethical use of various communication technologies to support a psychoanalytically oriented treatment of integrity in virtual reality. For most of us who are not expert in technology, it is hard to know what to believe, particularly when experts argue among themselves, and the various mental health professions have differing standards of practice. The silence of those who do not admit to using technology for communicating with their patients combines with the vocal output of those in favour and those against to create insecurity in all of us. We are simply looking for reputable ways to serve our patients' needs for access to and continuity of treatment. We certainly want to do no harm, and so we cannot afford to have false confidence in the privacy of the virtual setting. Yet we do not want to deny our patients access to care and continuity when they must travel or relocate.

Admittedly most therapists and patients, and that includes me, prefer to meet in person. But that is not a reason to avoid adapting ourselves to the current reality of our mobile society. Part of that reality includes the concern that technology may not offer the level of confidentiality that we expect in traditional in-office treatment. However, even in the in-person setting with double doors and excellent soundproofing, and even if there is a security guard in the lobby, security is not absolute. A session can be interrupted by a person with an emergency in the hallway, a private office can be broken into or bugged, and seductive behaviour on the part of the analyst is more likely to cause physical and emotional harm. Nevertheless we need to consider the invasion of privacy that could occur during treatment in virtual reality.

Security is a major concern. Cellphones are notoriously insecure. Landlines can be tapped. Skype, the free voice over internet service, may not be as secure as its claim to a strong security policy leads us to believe. Maheu (2012) states that, even though Skype offers encryption, it does not claim to be HIPAA compliant, and being a social media platform, it is not as suitable for telemental health assessment and treatment as videoteleconference supported by a videotechnology company with a medical-grade platform that claims to be HIPAA compliant (Maheu, 2012).

Nevertheless because Skype is readily accessible and free, young adult patients (who rarely have a landline) prefer it to the telephone. Psychotherapists and psychoanalysts are conducting teletherapy using Skype because they believe that encryption makes Skype secure or their patients find the level of risk acceptable and request the convenience. In Chapter Sixteen, Neumann, quoting from Snyder (2011) distinguishes three types of Skype: "Skype phone, Skype voice over Internet protocol (VOIP), and Skype computer-to-computer connections. Of these, only Skype computer-to-computer is secure" (Snyder, 2011). This is somewhat reassuring, and yet Skype may not be entirely secure because, even though Skype uses encryption that offers some protection, its proprietary software cannot be independently evaluated (Churcher 2012). Research on Skype has given evidence of leaks from which content could be inferred (Dupasquier, Burschka, McLaughlin & Sezer, 2011), and the literature on security studies reports "eavesdropping, interception, and modification" during Skype (Keromytis, 2011). Even so, such invasions are much more likely to occur on a national and international scale than to focus on an individual, except in certain vulnerable circumstances such as that of being a person of interest.

Even though we cannot give a guarantee of absolute security, we might consider providing teletherapy, if the patient who cannot attend in person requests it, provided it is not clinically or ethically contraindicated, and provided patient and therapist have considered the impact of technology and understand the experimental nature of teletherapy at this stage in its development. Patient and therapist need to understand that there may be interruptions due to interference on the line. They should evaluate the risk of conducting treatment over the telephone or internet at all levels, from inhibition of free association, and theft of information if the patient is in a domestic dispute, to harm if the potential patient is a person of interest in a culture of surveillance and persecution. They can discuss the level of threat of exposure, decide whether to proceed to treatment, and if so, continuously evaluate the effect of the risk on therapeutic integrity. This is true to the tradition of psychoanalysis which "questions itself and denies the existence of absolute truths" (Carlino, 2011, p. xix).

The field of technology is moving extremely fast and security measures are being developed as fast as hackers can demonstrate points of weakness. Technology will always be imperfect, but it is one way to provide outreach. If our technology is insecure, we may do harm, but by denying access to treatment we may also do harm. As Asbed Aryan says in Chapter Eleven, "At times, and under certain circumstances, the traditional setting has to be re-imagined to fit the demands of the modern world." Our professional associations need to work with us on weighing the benefits against the risks. As we build more experience with psychotherapy and psychoanalysis over the telephone and the internet, we will have more clinical reports in our professional journals, more correspondence, discussion at our association meetings, and systematic research as to whether teleanalysis can provide a secure setting and can meet the standard of being clinically equally effective.

Our main effort has been to show that teletherapy can be a useful resource for patients. But we have not forgotten the needs of mental health professionals in those communities that are far from training centres and cannot find treatment or advanced training in their local communities. Technology makes it possible for them to participate in individual treatment, clinical supervision, and group seminars on teleconference or videoconference. We hope to show that telemental health education can be as effective as in-person training programmes in producing well-qualified, independent clinicians who can provide outstanding service to patients while remaining in their local communities, and who can eventually become trainers for the next generation of mental health professionals.

This volume is an international collaboration by psychotherapists and psychoanalysts who consider the impact of cyberspace on our society and the value of communications technology for extending access to analytic treatment and to professional training and continuing education of therapists worldwide. We look at the impact of communications technology on mental health and relationships. We explore and compare experiences of analytic treatment conducted on the telephone and internet from the point of view of analyst, psychotherapist, and analyst as analysand. Reviewing its problems and possibilities, we provide a multifaceted view of it, an ethical stance in relation to it, and evidence from which to judge its effectiveness. Looking into the future, we imagine a time when technology-supported analytic treatment may be not only convenient as a supplement to in-person treatment but also preferable for some patients and therapists in various circumstances. We hope to jump-start a conversation that will invigorate the debate about technology and its responsible use in psychotherapy and psychoanalysis and in distance learning programmes for mental health professionals. Thank you for joining in this conversation.

References

Aryan, A. (2004). Cambios o transformaciones? Reconsideración del encuadre y de la transferencia-contratransferencia a la luz de las modificaciones tecnológicas. Paper given at workshop at 43rd IPA Congress, New Orleans, March.

Carlino, R. (2011). *Distance Psychoanalysis: the Theory and Practice of Using Communication Technology in the Clinic.* London: Karnac.

Churcher, J. (2012). On Skype and privacy. *Journal of the American Psychoanalytic Association*, 93(4): 1035–1037.

Dupasquier, B., Burschka, S., McLaughlin, K. & Sezer, S. (2011). Analysis of information leakage from encrypted Skype conversations. *International Journal of Security Studies*, 9: 313–325.

Keromytis, A. D. (2012, in press). A comprehensive survey of voice over IP security research. *IEEE Communications Surveys and Tutorials*. Also available online [accessed April 4, 2012] at: http://www.cs.columbia.edu/~angelos/Papers/2011/cst.pdf.

Maheu, M. (2012). Skype, HIPAA and Alternatives Webinar, *Telemental Health Institute*, accessed March 27, 2012.

Neumann, D. (2012). Psychoanalysis in cyberspace. *The Candidate Journal*, 5, January.

Snyder, E. (2011). *How Skype Video Works.* [Power Point slide presentation.] Paper presented at American Psychoanalytic Association winter conference, New York City, January 15.

PART I

TECHNOLOGY, PERSON, AND SOCIETY

CHAPTER ONE

The influence of social media and communications technology on self and relationships

Michael Stadter, PhD

A s patients enter my office, they commonly turn off their smartphones and electronic tablets, placing them on the table next to them. This actually and symbolically creates a space for reflection and intimate connection between us, uninterrupted by the intrusions of the internet, social media, and communications technology (calls, emails, texting). Some patients comment that this is the only place in their lives where they allow themselves to be free of technology, speaking to its nearly constant presence in their lives. It is a presence that can alter subjective and intersubjective space in a variety of ways and can be a third object in relationships between two people.

I have termed this presence the "e-third" (Stadter, 2012)—the influence of an electronic object in addition to self and other—and we are just beginning to understand its evolving effects for both good and ill. In studying the present and future of e-technology, Turkle (2004) writes, "What we need today is a new object-relations psychology that will help us understand such relationships and, indeed, to responsibly navigate them" (p. 28). The e-third is very different from Ogden's (1994) concept of the *analytic third* which is created by the individual subjectivities of the therapist and patient creating a third space, an intersubjective third space. In turn, the analytic third profoundly affects the subjectivities of the individual. This is a cyclical dialectic process between the influences of subjectivity and intersubjectivity and between the inner world and the external world of the therapy encounter. It is a space that exemplifies the psychodynamic sensibility of reverie (Ogden, 1997). The e-third also can promote reflection and curiosity. Yet, as illustrated in some of the vignettes that follow, it frequently encourages states of self and relating that can be rushed, distracted, shallow, and fragmented. In short, we need to study not only what this technology can do *for* us but also what it does *to* us.

In this chapter, I note a few of the diverse facets of the interactions between e-technology and us. I especially explore the impact on self and on intimacy, offering six brief clinical examples. While I note some of its remarkable benefits, I especially focus on some troubling effects. Consider the breadth of phenomena covered by the term social media. Kaplan and Haenlein (2010) state that the term has been applied to an array of technologies including these subtypes:

> Social networking (e.g., *Facebook, Google+*)
> Blogs and micro blogs (e.g., *Twitter*)
> Virtual social worlds (e.g., *Second Life*)
> Virtual game worlds (e.g., *World of Warcraft*)
> Content communities (e.g., *YouTube*)
> Collaborative projects (e.g., *Wikipedia*)

* * *

Overview

The contemporary practice of psychodynamic therapy involves many challenging elements (Stadter, 2012)—one of them is the impact of this technology. As the present volume demonstrates, there are many therapeutic and educational benefits that arise from e-technology but there are also potential dangers. We should study advantages and disadvantages, neither idealising nor demonising technology. From the time of the printing press, technological innovations have raised both extravagant hopes of utopian dimensions and intense dread that they will degrade culture, relationships, and thinking (Carr, 2010; Gopnik, 2011; Powers, 2010).

Some studies indicate that the internet has the positive effect of increasing users' social networks (e.g., Boase, Horrigan, Wellman & Rainie, 2006). Having an electronic intermediary can reduce social anxiety and anxieties about intimacy, enabling some people to reach out to others more easily (see below). Certainly, e-technology has made communication easy and inexpensive among many people and around the world. Therapists have been able to conduct therapy sessions remotely by either phone or face-to-face through video links. Other studies, however, show a deleterious impact such as a decline in family time of thirty to forty-five minutes for every hour spent on the internet (Nie & Erbring, 2002).

Even the casual observer would conclude that these technologies can powerfully affect those who use them, and now we are beginning to get some indication of that at the neurological level. For example, Small, Moody, Siddarth, and Bookheimer (2009) studied subjects' brain activity while conducting a Google search. Using brain imaging, an MRI, they compared experienced versus inexperienced internet users. Two findings were particularly interesting. First, the brain activity of the experienced users was much more dispersed than that of the novices. They then had the inexperienced users practise internet searches an hour a day for five days. In the repeat tests, six days after the first tests, the new users' brain activity was now dispersed like that of the veteran users. Small, Moody, Siddarth, and Bookheimer (2009) argued that the results suggest the human brain is highly sensitive to change through the environment of the internet—in this case after *only five hours* of practice. Carr's (2010) review of current research led him to conclude, "When we go online, we enter an environment that promotes cursory reading, hurried and distracted thinking, and superficial learning. It's possible to think deeply while surfing the Net, just as it's possible to think shallowly while reading a book, but that's not the type of thinking the technology encourages and rewards" (pp. 115–116).

These states that Carr notes are unlike those promoted in psychodynamic psychotherapy. The psychodynamic sensibility encourages reflection, patience, the suspension of judgment, the value of ambiguity, of not knowing and of tolerating uncomfortable affective states. As Scharff and Scharff (1998) note, therapists and patients give up the certainty of what they know for the uncertainty of what they do not *yet* know. This state of mind is also similar to that of "beginner's mind", or *shoshin*, a concept from Zen teaching (Suzuki, 1970) which refers to approaching experience with openness and eagerness, devoid of preconceived notions. Our psychodynamic sensibility can have two competing effects on the practice of therapy. On the one hand, it flies in the face of an e-culture that values speed, certainty, focus on the present, data that has been updated moments ago, and multitasking. On the other hand, it makes psychodynamic therapy a more valuable enterprise, given its evocation of states of mind that are not generally appreciated. One patient noted that she disconnected from her smartphone in our sessions so she could connect more with herself.

Among the many themes that could be addressed in this chapter, I have selected fragmentation of selves and objects and the co-presence of the e-third. The insightful work of Moreno (2010) and Turkle (2004, 2011) have been particularly influential in my thinking. In the following vignettes, all names and screen names are pseudonyms.

* * *

Fragmented selves and objects

Relating in social media environments need not be superficial, affectively dysregulating, or fragmenting but there can be a pull towards this, especially with individuals who have heightened vulnerabilities. This occurs in a variety of ways. With remarkable ease, a person can initiate or end contact, be highly selective, have a multitude of options, impulsively express primitive sexual or aggressive feelings, and keep contact limited (time, distance, anonymity, pseudonyms). Many questions arise. Do people who relate predominantly on the internet not know what they are missing in the real world? What are the neurological differences between contact that is in-person versus contact that is electronically mediated? Goleman (2007), among others, raised the point that internet-mediated relationships do not have the full array of social and emotional cues (unconscious and conscious) that in-person relationships have. How does the absence of part of this array affect the depth of the relationships? How does it affect empathy, aggression, and other behaviours or emotions?

* * *

The e-third as a facilitator of in-person connection

Warren, a twenty-seven-year-old astronomer, was intensely anxious in social situations and avoided them. He had little experience with people outside his family and, until college, was educated at home or in small rural schools. College and graduate school were difficult for him but he had handled them by being a recluse. He began seeing me in weekly therapy because of intense anxiety stimulated by his new job. It required that he work closely as a member of a project team that involved frequent meetings and presentations.

Concurrently he was a member of a weekly online scientific discussion as part of a professional networking site. He enjoyed and looked forward to this regular text-based, theme-focused group. In therapy we examined the nature of his anxiety which included fears of dependency, abandonment, and attack by others. Over a period of two years, he eventually began to meet in-person with two other members who were in the DC area as well, and these meetings subsequently led to friendships beyond their scientific interests. There was a synergistic effect between the therapy and the e-mediated social interactions. The e-third of the online group desensitised him to social interaction in a protected setting and facilitated more developed in-person relationships. In therapy, we worked on moderating his anxiety through understanding it better and through his experiencing it and gradually learning to tolerate it in our weekly face-to-face sessions, as we developed an increasingly intimate relationship.

* * *

The e-third as a narcissistic particle accelerator

Henry Seiden (Hanlon, 2001) used the term narcissistic particle accelerator to describe the internet's amplification of narcissistic trends by "magnifying the power of otherwise weak and tiny impulses supporting invention, inviting acting out, flattering grandiosity, supporting the spinning out of self-serving and potentially world-shaking scenarios" (p. 567). The next two vignettes illustrate the intensification of part and split aspects of self and its deleterious effects on marriage.

Barry is a married forty-five-year-old father of two who works as a foreman at a manufacturing plant. When I saw him for the first time, he said that he does not respect people who whine about their feelings and that he would never set foot inside a therapist's office unless his wife forced him to do so—which she did by threatening to leave him. Her complaints involved his generally irritable attitude and daily two hours or more (often much more) on a football website blogging as *Ultrafan* and engaging in spirited arguments with other fans. He has attended regularly for six months of weekly therapy but he says that he comes only because he is required by "marital law". His marriage has marginally improved but his connection to me is tenuous.

Barry has a passionate relationship to the website and says that he misses it terribly when he can't get his "daily dose" of it. He feels more himself there than anywhere else in his life. Barry is respected by a substantial subgroup of the site's users and his advice is sought by fans around the country. He feels like "the man" when he gets into verbal fights with others on the site and when he exhorts his supporters to "man-up". He described some of these fights and they are characterised by enraged, contemptuous, obscenity-laced "beatings" of his opponents. He has no empathy for these "stupid assholes".

Barry's offline life is very different. He is the only foreman at his plant without at least a community college degree. He believes he is not valued at work, has no chance of ever being promoted and is pessimistic about getting another job. His wife is dissatisfied with him and he feels inept in dealing with his children, aged ten and twelve. He has no friends other than from the website.

Barry has two identities: one online and one offline. As *Ultrafan*, he is wise, respected, decisive, powerful, and contemptuous of weakness. As Barry, he is demeaned, inept, and weak. *Ultrafan*'s world is simple and clear; there are good objects (his supporters, his team) and bad objects (fans who disagree with him, the other teams). Barry's world is complex with the messiness, frustrations, and ambiguity of real world relationships. Much of the challenge of therapy involves helping Barry to tolerate his external world, the difficulties and pain of offline living—and of therapy itself. Actually, Barry has grudgingly acknowledged such benefits. More fundamentally, therapy, if he stays with it, could facilitate the development of his internal world and the more cohesive self-embodying elements of both Barry and *Ultrafan*.

* * *

A virtual world and the fragmentation of a marriage

Simulation games take this issue of identity one step further. Two examples are *World of Warcraft* with 10.3 million subscribers (Cifaldi, 2011, November 8) and *Second Life* with one million active users (Singularity University, 2011, August 18). These are multiplayer internet games in which the participants interact with one another in virtual environments and the players construct their own identity or identities using *avatars* which often are very different from the player's real world identity (for example by choosing to be of a different gender, age, race, or status). An avatar may even be a non-human such as an animal.

Diane, a thirty-eight-year-old nurse practitioner, has seen me for two years of weekly therapy. She was referred by her couple therapist as she became more distressed and hopeless over the state of her marriage. She and her husband, Sam, also thirty-eight, had entered couple therapy with a colleague after he announced that he wanted a divorce. Both of them acknowledged that the marriage had been tense and distant following her miscarriage a year before, but Diane was surprised when Sam made up his mind without discussing it with her. Throughout their marriage, Sam had said repeatedly that he would work hard at repairing the marriage before giving up. Moreover, she had asked him a number of times if anything was wrong between them and he denied it, saying it was due to work stress and how much he was involved with "the game". The game was an internet simulation game in which he participated with a team of other players from around the world who generally knew each other only as avatars in this virtual world. Notably, in the context of Diane's miscarriage, an avatar in this game can die but be brought back to life.

Sam found the game to be extraordinarily compelling. Indeed, he would sometimes play for up to ten hours, often at night. As a self-employed consultant, he could set his own hours and would frequently go to bed at six in the morning, sleep until eleven and then meet with clients in the afternoon. Sam and Diane had rarely had sex during the preceding year and were often in bed together only for a few hours a night since he was so involved with the game. The couple therapy foundered and ended after seven months. Both Diane and the couple therapist viewed Sam as not invested in the process, and when conflict arose in the sessions he would emotionally withdraw or angrily walk out. The couple separated after a few months and subsequently divorced. Diane continued her individual work with me.

As their separation agreement was being finalised, Diane came across records from their joint credit card and saw charges to vendors that she did not recognise. She easily learned that a vendor sold sex toys. Hurt and enraged, she then checked the bill for Sam's cellphone and found that he had made many lengthy calls to a city thousands of miles from the DC area. When she confronted Sam he confessed that his avatar had fallen in love with another avatar as they had gone through "a lot of hard times together" in the virtual world. He invited the other avatar to connect outside the game. They did and had a passionate, sexual affair—she was a woman six years younger than him. He told Diane that he didn't know what would eventually happen but that it felt like a complete relationship. The woman and he were both very different from their avatars but they loved each other *and* their avatars.

A few final points. This is a couple that did not mourn—as a couple—the loss of their anticipated baby but each dealt with it separately. The absence of this process created distance between them and contributed to their separation. The game and the avatar-love served, in part, as a manic defence for Sam. The collapse of Diane's marriage shattered her trust in men and in her own judgment, especially since her first marriage had ended due to that husband also having an affair. Her anger towards Sam also helped her to let go of her attachment to him. She remains in therapy to further examine her part in these divorces.

* * *

Commentary

It is important to emphasise that the identity issues described in these two vignettes were not created by technology but rather were intensified by it. Certainly, humans have been experimenting with the question of "who am I?" long before social media. Indeed, trying on different identities is often seen as part of adolescence and of the transition from childhood to adulthood. The domains of social media, though, do provide a vast array of opportunities for trying out different selves. Gabbard (2001) wrote, "Virtual space has a lot in common with transitional space, in the sense that it is not truly an internal realm, but lies somewhere between external reality and our internal world. When we sit at a computer, we are both real and not real" (p. 734).

This touches on a central question: what is real and what is not real? Both Barry and Sam might say that they were more real online than they were in the rest of their lives. We could look at Barry and Sam as exhibiting adolescent behaviour—experimenting with different selves, playing with identities. Yet, how playful and how serious is it? Moreno (2010) questions whether the nature of play itself is transformed by virtual reality (the term itself is an oxymoron). The real world felt frustrating and flat in comparison to Barry's *Ultrafan* world and Sam's game world.

Turkle (2011) expresses concern that for many people, the simulated or virtual is no longer second best to the authentic. She goes so far as to say, "I believe that in our culture of simulation, the notion of authenticity is for us what sex was for the Victorians—threat and obsession, taboo and fascination" (p. 4). In a virtual world or in the part object blogosphere a person can try to find the perfect situation, the perfect other—uncomfortable elements can be easily jettisoned. Even identity can be discarded by adopting a new screen name or avatar. Identity also can be made multiple by simultaneously using many names.

Moreno (2010) holds that these forces in contemporary culture favour fragmentation of identity. Simultaneously, intrapsychic and interpersonal conflicts are avoided. Consider social networking. The ease and nature of connection on a site such as Facebook can enable a user to have hundreds of "friends" but what is the quality of the relationships? Also, if one has hundreds of "friends" it can be relatively easy to end a relationship quickly if conflict arises. The person simply makes new "friends". In interviews with adolescents, Turkle (2011) reports that many of the adolescents she spoke to admitted that their Facebook profiles were not totally accurate and were in fact more idealised versions of themselves. One girl described an avatar as "a Facebook profile come to life" (p. 191). Again, the questions arise: who am I?, what is real and what is simulated? Psychoanalytic theory acknowledges various experiences of self along a continuum from multiple and fragmented to unitary. A therapeutic and developmental goal is to allow these diverse expressions to form a complex well-integrated self rather than have them exist as split or dissociated identities.

Before closing this discussion, I want to at least note an enormous part of the internet that I have not yet mentioned (see also Chapter Four). It is estimated that there are 4.2 million pornography sites on the internet and, in the US in a single day, 40 million people log on to them (Lee, 2011, December 5). While pornography has been around for thousands of years prior to the internet, I have seen many patients whose internet use of it spiralled out of control while it had not done so previously with magazines and videos. The consequences have been devastating and have included marital strain, divorce, job loss, and arrest. The patients have reported the qualitatively different influence of the following characteristics: the ease and (apparent) anonymity of use, access without cost, sites making it difficult to log off, the power of the imagery, and the ease of searching for more and more stimulating images. One patient estimated that pornography had been part of his life for two to three hours a week prior to using it on the internet. With the internet, it was taking up twenty hours a week.

* * *

"Copresence"

Mobile technology permits people to almost always be connected. This frequent and reliable connectivity can have obvious benefits such as safety, emergency availability, and distance learning experiences. There are benefits for personal relationships as well. For instance, one study (Hoflich, Joachim & Linke, 2011) found that frequent texting between couples was associated with health in the relationship. Such usage can help partners feel "held in mind" rather than "out of sight, out of mind".

Alternatively, Gopnik (2011) and others have proposed that always being connected— "wrap-around usage"—can impoverish a person's internal world and relationships. Turkle (2011) refers to this as "copresence" and illustrates it with the example of people multitasking with electronic devices while with others. People believe that they can interact with an e-device while at the same time relating to a person who is physically present and that this can occur without diminishing the in-person connection (see below). Yet, there is a growing body of evidence (Jackson, 2008; Ophir, Nass & Wagner, 2009) that while people can successfully multitask, *every* task is performed less effectively than if attention had been focused on only one of them. While most of the research is on cognitive tasks, it is apparent that this is also true for relationships as well. Here are three vignettes of copresence.

* * *

The e-third as transitional object

A colleague offered the following vignette. Marilyn is a forty-two-year-old consultant who appeared anxious in her first session with her therapist Sandra, also in her forties. Marilyn described dreading an upcoming trip for her tenth anniversary. She sat on the edge of the couch, did not take off her coat, and held her phone in both hands. During this session it rang twice and she answered it once. When the phone rang again she glanced at it in her palm and did not answer. She did not comment on this call directly but said that when she went to dinner with her husband she always kept her phone on because she would regularly need to text with friends. Marilyn felt that she was disconnected from her husband and that he didn't understand her. She relied on texting or voice messages with friends for connection. Part (of course, only part) of her dread of the upcoming island vacation was that her phone and computer would not work and she would feel isolated. She also dreaded the intimacy of time with her husband without the copresence of the e-third.

Throughout the second session, Marilyn again held the phone tightly in her hands. When the phone rang mid-session, she glanced at the number but did not answer it. Sandra said that she guessed Marilyn must be concerned that someone would need to reach her during the fifty minutes. Of course, it went in both directions—*Marilyn* might need to reach someone else. Her parents had divorced when she was thirteen and she felt disconnected, even abandoned by her mother. Her connection with Sandra in this session enabled Marilyn to offer to have her phone only vibrate rather than ring while in session—still a presence but a smaller one.

As treatment progressed over the next few months, Marilyn took off her coat and sat back on the couch. She did, though, continue to hold the phone—always checking if it vibrated but rarely taking the call. Sandra thought of the phone as a transitional object. Holding the phone helped Marilyn feel safe by having a tangible, material connection to important others. It also helped her feel safe in the presence of Sandra who initially was an anxiety-provoking object. I would also suggest that holding the phone, as well as initially keeping her coat on, provided autistic-contiguous (Ogden, 1989) grounding for Marilyn—it kept her literally in touch, physically.

As Marilyn's anxiety began to lessen in therapy, she was slowly able to tolerate more physical distance between her phone and herself. She first placed it on the couch next to her and eventually kept it in her bag. Now, fifteen months into the therapy, she continues to check the phone when it vibrates. They are exploring this slow movement in her relationship with the phone. Marilyn told Sandra that being in therapy caused anxiety. Texting, emailing, and talking on the phone were much safer ways to interact. Sandra's patience and understanding concerning the phone-holding helped Marilyn trust that she could find containment within the therapy relationship.

* * *

The e-third as a constant, "silent" copresence

Paula, fifty-seven, CEO of an international non-profit organisation, and Tim, sixty-three, a managing partner of a large law firm, consulted with me because they were on the verge of separating. There were many issues in their eight-year marriage. One centred on the lack of couple time and the negative marital impact of their demanding work schedules. In an early couple session, they described a rare, beautiful walk in the forest together and the closeness they felt with each other. As I asked what had made this experience so exceptional, Paula said that she had left her phone at home and Tim hadn't answered his when it rang during the walk. I offered what I thought was an obvious comment: "You know, some couples set up technology-free time zones to create better couple time." They looked at each other and burst out laughing. I thought they had found my comment to be so obvious that it was absurd to say it. On the contrary, they went on to say *they had never thought of it*, although it was so obvious. Having such technology-free times (including our sessions), proved to be helpful for them but difficult to create. This also facilitated exploration of their phone use to avoid experiences of intimacy, conflict, and awareness of their different visions for the marriage.

* * *

The e-third as an intrusion

LeAnn, a fifty-five-year-old surgeon in weekly therapy, described a major fight she had with her husband, Sean, a college professor, also fifty-five. They shared an avid interest in football and were looking forward to spending time together watching a particular game on television. As the game progressed, LeAnn began texting a good friend of hers who was also watching the game in another city and did so throughout the game. Sean made a few comments about feeling like he was watching the game alone. She did not take the comment seriously and was surprised when he angrily walked out saying, "I might as well watch this by myself." The argument escalated and they did not speak with each other for two days.

It is noteworthy that she was shocked when Sean became so hurt and angry—despite his earlier comments and despite the fact that an important issue in their marriage was that Sean felt she took him for granted and did not value time with him. As LeAnn and I deconstructed what had happened, we examined why she had not seen this. She said that it never occurred to her. To her it was not like talking to someone else in the room or even on the phone. She said, "I was in the room with him, I was only texting." She came to see how it did take her away from Sean, why it was hurtful and why he would feel taken for granted. We also considered that the texting was an expression of unconscious hostility towards Sean as well as an unconscious identification with her busy, distracted mother.

In closing

My intent in this chapter has been to use clinical experience and a psychodynamic sensibility to explore some of the impact of the e-third. Clearly, the e-third will continue to be with us in our offices and in our lives in general. It can affect such core dimensions of experience as: identity, intimacy, awareness of the "otherness" of others, death and mourning, conflict, the perception of time, play, creativity, and privacy.

In his paper *Psychoanalysis and Virtual Reality*, Moreno (2010) argues that in the psychoanalytic study of these phenomena, "Perhaps our mission is, precisely, to promote the potential value of the intimate place. Contemporaneity, therefore, entails a unique relationship with our own time. We must stick to it yet distance ourselves somewhat from it so as to be able to 'see' it" (p. 6).

Turkle (2004) believes, "[N]ever have we needed the ability to think, so to speak, 'ambivalently' to consider life in shades of gray, consider moral dilemmas that aren't battles for 'infinite justice' between Good and Evil [such as in simulated or part object worlds]. Never have we so needed to be able to hold many different and contradictory thoughts and feelings at the same time. People may be comforted by the notion that we are moving from a psychoanalytic to a computer culture, but what the times demand is a passionate quest for joint citizenship if we are to fully comprehend the human meanings of the new and future objects of our lives" (pp. 29–30).

References

Boase, J., Horrigan, J. B., Wellman, B. & Rainie, L. (2006). *The Strength of Internet Ties*. Washington, DC: Pew Internet and American Life Project.

Carr, N. (2010). *The Shallows: What the Internet is Doing to our Brains*. New York: W. W. Norton.

Cifaldi, F. (2010, November 8). World of Warcraft loses another 800k subs in three months. http:www.gamasutra.com/view/news/38460/World of Warcraft_Loses_Another_800K Subs_In_Three_Months.php.

Gabbard, G. O. (2001). Cyberpassion: E-rotic transference on the Internet. *Psychoanalytic Quarterly, 70*: 719–737.

Goleman, D. (2007, February 20). Flame first, think later: new clues to e-mail misbehavior. *New York Times*.

Gopnik, A. (2011, February 14). The information: How the internet gets inside us. *New Yorker*, pp. 124–130.

Hanlon, J. (2001). Disembodied intimacies: Identity and relationship on the Internet. *Psychoanalytic Psychology, 18*(3): 566–571.

Hoflich, J. R. & Linke, C. (2011). Mobile communication in intimate relationships: Relationship development and the multiple dialectics of couples' media usage and communication. In: R. Ling & S. W. Campbell (Eds.), *Mobile Communication: Bringing us Together and Tearing us Apart*, (pp. 107–126). Piscataway, NJ: Transaction Publishers.

Jackson, M. (2008). *Distracted: The Erosion of Attention and the Coming Dark Age*. New York: Prometheus.

Kaplan, A. M. & Haenlein, M. (2010). Users of the world unite! The challenges and opportunities of social media. *Business Horizons, 53*(1): 59–68.

Lee, C. (2011, December 5). The sex addiction epidemic. *Newsweek*, pp. 48–55.

Moreno, J. (2010, January). Psychoanalysis and virtual reality. Paper presented at *Being human: psychoanalytic approaches to children and adults*. Weekend conference of the International Psychotherapy Institute, Washington, DC.

Nie, N. H. & Erbing, L. (2002). Internet and society: A preliminary report. *IT & Society*, 1: 275–283.

Ogden, T. H. (1989). *The Primitive Edge of Experience*. Northvale, NJ: Jason Aronson.

Ogden, T. H. (1994). *Subjects of Analysis*. Northvale, NJ: Jason Aronson.

Ogden, T. H. (1997). *Reverie and Interpretation*. Northvale, NJ: Jason Aronson.

Ophir, E., Nass, C. & Wagner, A. (2009). Cognitive control in media multitaskers. *Proceedings of the National Academy of Sciences*, 106: 15583–15587.

Powers, W. (2010). *Hamlet's Blackberry: A Practical Philosophy for Building a Good Life in the Digital Age*. New York: Harper Collins.

Scharff, J. S. & Scharff, D. E. (1998). *Object Relations Individual Therapy*. Northvale, NJ: Jason Aronson.

Singularity University (2011, August 18). Philip Rosedale, creator of Second Life speaks at Singularity University. http://www.youtube.com/watch?v=C04wwLjJ0os.

Small, G. W., Moody, T. D., Siddarth, P. & Bookheimer, S. Y. (2009). Your brain on Google: Patterns of cerebral activation during internet searching. *American Journal of Geriatric Psychiatry*, 17: 116–126.

Stadter, M. (2012). *Presence and the Present: Relationship and Time in Contemporary Psychodynamic Therapy*. Lanham, MD: Jason Aronson.

Suzuki, S. (1970). *Zen Mind, Beginner's Mind*. New York: Weatherhill.

Turkle, S. (2004). Whither psychoanalysis in computer culture? *Psychoanalytic Psychology*, 21(1): 16–30.

Turkle, S. (2011). *Alone Together: Why We Expect More from Technology and Less from Each Other*. New York: Basic.

CHAPTER TWO

Skype as the uncanny third

Irmgard Dettbarn, PhD

kyper, an acronym for *Sky peer-to-peer*, was the original name given to new software designed to make free phone calls possible on the internet in 2003. However, at this time, another domain with the same name already existed on the World Wide Web. So the "r" was simply deleted and *Skyper* became *Skype*. In Skype, described as a peer-to-peer network, "… resources and data can be simultaneously exchanged between two networked computers, however, both computers must be on an equal footing, as the name suggests. Using a microphone, the computer records the user's voice; it then converts this information into individual datagrams (or network packets) and sends it via the Internet Protocol (IP) to the respective receiving computer. Thus, the entire data exchange occurs via the Internet. The receiving computer puts the incoming datagrams back together and transforms the data back into language that is delivered via a loudspeaker" (www.voip-information.de/peer-to-peer.html).

In March 2011, Wikipedia reported that 30 million users, who were simultaneously online, could be reached through Skype (http://de.wikipedia.org/). As I am writing in May 2012, a few million more are surely using Skype. In fact, today I was one of these Skypers. I spoke to two separate analysands via Skype, each call lasting fifty minutes. So I carried out two analytic sessions today. Or did I? If the unconscious knows neither space nor time, then the answer is "Yes". If, according to Sandler, whatever the analyst does is "analysis", then "Yes". If one reads the International Psychoanalytical Association's definition of psychoanalytical treatment, the answer remains unclear. The question arises whether transference and resistance can develop in such a setting, sufficient to enable a genuine psychoanalytical process.

From 2007 to 2010, I had the opportunity to live and work as an analyst in Asia where I conducted in-person analysis with analysands who each had four sessions per week on average. Once back in Berlin, the question arose: would it be possible to continue the work as "shuttle" analysis with my returning to Asia only twice a year? A second question occurred to me: could Skype sessions bridge the time gap between my visits to Asia? Back in the 1990s, extensive discussions on the use of the telephone in psychoanalysis could already be found in publications of the International Psychoanalytical Association, and numerous other articles on "remote therapies" have been written since then (see Chapters Six and Twenty one). Personal discussions and conversations held among professionals have been quite controversial, often revealing very opposing viewpoints. On the one hand, some analysts have completely rejected the idea. On the other hand, some have enthusiastically highlighted their finding that analysts could not distinguish between the process notes of in-person sessions and those of analytic sessions conducted on the telephone or the internet.

I use Skype of necessity, but I have mixed feelings towards Skype. Doubt and fascination seem to go hand in hand, which has led me to think further about my experiences with this new tool. My thoughts revolve around what I have noticed and what has occurred to me when I am sitting (and just after I have been sitting) in front of my laptop, talking with the analysands who are thousands of miles away in another part of the world. I am very interested in finding out more about the influence of Skype on my analysands, on me, and on the analytic process itself. The two Skype contacts that I had on the day when I first started writing this text could not have been more different. The technical difficulty with Skype in each case was sometimes experienced differently depending on whether the context was a negative or a positive transference.

I bought my laptop specifically for Skype. It has particularly good speakers and a built-in camera. Every now and again, when starting up the computer, welcome messages from the software company pop up on my screen informing me that there will be an update of this or that program, and inquiring as to whether I want to download it now or later. I am faced with many questions calling for decisions and, unprepared, I am forced to answer them one way or the other, namely, with "Yes", "No", or "Later". My intellectual resources are diverted to making unwelcome decisions when I want to be in a state of reverie preparing for an analytic session. Carr notes the same: "Links have to be constantly evaluated and related decisions regarding the navigation made, while at the same time we are bombarded by an enormous amount of fleeting sensory stimuli … our brain is not only strained but also overwhelmed" (Carr, 2011, p. 18).

Today, I am able to log onto Skype straightaway, without encountering any difficulties. For me in Berlin the first session is at 7 am but for my analysand the local time is 1 pm. It is a beautiful sunny spring day in Berlin. Some 8000 kilometres away, it is lunchtime, and I have no idea if the analysand is looking out the window at smog, sunshine, or rain. Is it important to know this? Neither of us shares the same space nor the same time zone, and yet we are both in our own individual real time, both of us part of the media revolution.

On the screen I can see all the names and photos or icons of the people whose addresses are stored in my Skype address book. I can also see who is available on Skype right now and who is not. Although I do not know where my Skype contacts actually are, I am still informed as to whether they are currently available, busy, or not online. So every time I click on Skype or my Skype address book, I know who is online. Therefore, the Skype user can find out whether the other person is online or not, twenty-four hours a day. However, Skype also offers its subscribers the option of showing an "offline" message, when in fact they are still online, or they can activate a red icon requesting others not to disturb them. So, my experience of Skype has taught me that the information presented by the displayed icons does not always coincide with the facts. For example, the small "green cloud" beside my Skype address indicates that I am online, but the analysand's display may tell him something else. So neither the analysand in Asia nor the analyst in Berlin can be sure if either of us is online at the time of our appointment. When the analysand clicks on my Skype address on his computer, it should cause my laptop to ring. But here I am, sitting in front of my laptop, and it fails to ring.

Depending on the different types of computers being used, several essential preliminary actions have to be made before contact can be established via Skype. Instructions have to be followed and this task remains in the foreground of the analyst's attention until it becomes automatic. It is interesting to know that when Skype was first invented, intensive attention was being given to the place of the therapy room and couch in psychoanalytical literature (Guderian, 2004a and b).

With the great changes that have occurred in all aspects of life following the media revolution, the inevitability of being tied to traditional settings has been called into question. How significant will these new media opportunities become, how will they affect us and our society, and to what extent can they be put to use in psychoanalysis? In the 1950s, the media theorist Marshall McLuhan, author of the famous quote "The medium is the message" (McLuhan quoted in Grampp, 2011, pp. 175–218), noted the close connection man makes to the tools he has made to extend his capability and ease his life. As Carr puts it, "We shape our tools and thereafter our tools shape us" (2010, p. 323). Or as Krämer puts it, "Whenever we use a tool to gain greater control over the external world, we change our relationship to this world … The medium is not simply the message but it really perpetuates the message of the mark of the medium … as the unconscious is in relation to what is accessible to the consciousness" (Krämer, 1998, p. 81). But Carr warns, "If a carpenter takes a hammer in his hand, he can only do with this hand what the hammer allows him to do. The hand becomes a device to hammer in and pull out nails" (Carr, 2010, p. 323). So if as analysts we use technology, does this mean that we will find our analytic sensibility constrained by technology or that we will respond to technology with a creative, flexible adaptation of our technique in sync with the changing society in which we live?

The impact of information technology is one of the biggest changes that humanity has encountered since the invention of the clock, which fragmented our time, and the arrival of the printing press, which extended our knowledge and memory storage and heralded the age of industrial manufacturing and mass production which brought wealth to many. As we participate in the realm of technology, we are also changing the relationship with ourselves. The media revolution, expressed on radio, telephone, television, and film, and now burgeoning with the rapid development of cyberspace, has become a part of our conscious and unconscious experience. So imagine how it feels for analysts who are used to in-person analytic settings to read the Cyberspace Independence Declaration at the World Economic Forum in Davos on February 8, 1996 from the internet pioneer, John Perry Barlow:

> Governments of the Industrial World, you weary giants of flesh and steel, I come from Cyberspace, the new home of Mind. On behalf of the future, I ask you of the past to leave us alone. You are not welcome among us. You have no sovereignty where we gather. Our world is different, cyberspace transactions, relationships, and thought itself, arrayed like a standing wave in the web of our communications. Ours is a world that is both everywhere

and nowhere, but it is not where bodies live. Our identities have no bodies, so, unlike you, we cannot obtain order by physical coercion. (Barlow, 1996)

When I contemplate a matter-free world of thinking, I recall Freud's description of "magic and sorcery, the omnipotence of thoughts … all the factors which turn something frightening into something uncanny" (Freud, 1919h, p. 243). Is that what technology is? The writer Arthur C. Clarke thought so: "Any sufficiently advanced technology is indistinguishable from magic" (Herbold, 2012, p. 25). Before I continue with the uncanny and magical aspects of the new strange world we occupy, I would like to consider the influence Skype has on the setting and the analytic pair in psychoanalytic practice.

By eliminating the geographical distances created by locations spaced far apart, Skype can remove barriers to analysis for analysands who live in remote areas without access to analytic centres. However, Skype, with "its flickering screen" (Carr, 2011, p. 18) can be problematic and physically strenuous. At the same time, Skype connects the analytic pair by means of a machine. The vertical relationship (in the traditional setting) between analyst and analysand arises from the fact that the analysand actively seeks and then makes his way to the analyst. In turn, the analyst awaits the analysand and provides him with a safe room in which the analysand can enter a psychological space for work. With the advent of technology, this has all changed. Instead, a peer-to-peer communication is created. Both sit in front of the computer, both touching the keys. The similarity in the arrangements is that the analysand calls first.

Returning to an example, I am in my office waiting at the appointed hour for my analysand to call. The computer has yet to ring. In trusting the Skype icon, I assume that my analysand is present on his computer at the other end of the connection. I wonder why it does not ring. However, I know that the icons can sometimes be wrong or misleading! So I call him myself. Behold, the analysand had tried several times to reach me, but according to his computer I was not connected to Skype. The machine, a third party who suddenly determines the rules, becomes a part of our work. We are both affected by this: both of us are unprotected from the intrusion as we would be if the analysand who meets us in person has a road accident on his way to the analyst or the analyst's next door neighbour begins to play the piano or a handyman is drilling in the apartment above the practice. However, these disturbances come from a very understandable reality and we know what is to be done, whereas a malfunction in the computer is something that "very few of us would understand, even if the hidden codes were revealed to us" (Carr, 2011, p. 20). Unexplained computer malfunctions and broadband interferences that may interrupt and terminate the conversation at any given time, combined with the possibility that the person we are talking to may do so by happening to touch a key on the keyboard, leaves us questioning our reality.

This third party that not only participates in the Skype contact but also determines it to a degree is an inanimate object that is rapidly spreading itself throughout the world, especially among the younger generations and revolutionising their way of being. It is becoming an "evocative object" (Turkle, 2007). Here is a report of an intense relationship with a person's laptop:

My laptop computer is irreplaceable, and not just for all the usual reasons. It's practically a brain prosthesis. Besides, I love it. I would recognize the feel of its keyboard under my fingers in a darkened room …. I carried it on my back all over England, Cuba, Canada, and the United States. When I use it in bed, I remember to keep the blankets from covering its vents so it doesn't overheat …. It doesn't just belong to me; I also belong to it …. It just so happened that I had early romantic experiences with machines, and so computers make me think of love. (Newitz, 2007, p. 88 in Turkle, 2007)

When I read this text I am, of course, reminded of Winnicott's (1971) transitional object, and of Habermas's (1999) personal objects that accompany us in life. Newitz's descriptions of her relationship to her laptop provide an impressive and vivid example of Habermas's definition of personal objects. However, her text also reveals just how the object sets its own conditions; for example, when the author describes protecting it from overheating! Writing before Skype was invented, Habermas (1999) defined these personal objects as follows:

> Personal objects mediate not only between man and nature and between man and culture, but also thirdly, between the individual and his fellow man, especially his significant other(s).
>
> A) Personal objects can remind us of a significant other and therefore the relationship with him or they can even represent him. Personal objects help to symbolically maintain the connection to another or others; they make him present, even when he is no longer there following separation or in situations of separation.
>
> B) Personal objects can also serve as a medium to connect with others by acting as a common object, organizing joint activities or by making communication over long distances possible, i.e. technology such as the telephone and car. (Habermas, 1999, p. 500)

The device that is programmed to use Skype, whether it is a computer, laptop, notebook, or iPad, fulfils these personal object functions. In its technical existence, it mediates between man and culture, and when used as a means of communication, it not only links the analyst to the analysand during sessions but it can symbolically make and potentially maintain the connection eternally, as when a Skype participant looks to see if his analyst is online around the clock.

The beloved object has, as it were, become a living object, having settled somewhere between living and dead matter. Once again, I hear the ring of the magical and uncanny. The uncanny is that which exists between life and death and creates the impression of living. Why do we treat or deal with dead matter as if it were "alive"? In addition to psychological explanations, perhaps the neurosciences can be materialised too? According to John Mitchell, "Evolution has imbued our brains with a powerful social instinct … a set of processes for inferring what those around us are thinking and feeling … Recent neuroimaging studies indicate that three highly active brain regions—one in the prefrontal cortex, one in the parietal cortex, and one at the intersection of the parietal and temporal cortices—are specifically dedicated to the task of understanding the goings-on of other people's minds … As we have entered the computer age, however, our talent for connecting with other minds has led to an unintended consequence!" (Carr, 2010, p. 213). Mitchell says: "Chronic overactivity of those brain regions implicated in social thought … can lead us to perceive minds where no minds exist, even in inanimate objects" (Carr, 2010, p. 213).

Inanimate objects may be thought to assume the functions of human abilities. The creepier they seem, the more we project vitality into the inanimate object, and the more perturbing it is to us. Just as the child with the help of the transitional object in imagination learns how to bear the absence of its mother, the adult tries to bring the mighty inanimate object to life, and in doing so, hopes to evade the uncanny, the terrifying absence of life, and the imagined encounter with death. "In addition, there is mounting evidence that our brain naturally imitates the spirit of those with whom we interact, whether real or imaginary. Such 'neural mirroring or reflections' explain why we so quickly ascribe human characteristics to our computers and computer properties to ourselves" (Carr, 2010, p. 213). "Even as the larger system, into which our minds so readily meld, is lending us its powers, it is also imposing its limitations on us" (Carr, 2011, p. 19).

Let us return to the Skype session: the computer has given us the power to overcome a seemingly insurmountable distance for a short time but its technical possibilities have limitations, such as presenting false information concerning the presence of the Skype user. The computer has created a relationship of equality, as previously described. It has also put us into the realm of disembodiment. Do our voices become disembodied on the computer? Are they ghostly voices? But who still believes in ghosts? Surely we have long since left this notion behind us. Or have we? Perhaps technology throws us back into an encounter with the uncanny "when infantile complexes which have been repressed are once more revived by some impression, or when primitive beliefs which have been surmounted seem once more to be confirmed" (Freud, 1919h, p. 249).

As the normally vibrant mark of our presence, does the voice lose its vitality in the absence of the body or does it lead us into an emotional area between the living and the dead? A witness to history in the making impressively describes his feelings about the disembodied voices of the first talking machines:

> You can't believe it dear friend, what a strange sensation and impression it made on us; hearing a human voice and human speech for the first time ever which did not seem to come from a human mouth at all. We looked at each other in stunned silence, and afterwards we openly admitted that during those first few moments a secret little shiver had run down our spine. (Macho, 2006, p. 136)

In 1878, Edison enthused about the voice of a dog which he had recorded:

> One day, a dog came passing by and began barking in the hopper, and … this barking was reproduced in such fantastic quality. We have removed the roll well and now we can let him bark at any time. As far as I'm concerned this dog may die and go to dog-heaven … but we have him—everything that has a voice survives … This dead apparatus presented the dead voice as the overcoming of death. (Edison, 1878, quoted in Macho, 2006, p. 139)

"Since time immemorial, human beings have tried to use voices to humanize inanimate matter. Animals, plants, objects, dead people or abstract entities were given a voice, so as to provide them with human characteristics" (Macho, 2006, p. 139). The lifeless should be brought to life and technical inventions are supposed to refute the statement that all of us are mortal. "[B]ut no human being really grasps it, and our unconscious has as little use now as it ever had for the idea of its own mortality" (Freud, 1919h, p. 242). This is the deadly sinister side of technology, laptops, notebooks, or Skype.

Computer technology puts us at the mercy of an apparatus that we do not properly understand: it functions according to its own laws and, therefore, it can be controlled only to a limited extent. When the connection fails in a Skype session, this may be a minor obstacle for some people. However, for others it might mean the reactivation of a trauma, or it might even cause a trauma with associated feelings of powerlessness, helplessness, and vulnerability. Both analysand and analyst are equally exposed to this: maybe there is even the risk of a seductive symbiotic "joining of forces" against the uncanny third. In turn, this can prevent the working through of conflicts within the analytical process. The ensuing potential aggression and fear should not be underestimated. It can be a relief not to be left alone at the mercy of unpredictable technology. In terms of the analysand, this can also mean disillusionment, if he has attributed magical powers to the analyst. On the other hand, this traumatic situation can lend support to mutually complicated and negative feelings being experienced in the transference: If the analyst is experienced as a bad object, malfunctions or disruptions in Skype are interpreted as confirmation of the analyst's aggression towards the analysand. Since the technical problems with Skype cannot really be controlled, the field of magic and the uncanny is activated.

In another Skype session, a patient raised a very touching but also troubling issue. My eyes are closed as I listen to him. I often do this during in-person sessions to tune in to my analytic reverie. I realise that I am deeply moved by what he is telling me. When I open my eyes again and look at the Skype images on the screen, I see that the patient is crying. I do not doubt the sincerity of his or my own emotions for one moment; the closeness and proximity between him and me, which, with the help of technology in a virtual world, happened at this very moment, even though we are far apart. I am not only surprised but positively impressed by the possibility of this experience of emotional presence in a Skype session.

A few hours later, it is now early afternoon in Berlin and late evening in another analysand's city. The connection is established without any initial difficulties, until a text bubble from Skype appears on the screen, announcing that it has found a fault and is trying to reconnect. Even so, the conversation continues. I endeavour to understand what the analysand is saying. But despite all my efforts, I often have to ask him to repeat or explain himself again, because our words are being lost somewhere in cyberspace. I cannot quite connect to what he is saying. Both of us are really annoyed. Alternately, we try to call each other again and again. The analysand asks me to stop asking him to repeat himself so often. He suggests that we should try to guess what each other has meant. I understood this as an attempt to install an illusionary symbiotic form of communication, rather than submit to the dictates of technology. Needless to say this particular session took place with a negative transference in the background. The problems are piling up: The computer forces us to constantly focus on restoring the connection, and we are both upset at the lack of continuity. Should we stop or just switch to the telephone? But on this occasion the phone also fails to work properly. The analysand, who already would have preferred to do anything else other than have a session, is now full of anger. To me it seems very much like the uncanny third party has become his ally! Neither of us can change the situation. By the time the session comes to an end, both of us are angry. We are in a state of "double negative transference". "That's unfair," he says, "I was waiting the whole time when we weren't connected." I also think it's unfair: technology is simply unfair. When I found the term, "machine-loathing" (Ziemann, 2011, p. 116), I could only confirm that someone had found the right name for my current feelings.

With regard to the voice, silence is also a part of speaking. In the last session described, the troubled or malfunctioning technology made it impossible for any "sense-perceptible silence" to occur (Gehring, 2006, p. 91). In any case, Skype makes it difficult for any "silent understanding" to take place. If neither the analyst nor the analysand is speaking on Skype, we cannot tell whether the silence is due to a technical problem or if it is an active silence on the part of one of us. This can result in an unwanted "forced-to-speak" situation for both parties. A poor internet connection can create distortions of the voice so that it repeats like an echo. In her article on the repeating voice Gehring describes the story of the nymph Echo who needs to speak, but can no longer say anything other than repeat the words of others. "An echo loses its ability to remain silent, it loses all semantic scope (or space), sentences are also truncated and the echo is robbed of the dimension of listening" (Gehring, 2006, p. 106). The voice cannot communicate any sense. It can neither really "live" nor "die". Skype guides us back into the uncanny space between life and death.

The next day, I have another Skype session, also of poor technical quality. So we change to the phone without difficulty. During this session there is a positive transference mood and any technical problems with Skype are irrelevant. Although the patient finds the change of media somewhat distracting, he is so intent on his thoughts and feelings that not even this change seems to cause any kind of disruption, even though, for this particular session, he was away from his usual location. This begs the question, what role does the room or space play? Gumbrecht addresses this as follows:

> [This is] the most difficult existential consequence of the electronic age; … eliminating the spatial dimensions at various levels of our experience, our behavior … Thereby, we encounter a fascinating paradox: With the help of electronics, globalization has, on an unimaginable scale, expanded and strengthened our control over the space on earth and at the same time, it has almost completely excluded this space from our existence. (2010, p. 42)

With the elimination of space and distance comes dislocation. According to Attali (1992), the highly mobile residents of the global village seem to live like nomads equipped with communication devices that he refers to as nomadic objects.

> To use these devices, they only need to be connected to global electronic information and trading networks, the oases of the new nomads … It does not matter where you come from; a number or name is enough to identify the nomads of the Millennium. (p. 26)
> Like the objects of pagan antiquity, the nomadic object of the future will be an inanimate object, however, they will embody the life, spirit and values of those who develop and use them. Basically, they are branches of our senses and our bodily functions. For example, computers supplement the human brain. (Attali, 1992, p. 107)

When Attali continues to develop his ideas about the future, he places future technical developments in the area of the horrific and the uncanny:

> One could imagine that man also becomes a nomadic object subsequent to this cultural mutation. ... One day, you will be able to create an inventory of yourself or others; browse and rummage in the organ department store, consume other people as objects and change into another body or spirit. (1992, p. 116)

Now I would like to go back to the beginning of this text, to Skyper, the word that dropped its "r" so that it could enter the stage of the World Wide Web. We can use Skype to overcome distances and hold real-time conversations with the intense quality of analytical sessions. Then again, a disrupted Skype contact can remind us of Echo's punishment; namely that she is forced to speak the words of others again and again, however senseless this may be; her never-ending repeating voice preventing her from taking or giving any comfort or relief from silence.

Just as an echo must repeat itself and cannot be silent, the punishment's distinguishing feature is its immortality: It never ends. Using this metaphor it seems Skype is becoming a punishing superego. In any case, a man-made machine superego cannot be merciful to the human ego. Do we submit because "the digital revolution is irreversible" (Schirrmacher, 2010, p. 1) and because we can no more hold back the impact of technology than we can dismiss the sun or the sky? Talking metaphorically of sky, reminds me of another metaphor—the cloud, a name for repositories of data that are stored in geographically remote data centres that can be accessed via the internet. Again, to the technology neophyte, it sounds uncanny.

Before communication satellites appeared on the scene, stars, angels, spirits, and the gods were to be found in the clouds. In *Clouds*, a comedy by Aristophanes (423 BC) a middle-aged Athenian tells Socrates that he wants to know the truth of the divine and communicate with the deities in the clouds. In the post-modern Western world, we are caught between the clouds of Aristophanes and the clouds of the computer world. Although they are separated by more than 2,000 years, they still have one thing in common. They are there where "... it often seems to be uncanny, when the line between fantasy and reality is blurred, when something real steps out in front of us, which we hitherto had considered fantastic" (Freud, 1919h, p. 244).

Skype, a representative of a man-made digital world that is based on the number line between 0 and 1, is programmed to decide automatically between right and wrong. In contrast, psychoanalysis addresses ambivalence and the constant inner conflict between right and wrong. The computer can only function when the user makes a clear decision: Yes or No. This is in complete contrast to the unconscious, which does not differentiate between contradictions. Yet a function so binary as Skype is asked to support the complexity of psychoanalytic process.

Unlike analysis, Skype guarantees a special identity for eternity. A Skype address is unique and never deleted. Even though there can be anonymity on a large scale, there is also eternal life. Does this give us some narcissistic gratification? Or does its virtual reality abandon us to a new kind of solitude? We can be reached on Skype at all times and everywhere, but we are not actually together, physically present in the same room.

We have lost not only the "r" in Skype but also the bodily presence of analyst and analysand. This negative can also be a positive in some cases in that it can eliminate the threat of physical aggression or potential sexual attacks. "When two bodies come close to each other geographically, this reinforces the sexual (or aggressive) attraction, and simultaneously the visual perception of the overall shape of the other person begins to blur .... Close spatial proximity implies emotional closeness" (Habermas, 1999, p. 64). The gain of reduced threat is countered by the loss of closeness. In analysis by Skype, is it "a dangerous illusion, if in a 'broad present', we are robbed of our physical presence?" (Gumbrecht, 2010, p. 130). It seems that there is danger and opportunity whether the body is present or not. Extreme acts of physical violence including sexual abuse and murder are not a literal possibility as they are in traditional in-person analysis. Skype provides a particularly safe setting that may eliminate the stimulus for passionate declaration, or it may facilitate its expression because there is no possibility of actual violence.

Although we do not share a common physical space, now we can always be reached. Does this spare us the pain of separation? Gumbrecht suggests that "We have replaced the pain of loneliness caused by physical absence with the permanent semi-loneliness of unlimited availability" (2010, p. 130). Does this affect the process of mourning?

Technology as a tool reduces the workload and increases possibilities: it leads to experiences and facilitates processes that without devices would be not simply weakened but would not exist at all. On the downside, the goal of media technology seems to be global reach rather than improved performance (Krämer, 1998). So much interaction across distance in real time is now possible, but what if, sitting at our computers and speaking to each other on Skype, "everything merges into one another, everything is fusion" (Gumbrecht, 2010, p. 130)? How do we differentiate and adapt the technology to our use without fooling ourselves? Turkle (2007) suggests: "As we begin to live with objects that challenge the boundaries between the born and created and between humans and everything else, we will need to tell ourselves different stories" (p. 326). Until then, does technology, the third uncanny party, remain a threat? Technology as a device or apparatus, however useful in some ways, creates artificial worlds. Can and do we want to use this newly created world for psychoanalysis?

References

Aristophanes (423 BC). *Clouds*. http://records.viu.ca/~johnstoi/aristophanes/clouds.html.

Attali, J. (1992). *Millenium*. Düsseldorf, Germany: Econ.

Barlow, J. P. (1996). Cyperspace Independence Declaration. http:www.eff.org/~barlow.

Carr, N. (2010). *The Shallows—What the Internet is Doing to Our Brains*. New York: W. W. Norton.

Carr, N. (2011). Wie das Internet unser denken verändert. In: *Du, 815*, April 2011, pp. 14–21. Zürich, Switzerland: Oliver Prange.

Ellrich, L. (2011). Phänomenologie des Mediengebrauchs. In: A. Ziemann (Ed.), *Medienkultur und Gesellschaftsstruktur*. Wiesbaden, Germany: Springer.

Freud, S. (1919h). The uncanny. *S. E., 17* (pp. 217–256). London: Hogarth.

Gehring, P. (2006). Die Wiederholungs-Stimme. Über die Strafe der Echo [The repeating voice. On the punishment of Echo]. In: D. Kolesch & S. Krämer, *Stimme* [*Voice*]. Frankfurt, Germany: Suhrkamp.

Grampp, S. (2011). *Marshall McLuhan*. Konstanz, Germany: UVK.

Guderian, C. (2004a). *Die Couch in der Psychoanalyse*. Stuttgart, Germany: Kohlhammer.

Guderian, C. (2004b). *Magie der Couch*. Stuttgart, Germany: Kohlhammer.

Gumbrecht, H. (2010). *Unsere breite Gegenwart* [*Our Broad Presence*]. Berlin: Suhrkamp.

Habermas, T. (1999). *Geliebte Objekte* [*Loved Objects*]. Frankfurt, Germany: Suhrkamp.

Herbold, A. (2012). Bezaubernde Siri [*Enchanting Siri*]. In: *Der Tagesspiegel*, January 8, p. 25 (Berlin newspaper).

Krämer, S. (1998). Das Medium als Spur und als Apparat [The medium as trace and apparatus]. In: S. Krämer, *Medien Computer Realität* [*Media, Computer, Reality*]. Frankfurt, Germany: Suhrkamp.

Macho, T. (2006). Stimmen ohne Körper. Anmerkungen zur Technikgeschichte der Stimme [Voices without body. Comments on the technical history of voice]. In: D. Kolesch & S. Krämer, *Stimme* [*Voice*]. Frankfurt, Germany: Suhrkamp.

Newitz, A. (2007). My laptop. In: S. Turkle (Ed.)., *Evocative Objects* (pp. 88–91). Cambridge, MA: Massachusetts Institute of Technology Press.

Peer-to-Peer-Technik, VOIP DSL-Wlan-specials www.voip-information.de/peer-to-peer.php.

Schirrmacher, F. (2010). Preface. In: N. Carr, Wer bin ich, wenn ich online bin … und was macht mein Gehirn solange? Wie das Internet unser Denken verändert. (German edition of *The Shallows*.) Munich, Germany: Blessing.

Skype—http://de.wikipedia.org/w/index.php?title=Skype&oldid=97893968.

Turkle, S. (1995). *Life on the Screen: Identity in the Age of the Internet*. New York: Simon & Schuster.

Turkle, S. (2007). *Evocative Objects*. Cambridge, MA: Massachusetts Institute of Technology Press.

Winnicott, D. W. (1971). *Playing and Reality*. London: Tavistock.

Ziemann, A. (2011). *Medienkultur und Gesellschaftsstruktur* [Media culture and the structure of society]. Wiesbaden, Germany: Springer.

CHAPTER THREE

The computer as metaphor for state of mind

Karen Sharer-Mohatt, PsyD and Jill Savege Scharff, MD

We will present clinical material to show how computer technology that is a substitute for relating can become a vehicle for being understood. Describing frustrating work on the computer reveals the patient's dynamics, his defences, and his relationship to his analysis. As the analyst listens and interacts with him in the language of technology, she sees the computer as a metaphor for his state of mind and his feelings about his treatment and her.

Mr. X is a depressed, divorced man whose only affectionate relationship is with his cat. He has not had a relationship or even a date with a woman since he broke off with a woman he still longs for, but has not contacted since she married another man. An electronics technician, he works too many hours in a boring job repairing electronic equipment in communication devices, and feels too tired and overwhelmed to keep up with the repair projects in his own home. He spends his time on computer programming and games instead of dating and taking care of his home. His greatest pleasure is to retreat into sleep, sometimes for a whole day. He acknowledges how depressed he is, and how hopeless he feels, and having been in therapy twice, he is convinced of the need for analysis but unsure of its value. A man who spends money frugally and mainly on computer products, Mr. X had to calculate his finances and his analyst's worth before making a commitment to analysis. He meets her four times a week, attends regularly, and is now in the early middle phase of analysis. We will now provide vignettes from a series of sessions to show how Mr. X expresses his issues in the language of technology—programs, text, chat, and rebands (changing the frequency on a radio). The analyst will now take over in the first person to present relevant parts of the analytic dialogue interspersed with her unspoken thoughts in italics.

Expressing defence and conflict in computer terminology

Mr. X arrived late for the first session of the week, one week after I had returned from my two-week vacation. I had been surprised at how little reaction there had been to my absence, but in the following sessions I can see that anger is gathering in the transference. In the first session, Mr. X displaces the transference into anger at a missing employee whose assignment on rebands Mr. X must do, in addition to his own repair work. In the second session, he displaces his own despair into the hopeless case of a friend. And in the third session, a dream about a computer helps us get to the point.

Mr. X: Yesterday another person at work was supposed to do rebands, and it looked like it didn't get done. No rebands since Monday of last week. So we've got all the rebands to do now because there's no one on rebands. Tomorrow I'm supposed to talk to the boss about having another guy work on rebands, as it's the first priority to fill in for the person who's gone, the one that does the rebands. And then I still have to do repairs! So I guess it kind of annoyed me. Probably two of us could do it faster than one, but it just kind of annoyed me. Then we got two rush orders, and they want their product back by tomorrow, and that's not going to happen because we haven't even started the order, and I'm covering for the reband guy too! I guess it's bothering me. I feel like one person's trying to weasel his way out of the order. And there's no cost set for it, and so I'm wondering if he doesn't want to do it.

Mr. X is annoyed, apparently by work, and especially at someone who is not there to do his share of the work. Mr. X might well be annoyed at my absence. Thinking that the term rebands may have unconscious significance, I ask him to clarify.

Analyst: What are rebands?
  Mr. X: Basically just changing the frequency the radio operates on. Last year the government decided you can't use that frequency any more. So, people are sending in radios to be changed to a frequency that they can legally use.

I stay with the displacement.

Analyst: So it seems like you're saying things are behind at work.
  Mr. X: Well they are behind! It gets annoying to tell someone when the work will be done and then the variables keep changing on you. And it gets annoying when like last week I was gone, and the other guy didn't do anything with it but watch it pile up. [Pause.] His wife's friend is interested in me again but I'm not interested because I heard she was dating someone just to get money out of him, and that's not right. If you want to date someone just for money, I'll move on.

Mr. X is talking about another woman who is interested, as if to say he is afraid that I am not interested in him, only in his fee.

Analyst: You're talking about variables changing at work and a potential date, but I'm wondering what you might feel is changing here that is annoying to you?

Mr. X: Um, no. I suppose about the only variable here that changes is—when you're out of the office. No, I suppose about the only thing I'd say about that is maybe the variables don't change enough—meaning that, uh, maybe there's a different way to approach this, maybe try something different.

Mr. X gets to the point, and raises the spectre of retaliation because I have been away and he feels that the analysis is not helping him enough and leaving him with too much to do alone. I throw it back on him, feeling a bit retaliatory.

Analyst: Perhaps you're speaking about variables in you that you'd like to change or do differently.

Mr. X: Well, there's things I'd like to change, it's just that, uh, changes take a lot of work and it takes a long, long time to make any changes. And when I'm working more, there's less opportunity to make those changes. [Silence.] Well, I guess I got all quiet on you.

Analyst: Where did you go?

Mr. X: I don't know, just feeling frustrated about things, and talking about it.

Analyst: Well, I hear you saying you're frustrated with these variables in yourself but don't know how to change or don't want to change, which just leads you back to a frustrated place, a stuck-ness, not exciting.

Mr. X: I guess I'm feeling more frustrated about it because I'm just thinking about the things that I could or should do that would not waste money right now but to get there takes time, and nobody else is going to do it for me.

Mr. X gets back to the transference. He is annoyed that he cannot get me to do more for him. Then it is time to stop.

In the second session, Mr. X stays away from the transference. He reflects on the problems he sees in his friend who gambles, wastes money, and does not act on the help he receives, which is annoying to Mr. X. I realise that Mr. X is displacing his feelings about himself onto his friend.

Mr. X began the third session saying that his dreams were telling him that his unconscious was not in favour of his way of dealing with his work issues.

Mr. X: I could remember at least one dream. I remember some kind of object of some sort, either right by my head or my brain, and there might have been multiples of me or this device. I remember trying to use some kind of program on the computer that felt like an old program I was trying to use to text with others and chat with a particular person. It had to be later at night. It almost seems like at a store. I was having issues and it wouldn't let me use it after a certain time frame. I know the cat came up on the bed twice and wanted to be petted but I didn't because I wasn't awake. I remember at one point, like I was holding my breath which caused me to breathe heavily in short breaths, kind of like huh, huh, huh, huh, something like that. [Mr. X associates to the dream for some minutes.]

Analyst: I'm thinking I'm the object in your dream since I sit right by your head, and you're trying to figure out a way to "chat" here and understand what's going on in your mind.

Mr. X: Perhaps.

Analyst: Then you find yourself interrupted by your cat being needy, and then you begin to panic.

Mr. X: Well, I don't know if I panic with the shortness of breath. It's more like a sense of punishing myself. I just feel frustrated and can't do anything about it, and so I get frustrated and angry and sad, and typically it leads to more sleep.

Analyst: Well, sleeping does help you to avoid how needy you might feel.

Mr. X: Yeah. [Silence. He's so still that I wonder if he's asleep. Mr. X sighs, and folds his hands.] Well, I guess I'm sorry. I'm getting angry over the last thing you said.

Analyst: Why would you feel angry about that?

Mr. X: I'm building anger and frustration toward you, and I don't want to do that, and I'm sorry.

Analyst: It's more important that we try and understand it.

Mr. X: Well, yeah, but let's quit tiptoeing around something we've already established, and just whip this thing in the butt instead of going back over what's un-needed.

Analyst: You're right. We need to quit tiptoeing around.

Mr. X: That makes me think *you* think *I'm* tiptoeing around where this thing is going! I suppose it makes me more frustrated because I don't know which way to go with it, so I feel frustration and confusion building, and it's quite annoying. I get enough of that feeling at home, and I don't need that here.

Analyst: Well, the frustration and annoyance and anger you feel have something to do with whether you feel productive at home, and it has to do with what you needed and felt you weren't getting here.

Mr. X: Well, yeah, I agree. What I needed was to be listened to right now, the here and now.

The dream has moved us into the transference. I appreciate that Mr. X has gone from expressing anger at the computer to telling me that he is not getting what he needs from me. He is being much more direct, more able to relate to me as a person rather than to a listening device to receive information about a machine. I am more able to listen to him now.

A device for getting the analyst to take him in while he imagines doing without her

Mr. X moved on from talking about technical problems at work to technical problems at home. He is working with an old system, continually trying to update it to make it current and as functional as possible but runs into difficulties. He longs to have a well functioning integrated computer system, but he is constantly frustrated in his attempts to achieve that. The most recent problem is a glitch in the new data redundancy program. Mr. X cannot leave it alone; and he cannot get it to work. Similarly, he longs to have a relationship with a woman, but he cannot make it work. He got a coupon for a set of free callipers, an instrument he might use to measure the distance between two points. I thought he was using this technical device to refer to gauging closeness and distance in his relationships at work, with friends, and with me. He agreed that he doesn't feel close to people, or to me.

In the next session he was reluctant to speak. At last he spoke of his regret that he cannot be with the woman he loved or any other woman, or feel close to me. His previous therapist had left him in the lurch and a psychiatrist who had given him medication at that time had relocated and transferred him to his replacement. So I said that he had been hesitant to speak, because he feared I would leave also. He agreed.

The next week, Mr. X talked about unsettling physical changes at his place of work. I explored this in the displacement, and then I said that he must have noticed physical changes in my office, which had perhaps left him insecure and hesitant. My desktop computer had crashed and I had placed it in the outer office secretarial space, purchased a new laptop and iPad, and had them installed on my desk. I had seen him looking at the equipment over a couple of days, and it had occurred to me that, given his affinity for computers, he might have had a reaction, but he had not said anything directly about the change. He had, however, been talking about spending hours installing a game from his desktop to his laptop. Mr. X became irritated when I took occasional notes, and asked me to use a digital tape recorder instead of pen and paper, to be sure I got everything down. The following week he referred back to his suggestion concerning the tape recorder.

Mr. X: What happened to the tape recorder idea? A digital recorder works like this. [He described it in such abstruse technical language that I could not get it.] You could use an Apple product instead. I guess they're reliable, work easy, slick, eye appealing. Well I'm definitely not the type who buys the latest technology to look cool. They seem to be more popular than they're worth in my opinion.

This seems aggressive (and perhaps envious) towards me since he must have noticed my new iPad and iPhone.

Mr. X: The iPhone is overpriced for what you get, and the iPad is overpriced and I don't see an application for it. It can't replace the pc laptop or desktop. So that's what I think about it.
Analyst: I wonder if you're waiting for me to pick up more from you to help you, and you feel a bit angry that I haven't.
Mr. X: Yeah, that's a valid statement. I guess my mind is stuck on your Apple products, which should have recording capability. I know my 20.00 mp3 has a recording function. [*He takes his out of his pocket and looks at it.*] Well, this thing looks like it can record over twenty-eight hours' worth. I bought this thing to play music on, and then I can just toss it. I'm not the big fan of listening on headphones. I prefer listening on the full range of speakers for surround sound, but I have really old speakers. The speakers are downstairs, but I'm usually upstairs, and so I don't really listen to it that much.

I'm thinking he is telling me about his resistance to what is in the depths of his mind.

Mr. X: When I moved out of the parents' house and into the duplex, I didn't want to bug the neighbours, and so I put it all downstairs so it would be more containing.

Analyst: Yes, you seem to enjoy the experience of the full range of the music, the sound and volume and the feeling of the music, but then your life changed and you put both it and yourself away and haven't been able to get it back to enjoy.

Mr. X: Well yeah, I've got all the parts. There are lots of adjustments to make with the wiring set up.

I feel encouraged that he is going to try to reintegrate the parts of himself that might bring him satisfaction. I listen to see how he will do this.

Mr. X: I may need to retune or recalibrate with the sound and the laser power. The play station connections are kind of intermittent. I may need another optical cable, and I know the sub has a function on it and basically I'd have to have it in standby mode to connect from the receiver. I usually have to re-plug the power to use it. So there's another little problem, and another problem is hooking to the television because the picture is fuzzy, and I have to figure that out at some point.

Analyst: Like dealing with electrical equipment, you were working on the fine tuning of your mind to help you understand and function better.

Mr. X: I can't see myself getting to do it, especially when that would be on my own.

Analyst: You say "on my own" but I'm sitting right here!

He throws cold water on my formulation, and I feel pushed away. I am glad he is working on putting his mind together, but I notice that he wants to feel independent of me and my ideas or perhaps he wants to defeat them.

The use of a computer to deny loss and reorganise the mind

Some months later, Mr. X came for his Friday session visibly distressed. He had a call from his mother warning him that his grandmother's health had deteriorated and that she had been transferred to a hospital, where it was expected that she had very little time left before her death. Mr. X sounded very sad, and fell silent through the remainder of the session. I got the impression that he, thinking that he was wasting my time, couldn't believe that I would sit with him in his sadness and grief. I said that the loss of his grandmother was bringing up some powerful feelings. Mr. X explained curtly that it was pulling up the loss of the woman he loved. He didn't want to feel the feelings. He would prefer to go home to sleep away the day.

On Tuesday (his first session after the weekend) I learned that, over the weekend, Mr. X's grandmother had died. His employer gave him three days of compassionate leave. Mr. X came to his first session of the week, which came after the funeral, formally dressed. He had obviously been crying. There were many silences throughout the session. When I asked him where his mind was, he said that it was with the woman he had lost to another man. He told me more about her than he had until then. I felt that he was closer to me than usual.

On Wednesday he reported on a breakfast with family members. He was surprised and embarrassed to note sexual feelings towards his first cousin, a woman he had not seen since childhood. He felt that his conversation was forced as he tried to deflect this feeling of arousal. I thought that he was surprised to be drawn to life and longing for closeness to this cousin and to his lover. I thought he felt similarly drawn to me but I was not ready to interpret the positive transference.

On Thursday Mr. X did not show for his session, and he did not call or leave a message.

From relationship with computer to personal relationship via mourning

On Friday of the same week, Mr. X referred to the missed session.

Mr. X: Well, I think I erred. I basically forgot all about it. I had to get my licence renewed, did that, and basically sat in front of the computer all day. So there's no reason I wasn't here yesterday. I had things with the computer I wanted to accomplish, so yeah, that was about it. He fell silent.

Analyst: What did you accomplish with the computer?

Mr. X: [Speaking excitedly] I guess there were a couple things I wanted to do. I wanted to get up and running on the laptop an old game program I used to enjoy. A long time ago, I wanted to do it on the other computer, but I wasn't able to do it. The operating system wouldn't work. I needed it to get it fixed so that the game could run. I wanted to see if I could tell the system to delete one game off the hard drive and then bring back up the old game I needed. So, that's what I had in mind. Pretty much what I did yesterday was work on the computer, and I got a lot accomplished.

Analyst: So you feel more organised now.

Mr. X: Well, nobody else can see it, though. Do I feel more organised? No, not really. Huh … um … well, I guess I feel spent with that subject.

Analyst: Well, certainly the loss of a loved one has a big impact on your emotions and on your mind. So you used your leave to reorganise your computer, and I think to reorganise your upset mind.

Mr. X: Well, yes. [Silence.]

Analyst: I also wondered if experiencing your sadness here with me on Wednesday night made you feel close to me, and if that made it difficult to come back here the next day?

Mr. X: I don't think so. I don't think I was thinking of anything else but the computer, and so everything else was out the window. I hadn't planned on skipping yesterday. I guess I feel stuck on what to say next.

Analyst: Take your time, and let's see what comes to your mind.

Mr. X: Well, the thing that comes to mind is, listening to the conservative Republican bias I get at work. That is annoying at times. I wish we could get rid of money problems. Maybe society wouldn't have to put a man-made burden on ourselves and suffer through economic cycles. I was thinking, when everything is paid for, how much better life felt.

Analyst: I wonder if you felt unburdened yesterday?

Mr. X: Well, at times the burden wasn't there. I guess that was about the only burden I felt less of yesterday. I was thinking if I had to deal with the government debt issue, how would I proceed with it? I'd probably push for increasing taxes and cutting every area of spending. And I guess earlier today I was thinking about finding somebody in life I could do things with. I don't know if there's another person out there that would fit that description for what I'm thinking of, or I don't have any idea of how to look for such a person.

Analyst: I think you're talking about unburdening yourself of the emotional debt you've been carrying so you can get out there and make yourself available to someone who might want to spend time with you.

Mr. X: Well, I know work won't ease that burden type feeling, just make it worse. Hmm. I don't know if getting out there would really solve it, but that's one thing I'm thinking of.

Analyst: I think Wednesday night you began to get in touch with something very powerful, something that was burdening you emotionally and you had to move away from it and reorganise yourself before you could come back here.

Mr. X: Wednesday, I guess I had a little bit different feeling than I've had for a while. Now I am asking if there's another person out there who is basically in search of somebody like I'm in search of somebody, a person who wants to accomplish something, give and receive. I'd help them as they would help me. Instead of sitting in front of the computer by myself and not doing much, I could accomplish something that would actually have some meaning.

Regression to the defensive relationship to the computer

A month later, Mr. X is again preoccupied with his computer problems.

Mr. X: Since I screwed up on the one computer, this weekend, I'm going to have to redo everything again. Sometime last week I found this one driver that actually would work with a new version of DOS [Disk Operating System]. The DOS I had on there didn't work for some reason. So then I thought I'd just switch to the other DOS, and in doing that I did a couple things I didn't think would cause any issue but it screwed up and booted into Windows, and, long story short, I couldn't get into Windows, and basically I ended up having to reload everything that I've kind of been doing on and off for the last three to four months. [Pause.]

Analyst: It sounds like you've been trying to find the most effective disk operating system to organise your information, and from time to time information changes, so then you feel perhaps another system would work better. That is like what we do here. We are looking at the DOS of your mind and working with it to understand how it's operating, and how it's going to operate the best.

Mr. X: Well. I couldn't make it perfect but only as clean as possible. With the computer, I just feel like I'm restarting all the time. And I've had this computer since 2005, and I've had in my mind exactly what I wanted to do with it but I screw it up and keep on restarting. I want to have these different operating systems on there so that this operating system can interface with that operating system, and I can say this works with that, and that makes it the hub for everything else—not a server but something like that. I have all my files on it so basically all my computers can access all the files.

Analyst: I'm thinking that it's actually a server that you've been trying to access or create for some time now. What do you see is the function of a server?

Mr. X: A server is basically to store data, and send data out to computers.

Analyst: I'm thinking that a server is like a mother that stores up a lot of information and then dishes it out to her kids, spouse, or family members when they need it.

Mr. X: Sure.

Analyst: And I'm thinking that you've been disappointed with some of the servers in your life, whether it was your mom, or the computer, or the woman you loved and lost, or even me at some times when the information we need hasn't been shared so you could access it and use it.

Mr. X: Well I'd say that's valid.

Analyst: And when that happens, I think you really experience the loss and the emptiness and despair that you were talking about yesterday because you can't access what you really want to get from the server.

Mr. X: Yeah, that's … I can see that, but is there any point to what you're saying? It's not stimulating anything in my mind. I just don't see what to really do with it. I guess it just doesn't do much for me.

Analyst: I think you are anxious about not being able to access, for example, what the server can give out.

Mr. X: I'll accept what you're saying. Right before you talked about that, I was responding to a couple of images from unpleasant dreams last night that popped up in my head and could be a part of it. The first part that popped in my mind is moving sets of scenery with Christmas lights. When I was younger I wasn't able to participate in that because my parents didn't let me. In the next image, I was frozen and then I was trying to get to this certain place in the next state. A man who tried to help me thought the only way to do this was to break into this old radio station that I used to work at, but it was closed. Then we got arrested, and I was like in jail for a long while. Then I was running to a city by a lake, running for some reason, and I got into a bad part of town, running and getting shot at.

As we worked on the dream, Mr. X's association led us to think of the first dream with the holiday scenery as an expression of his feeling that his parents would not let him be a part of something he wanted to fill himself up with but could not. In the next dream he was frozen, but with help he could move into another state.

Mr. X: The man thought that a break-in was the only way to get into the other state. I don't think I ever made it in the dream, and tonight I'm not really getting anything out of this. I'm trying to think about what you're saying that I can apply to my issues in life, but as we've been going along here I've been—not really dismissing you but—not really taking it with me and doing anything with it.

Analyst: You feel that you just can't access it, can't make that function work to get to a place of sharing joy or getting to a new state. You're also talking about how you do access what I give you here, but it doesn't connect in a way that you can use. You've been telling me for the last few months about how difficult it is to connect and how painful it is when you can't feel a sense of connection or aliveness.

Mr. X: It's there basically every day.

Mr. X now has three computers that he has been working on trying to enable them to communicate with one another. One computer is a remote access computer, one is a central processor, and one is the data gatherer/organiser. To me these computers represent three parts or aspects of his self. I feel that the data organiser/gatherer is more present than the remote access computer part of him, both of them controlled by the central processor. Mr. X believes it is the remote access computer that is here with me in sessions but I think that it is a vulnerable and fearful part of him that must be protected through distancing.

I said to Mr. X that I thought this set-up represents three parts of him and that the part that I present in the session is really the data gatherer whose function it is to collect and organise data about his life circumstances so he can progress. This is what he thinks he wants from me—ideas or data. But his efforts have been frustrated by me because that is not what analysis deals with. I told him that I am trying to understand the central processor and that his struggle with me has been like a negative feedback loop created by the data gatherer/remote access part of himself. So there we are again talking about our relationship in the terms of computer technology. Mr. X makes progress towards human relationships and engagement in his domestic life at home and with friends, but at this stage of analysis, he slips back to the safer world of the computer.

Summary

Vignettes in narrative and dialogue illustrate the frequent use of computer terminology in an analysand's discourse. The analyst responds to the terminology as a metaphor for the analysand's defensive structure, his difficulty with the organisation of his mind, his expectations of analysis, and his way of relating in the transference. The analyst interacts in the language of technology, works in the displacement, and gradually interprets the unconscious parallel between aspects of the computer and parts of his mind.

In the year after this vignette was written, the analytic work would continue moving back and forth from Mr. X's defensive retreat of immersion in his computer and greater awareness of and connection to his analyst. Mr. X moved from the computer as the source of his frustration, to his parents, analysis, and analyst as disappointing objects. As the analyst accepted and contained Mr. X's negative maternal transference, he could access positive feelings for her, which brings hope for his eventually feeling able to express complex feelings in relationship to a woman friend with whom he might hope to develop an intimate relationship.

CHAPTER FOUR

Internet pornography as a source of marital distress

Sue Cebulko, PhD

The relationships married women have with their pornography using husbands are complex and complicated. Wives and husbands engage in a continuous cycle of discovery, confrontation, demands for change, ultimatums, extraction of promises of change, forgiveness, and return to relative peace. Husbands and wives maintain a state of denial, except when crises of compulsion, discovery, and betrayal break through until reassurance and forgiveness re-establish the status quo and the cycle is reinforced. All the women struggle internally and externally with this issue. It impacts their spiritual, emotional, sexual, intellectual, and relational lives.

When I made my study of these relationships (Cebulko, 2007) I focused on wives of pornography using men, and I employed a psychodynamic perspective to study and increase the depth of my understanding of the experiences of wives whose husbands use the internet for pornography. I found that many of these women had experiences of traumatic developmental interferences that seemed to hinder their efficacy in managing their lives. From the beginning of the relationship, the women managed not to acknowledge early indications of their partners' sexual proclivities and other compulsive activities. Untreated trauma and individual personality characteristics influenced both the choice of spouse and the inability to disengage from problematic marital dynamics. Once married, and faced with the reality of pornography, the wife tended to focus her concern specifically on the husband's internet pornography use, even when he was engrossed in other sexually related activities and numerous other compulsions.

Characterological issues contribute to each individual's inability to alter the marital dynamic. The couple converts a multifaceted, long-standing emotional, intrapsychic, and interpersonal problem into a concrete symptom. Compulsive internet pornography combines individual vulnerability and marital dysfunction and affords one half of the marital couple an opportunity to categorise the other as the identified patient. Like any obsessional symptom, compulsive internet use needs to be unpacked and understood in terms of the individual dynamics of each member of the couple and its function for the couple. Falling for the couple's focus on internet pornography as the central problem distracts the therapist from exploring and understanding the underlying issues.

On pornography

Pornography refers to any "written, graphic, or oral depictions of erotic subjects intended to arouse sexual excitement in the audience" (Microsoft Encarta Encyclopedia, 1997). Stoller (1991) defines pornography as "material produced with the intent to excite erotically" (p. 1984). Less obviously pornographic romance novels qualify as pornography under this definition because women use them to excite themselves. Pornography is not about intimacy, but about a physical manipulation of one's body and the other's bodily organs (Khan, 1979). Cybersex refers to individual sexual arousal through the use of the internet. Cybersex behaviours include viewing and downloading pornographic material and/or illegal or deviant sexual images, visiting sexually oriented chat rooms, exchanging sexually explicit email, exchanging visual images via digital cameras, and engaging in interactive online affairs. The cybersex consumer may be involved in activities with opposite sex or same sex individuals.

Pornography has existed in Western civilisation since the Greek and Roman periods. The contemporary heterosexual pornography business began with the publication of *Playboy* in 1953. With the growth of the internet, pornography has mushroomed into a multi-billion dollar industry. Between 2005 and 2008, 75 million viewers accessed adult websites (http://theweek.com/article/index/204156/the-internet-porn-epidemic-by-the-numbers, accessed January 10, 2012). Pornography use has been considered from the perspectives of morality (Perkins, 1997), domination and oppression of women (Dines, Jenson & Russo, 1998), and violation of women's civil rights (Dworkin, 1989), all of which assume that women are victims and men are unable to control their sexuality. With the rise of internet pornography, most research that examines the issue from an addiction perspective (Carnes, Delmonico, Griffin & Moriarty, 2001; Schneider, 2002a) argues that individuals become addicted to the sexual stimulation of the internet much as one becomes addicted to drugs or alcohol. In this model there is an addict and a co-addict. Treatment is prescribed for both addict and co-addict based on recovery from the addiction.

The majority of the focus has been on the male compulsive user (Carnes, Delmonico, Griffin & Moriarty, 2001; Schneider, 2002), on particular types of sexual behaviour (Almodóvar & Yanof, 2005), and on negative effects on spouses and families (Manning, 2006; Schneider, 2000a, 2000b). Most studies have examined the interest in internet pornography using an addiction model (Carnes, Delmonico, Griffin & Moriarty, 2001; Schneider, 2000a, 2002; Young, 2000).

Studies which focus exclusively on internet pornography as an addiction do not provide an in-depth understanding of individual human behaviour, unconscious motives, or the role that compulsive use of internet pornography may play in a marital relationship. The studies expand and enhance the role the brain plays in understanding cybersex use. However, centring on compulsive sexual behaviours as addictions may obscure other important information such as each individual's underlying pathology and untreated trauma associated with sexual, emotional, and physical abuse related to developmental failures and parental deficits.

Recently, researchers have begun to examine cybersex from a systemic perspective (Bird, 2006; Whitty & Quigley, 2008). These studies expand the inquiry to consider the individual in the context of the family as an emotional unit, use a psychodynamic approach, and provide options for clinical interventions. Other researchers are investigating therapists' perceptions of the problem (Goldberg, Peterson, Rosen & Sara, 2008), and therapists' treatment decisions (Hertlein & Piercy, 2008).

More psychodynamic investigation is taking place as theorists seek to understand the complexity of compulsive internet use. Dryer and Lijtmaer (2007) analyse a clinical case from a psychodynamic perspective on intimacy, separation, and sadomasochistic object relating in order to understand the meaning and function of cybersex for the patient. Wood (2006, 2011) argues that a psychoanalytic perspective brings insight into the aetiology and psychodynamics of individuals. She traces the escalating trend in accessing cybersex, and explores what internet sex offers to the unconscious mind. In agreement with Dryer and Lijtmaer (2007), she notes that internet sex offers a flight from the anxieties of intimacy, invites part object relating, and becomes a vehicle for the expression of sadism. She adds that internet sex fuels manic defences.

Kalman (2008) is also interested in an analytic understanding of internet pornography as seen in individual male users in the clinical population. He reviews the relevant psychoanalytic literature on pornography with a special interest in Stoller (1975, 1985, 1991). He reports on four cases that emphasise the subjective experience of the male users but he does not offer an analytic understanding of the unconscious mind. He notes the destructive effect of internet pornography on the marital relationship but he does not expand on understanding. Miliner's study (2008) focuses on couples who seek both emotional and physical intimacy. The study is interested in the male user and his internal dynamics, but does not explore the internal dynamics of the woman or the function of the symptom in the relationship. These studies broaden the dialogue beyond the addiction perspective, yet remain focused on the individual user. With exceptions, few studies examine internet pornography and the marital relationship from a psychodynamic perspective.

Women's experiences of husbands' internet pornography use

Women in the study and in my clinical practice express a feeling of being helplessly entangled in their husbands' use of internet pornography as though something is happening to them. They try various means to effect change, usually to no avail, and experience themselves caught in a repetitive cycle of conflict over which they feel a loss of control. This cycle consists of numerous discoveries of pornography, confrontations with husbands, demands that the men quit, and being appeased. However, the husbands are unable to keep their promises and the pornography use continues. Some wives attempt to ignore the behaviour. Others monitor the computer history, argue about the material, and bargain with the husband. Some go into investigative mode, using detective software to reveal cybersex activities, while others control computer access and police the porn websites. Some wives increase the frequency of sexual activity and their repertoire of sexual activities, but many withdraw from the relationship. Some wives retaliate by spending money or engaging in extramarital affairs, and others generate conflict about issues seemingly unrelated to their husbands' internet activity. Many women confront their husbands directly only after the children are exposed to the material. Rarely do women confide in others due to intense shame about their spouse's use of pornography.

Often women defend against any knowledge of their husband's behaviours by denial. Others know of their husband's internet behaviours, but disavow that knowledge (Goldberg, 1999), which allows them to tolerate their husband's activity and continue in the relationship. Many women describe what is happening to them in the language of addictions treatment and so they believe that the husband has the problem, over which husband and wife have no power. The individual will attend a twelve-step programme for support, but these programmes produce mixed results.

The women in my study (Cebulko, 2007) reported histories of early trauma, some pre-Oedipal and some Oedipal. They and their husbands came from chaotic families with physical, sexual, and emotional boundary violations, infidelity, divorce, alcohol and drug use, and parents who were absent because of divorce, death, mental illness, or preoccupation with careers. Parents were emotionally or physically absent, over-involved in children's lives, abused alcohol or drugs, had extramarital affairs, and exhibited violent behaviour. In short, their parents were unable to establish optimal conditions necessary for normative development.

Each time a wife discovers pornography she finds herself caught in a cycle of confronting, extracting confessions, threatening the spouse with ultimatums, and obtaining promises of change. It is a sadomasochistic dynamic (Akhtar, 2003). Wanting to feel hopeful about transformation, wives tend to forgive their husbands prematurely (Akhtar, 2003) before the trauma has been internally processed In other words, forgiveness is used as a defence against trauma and as a way to bind anger. Forgiveness appears to be a compromise formation that helps to manage aggressive impulses and superego prohibitions. The women in my study and in my clinical practice absolve their husbands multiple times believing this would eventually transform a disappointing relationship into a good relationship. This forgiveness gives rise to increased hope which then drives repeated attempts at forgiving perceived injuries.

Hope can be a positive attribute as it contributes to meaning in life and inspiration but hope is pathological when it serves a defensive function and impedes the executive function of the ego. Hope is "permeated with ambivalence, with conflict" (Searles, 1979, p. 479), and is often devoted to destructive ends. Just as too little hope leads to despair, too much hopefulness can be maladaptive. Pathological hope is an attempt to hang on tenaciously to the idealised, embellished vision of one's mother, longing for a return to the symbiosis of the mother-infant relationship (Akhtar, 1999). Women's inabilities to extricate themselves from the cycle may be interpreted as an unsuccessful search for a responsive object that can fill a void. The repetition of the cycle and the behaviours involved can be seen as hopeful attempts by the wife to find an object that will mitigate previous disappointments, meet the unmet needs, and help resolve the conflict.

Clinical examples

I will present two cases of couples dealing with a husband's use of internet pornography. The first example comes from a couple treated in weekly marital counselling over a period of five years, while the second case, in which there was additional sexual symptomatology, comes from individual therapy with the wife, augmented by occasional couple sessions. Both cases demonstrate that while internet pornography was the initial problem, each individual had untreated early trauma, disrupted psychosexual development, and personality characteristics to be factored into the marital dynamic. In each case, the woman's individual perversions aligned with the husband's interest in pornography and other perversions.

Jack and Leslie

Jack and Leslie, a couple in their mid-thirties, have been married for fourteen years and have three children under the age of seven. Both parents work full time, Leslie weekends and Jack weekdays, which means that opportunities for being together are restricted. Periodically Jack surfs the web looking for internet pornography. Several times Leslie has stumbled onto his pornography and each time has been furious. After many discoveries and confrontations over the years, the couple came in for marital therapy. Leslie claimed she was ready for a divorce while Jack was desperate to save the marriage. For Leslie, Jack's behaviour was felt to be as much of an affair as the many extramarital affairs her father had.

As children, Leslie and Jack had both been exposed to sexual material beyond their capacity for understanding: Jack had been sexually molested and Leslie had to endure her father's numerous affairs. Jack's childhood was marked by having a critical mother who kept her cancer secret and who attempted suicide, and by being subject to bullying at school. His parents were absorbed in each other. Leslie's father was emotionally and physically absent and her mother was preoccupied with her own problems and depression. Leslie was a disappointment to her father as she was not a boy. Jack was a disappointment to his mother for being a boy. Their parents were preoccupied with their own concerns and unable to attend consistently to their children's psychosexual developmental needs.

Jack and Leslie each wanted to avoid the pain of earlier neglect and trauma. Jack was lax in assuming household and parental responsibilities. It was Leslie's job both to encourage him to be assertive and to keep him in line. Like the women in the research study, on discovering Jack's porn use, Leslie immediately took charge of his behaviour and insisted that he get help at their church. She password-protected the computer, frequently checked the history, and installed software to monitor his computer activity. Jack's porn use afforded Leslie the opportunity to demonstrate her competence and his incompetence.

Treating Jack like a naughty child and frequently expressing her displeasure at his passivity and incompetence, Leslie carried the overt aggression for the couple, while Jack expressed his aggression in a passive manner, leaving pornography in prominent places for Leslie to discover and refusing to talk about her reactions. Leslie was the seemingly powerful phallic woman while Jack seemed emotionally castrated by her power.

Leslie and Jack had a moderately successful treatment. The major dynamic of Leslie's domineering attitude towards Jack and his retreat into helplessness did not completely evaporate. However, the couple was able to begin to recognise and then talk about the pattern. Interestingly enough, the pornography problem only surfaced one time during marital therapy. Leslie desperately wanted to get pregnant and have a fourth child. Despite Jack's financial as well as emotional concerns, she decided to remove her IUD and get pregnant. The night prior to

Leslie's appointment with her gynaecologist, Jack once again accessed pornography. This time Leslie heard Jack very clearly and she did not keep the appointment. We processed Jack's desperate attempt to get Leslie to listen to him and Leslie's difficulty in responding to words rather than behaviour. Eventually the couple agreed to a fourth child and Leslie gave birth.

Sam and Maya

Maya and Sam, both in their early forties, have been married for fifteen years. They are raising three children, and they both work long hours in sales. Maya and Sam met on vacation and immediately began a sexual relationship. Returning from vacation they moved in together and within a year were married. Then they found that they had infertility issues and Maya had to endure numerous invasive procedures before she could conceive. They now have three children in elementary school. The youngest child has serious food allergies that require rigid dietary restrictions and frequent trips to hospital as an emergency.

Nine years ago Maya discovered that Sam had been accessing pornography on the internet. This was not the first discovery of his interest in porn, but the timing of this one was devastating to her. Before she could confront him, Maya went into labour. The day after the birth of her child, her father died. She reports that she was in shock throughout the week of the funeral. Later Maya spoke to Sam about the pornography, but he reassured her that it was not a problem. Wanting to believe him, Maya put the incident out of her mind just as she had done on previous occasions. Over the years the pornography problem resurfaced and each time Maya was able to disavow it. Not until Sam's arrest for soliciting did she begin to allow it to register more clearly. Maya and Sam went to their parish priest and for the first time she disclosed sexual abuse that occurred between the ages of four and nine. Sam and Maya began couple therapy with a sex addiction specialist. After several months of conjoint sessions, the sex addiction therapist declared that the marriage was fine and that each partner should continue individual work. Once in individual therapy with me, she disclosed that she had been sexually abused from the age of four to nine, and date raped twice while in college. She feels responsible for all these sexual encounters. The sexual assaults had never been thought or talked about in the intervening years. After disclosing these traumas in therapy, Maya began drinking excessively and taking Xanax to manage anxiety. While intoxicated she was able to write in her journal about her traumas. Within several months of treatment she stopped both the drinking and the prescription medication.

During the past six years of therapy, more and more details have emerged about the rapes and the molestation. At age four, Maya told her mother that a relative touched her inappropriately. Her mother spoke to the relative and the molesting ceased temporarily, only to be resumed at a later date. The two families continued to socialise on a regular basis. Her mother's neglect and the continued abuse meant that Maya learned to pretend that nothing was out of order and she withdrew.

Maya is closed off to her own affect, unable to put into words what she is feeling. She sits rigidly on the couch, often holding her breath. Several months into therapy she began noticing that she was "not there" during sex. Dissociating to a corner of the bedroom ceiling, Maya goes through the motions of sex, unable to be present. She has never been orgasmic and wonders what it is like. Maya does not think that Sam notices her "not being there". Retrospectively, she realises that she also dissociated during previous sexual encounters, lying passively waiting for the sexual encounter to be done, as she did when waiting for the sexual molestation to be over.

Periodically Maya and Sam come in together to talk about a specific issue in the marriage. In the first joint sessions, Sam sat miserably slumped on the couch. He was open about his problems and took responsibility for the state of the marriage. He expressed the wish that Maya would be more passionate with him, indicating that he knew she was not present during sex. Sam also suffered early trauma from an alcoholic, abusive father, early exposure to his father's pornography, and an emotionally absent mother who denied his father's alcoholism and abuse, and molestation. Two of his siblings have substance addictions. Sam self identifies as a sex addict and periodically attends a twelve-step programme. The marital therapist suggested that Maya attend a twelve-step for spouses of sex addicts but she found these meetings more traumatising than helpful.

Neither Sam nor Maya has been able to deal with the early childhood trauma. Maya's dissociation and repressed affect feels like abandonment to Sam and re-creates his early maternal experiences with a mother who was not emotionally present. His desperate attempts to get a response from Maya are seen in his accessing pornography and engaging in other sexual enactments. Indeed, his arrest generated a dramatic response from Maya; she kicked him in his genitals and punched him viciously in a shoulder that was already injured. Sam's arrest appeared to be the impetus for Maya remembering her own trauma. Maya focuses more on Sam's problem than on her own trauma, believing that if she can control his activities, she will be safe.

Discussion

Both couples presented with internet pornography use as the dominant problem. Leslie and Jack used the incidences of Jack's internet searches as another way in which to avoid the pain of earlier trauma and experiences of intimacy. The internet pornography problem for Maya and Sam was more pathological as Sam's interest expanded beyond internet activity and included actual contact with prostitutes. Like Leslie and Jack, they too used Sam's perversions as a way to avoid the pain of earlier trauma as well as current opportunities for intimacy.

Leslie and Jack are unable to come together and form an intimate connection. Leslie is frightened of her own dependency needs, projecting them onto Jack who then acts in irresponsible ways. Both Leslie and Jack are able to disavow painful childhood trauma and neglect by sustaining marital disagreement. However, this also means they remain immobilised in a conflicted arrangement and perpetuate trauma on each other.

The early sexual trauma experienced by Sam and Maya is far more severe, thus hampering their ability to experience marital connection. Maya closes off her painful affect through dissociation, while Sam avoids pain and depression by engaging in sexual enactments. Sam holds the couple's desire for passion, while Maya contains the split off affect for both of them. Prior to any discovery of pornography, Sam and Maya never fought. Not only did they not argue, they failed to discuss any problems in the relationship. For the offence of viewing pornography, Maya ejects Sam from the bedroom. For soliciting a prostitute and being arrested, Maya evicted Sam from the house—only to let him return home and into the bedroom. Maya struggles with the question of staying married or obtaining a divorce as if that were the only answer. For Sam and Maya, there is a behaviour and a consequence, but no discussion of their issues.

For all four individuals, pre-Oedipal and Oedipal disruptions affect their ability to develop intimacy, self efficacy, and the capacity for whole object relatedness. Neither Leslie nor Maya believe they can significantly influence their husbands. They both view their spouses as having all the control. Both report feeling victimised by their spouses. In turn, the husbands feel mistreated by their wives—Jack by Leslie's anger and control and Sam by Maya's lack of passion and withdrawal.

The internal object relationships of each individual in the marital dyad affect and colour the couple's present interactions. Both couples grew up in families where their primary caregivers failed to provide good enough care and thus affected psychosexual development. For Maya and Sam, pre-Oedipal development was compromised, while for Jack and Leslie, Oedipal development was adversely affected. The relational template laid down in early infancy and childhood became the foundation for future adult relationships that did not offer any of the individuals fulfilling marriages.

Both couples struggle with intimacy. Deep and lasting relations between two people require that both have the capacity for empathy and understanding for one's self and for the other (Kernberg, 1995). Intimacy is a component in mature sexual love in which each partner can experience and maintain an exclusive love relation with the other. None of the individuals in these marital dyads seemed able to connect in deep and lasting ways. Failure in development complicated the ability for object relatedness, closeness, and intimacy. Intimacy in the marital dyad increased after each disclosure about internet pornography use. The wives were furious with their husbands, but at least they were talking to each other in more real ways than they could do prior to discovery. The gratification of these moments of connection around discovery and confrontation preserved and perpetuated the cycle.

As a defence against authentic contact, the couple relationships take on a sadomasochistic organisation. Sadism is the "most common and the most significant of all the perversions" (Freud, 1905d, p. 157). The aim of the sadistic impulse is the gratification of the unconscious need for self-punishment stemming from guilt over forbidden sexual impulses. Freud (1933) links sadism with masculinity and masochism with femininity, but they occur together in the same individual. Although it is tempting to view the female half of the couple as masochistic in tolerating the acting out behaviour in the spouse, this view is incomplete. There are sadistic and masochistic elements in husband and in wife. For instance, when Leslie criticises and punishes Jack, she is in the sadistic position, and when he retaliates by leaving pornography around to upset Leslie, he is in the sadistic position, the other partner in each case being required to submit to the sadistic attack. Maintaining this sadomasochistic cycle the couple can continue to flee from the anxiety of the relationship and their own emotional pain. Sam experiences Maya's lack of passion as abandoning and harsh. He turns to sexual acting out as antidote to the resulting depression and as retaliation against the abandoning object (Wood, 2011). However, Maya's response to most of his behaviours is to shut down and withdraw, which only aggravates his feeling of abandonment and drives him to further solace. Not until Sam was arrested for soliciting did Maya respond with anger, thus providing him with the passion he longed for.

Maya's physically sadistic action towards Sam actually brought him satisfaction, as it secured an intense reaction from a woman who was generally disengaged.

Wood (2011) comments that compulsive use of the internet fuels manic defences. Agreeing with Segal (1975), Wood states that when manic defences are used, "… feelings of dependency and vulnerability are replaced by control, triumph and contempt" (p. 130). The women in my study and in my clinical practice use the manic defence in a similar manner. While focusing on husbands' behaviour, spying, collecting evidence, and monitoring internet activity, the wives can avoid attending to their own trauma. Leslie and Maya, like many of the women in the study, are depressed. Focus on the husbands and manic activity (Leslie's arguing and Maya's computer spying) temporarily ward off depression.

Leslie and Maya feel betrayed, as if their husbands had engaged in affairs. Both focus on the lack of ability to trust. Yet neither woman has experiences of truly trusting another. They could not trust their parents, and now they cannot trust their husbands. They project their original distrust onto the new object in the marital relationship. Like the women I interviewed for the study, Leslie and Maya have hidden perversions of their own which are parallel to those of their husbands. The concept of perversions has expanded in the last two decades and now defines particular types of relationships or psychological organisations. It is no longer seen as an individual issue but a relationship issue, a defence against object-relatedness (Parsons, 2000), and a "sexualization of the avoidance of mutuality" (Parsons, 2000, p. 46).

In perverse relationships one sees a lack of respect for the other (Parsons, 2000). People are related to as if they are simply part objects (McDougall, 1986). In perverse relationships harm to the other is either consciously or unconsciously entertained (McDougall 1986; Stoller, 1975). Sexualisation of relationships is a feature of perversion and can be used to defend against painful affect (Blos, 1991). Addressing perversion in an individual, Glasser (1986) discusses its function.

Clinical and social observation shows us that both sadism and masochism engage the object in an intense relationship, but on the uncompromising condition that intimacy and union are never present. Through sadomasochism, the individual establishes a firm grip on the object, but this grip also entails keeping the object at arm's length (Glasser 1986, p. 10). The sadomasochist aspect of the perversions for each member of the couple appears to be to keep the object at arm's length. The women perversely attempt to control the object and thus the relationship, and at the same time maintain distance. The husbands engage in the perverse behaviours with a virtual object as a way to avoid actually being in a relationship with an actual object.

The focus of treatment is not to control the symptom, but to understand how the defences work and to help the couple understand and talk about the relational pattern. The women in the study and in the clinical cases were embroiled in the cycle "that just keeps happening". The theoretical implications of the study strongly suggest that an inability to effect change in the marital relationship is grounded in early infant caretakers' failures to meet essential needs. Furthermore, later childhood traumas caused by boundary violations negatively impact development. Derailed development and trauma impede self-agency, that ability to take responsibility for one's own behaviours, make decisions, carry out actions, and expect consequences. Intimacy is impaired by these developmental challenges. Participants use defences of dissociation, pathological hope, and premature forgiveness in their attempts to manage and cope with the marital situation.

The wives in the study and in clinical practice find that their husbands' use of internet pornography causes intrapsychic distress and is a major disruption in the marriage. Drawing on clinical experience to augment my research study findings gives a more complex understanding of the marital relationship and the contribution of each individual's dynamics. In the case of the two couples, pornography was the symptom that was used to maintain the status quo for the individuals and the marriage and avoid a more intimate connection. Compulsive internet use is a conversion by the couple of a complex and longstanding individual and combined emotional problem to an apparently individual symptom. To focus exclusively on the compulsion hampers understanding of the couple's dynamics and obscures underlying difficulties. The therapist who would treat compulsive pornography use needs to retranslate the language embedded in the symptom and connect it to the marital dynamics and childhood histories of the couple. Compulsive pornography use must be understood within the complexity of the marital relationship.

References

Akhtar, S. (1999). *Inner Torment: Living between Conflict and Fragmentation*. Northvale, NJ: Jason Aronson.

Akhtar, S. (2003). *New Clinical Realms: Pushing the Envelope of Theory and Technique*. Northvale, NJ: Jason Aronson.

Almodóvar, P. & Yanof, J. A. (2005). Perversion in *La Mala Educación* [*Bad Education*] (2004). *International Journal of Psychoanalysis*, 86: 1715–1724.

Bird, M. (2006). Sexual addiction and marriage and family therapy: Facilitating individual and relationship healing through couple therapy. *Journal of Marital & Family Therapy*, 32(3): 297–311.

Blos, P., Jr. (1991). Sadomasochism and the defense against recall of painful affect. *Journal of the American Psychoanalytic Association*, 39: 417–430.

Carnes, P., Delmonico, D., Griffin, E. & Moriarty, R. (2001). *In the Shadows of the Net: Breaking Free of Compulsive Online Sexual Behavior*. Center City, MN: Hazelden Education and Publishing.

Cebulko, S. (2007). *The Impact of Internet Pornography on Married Women: A Psychodynamic Perspective*. New York: Cambria Press.

Dines, G., Jensen, R. & Russo, A. (1998). *Pornography: The Production and Consumption of Inequality*. New York: Routledge.

Dryer, J. A. & Lijtmaer, R. M. (2007). Cyber-sex as twilight zone between virtual reality and virtual fantasy. *Psychoanalytic Review*, 94: 39–61.

Dworkin, A. (1989). *Pornography: Men Possessing Women*. New York: E. F. Dutton.

Freud, S. (1905d). Three essays on the theory of sexuality. *S. E., 7* (pp. 135–245). London: Hogarth.

Freud, S. (1933). Femininity. *S. E., 22* (pp. 112–135). London: Hogarth.

Glasser, M. (1986). Identification and its vicissitudes as observed in the perversions. *International Journal of Psychoanalysis*, 67: 9–16.

Goldberg, A. (1999). *Being of Two Minds: The Vertical Split in Psychoanalysis and Psychotherapy*. Hillsdale, NJ: Analytic Press.

Goldberg, P., Peterson, D., Rosen, K. & Sara, M. (2008). The impact of a contemporary problem on the practices of marriage and family therapists. *Journal of Marital & Family Therapy*, 34(4): 469–480.

Hertlein, K. & Piercy, F. (2006). Internet infidelity: A critical review of the literature. *Family Journal*, *14*(4): 366–371.

Kalman, T. (2008). Clinical encounters with internet pornography. *Journal of the American Academy of Psychoanalysis and Dynamic Psychiatry*, *36*(4): 593–618.

Kernberg, O. (1995). *Love Relations: Normality and Pathology*. New Haven, CT: Yale University Press.

Khan, R. M. (1979). *Alienation in Perversions*. New York: International Universities Press.

Manning, J. (2006). The impact of internet pornography on marriage and the family: a review of the research. *Sexual Addiction & Compulsivity*, *13*(4): 131–165.

McDougall, J. (1986). Identifications, neoneeds and neosexualities. *International Journal of Psychoanalysis*, *67*: 19–30.

Microsoft Encarta Encyclopedia. Redmond, WA: Microsoft, 1997.

Miliner, V. (2008). Internet infidelity: a case of intimacy with detachment. *Family Journal*, 16(1): 78–82.

Parsons, M. (2000). Sexuality and perversion a hundred years on: discovering what Freud discovered. *International Journal of Psychoanalysis*, *81*: 37–49.

Perkins, B. (1997). *When Good Men Are Tempted*. Grand Rapids, MI: Zondervan.

Schneider, J. P. (2000a). A qualitative study of cybersex participants: Gender differences, recovery issues, and implications for therapists. *Sexual Addiction and Compulsivity*, 7: 249–278.

Schneider, J. P. (2000b). *Effects of cybersex addiction on the family: results of a survey.* Retrieved November 11, 2003, from http://www.jenniferschneider.com.html.

Schneider, J. P. (2002). The new elephant in the living room. In: A. Cooper (Ed.), *Sex and the Internet*. New York: Brunner-Routledge.

Schneider, J. P. & Weiss, R. (2001). *Cybersex Exposed: From Fantasy to Obsession*. Center City, MN: Hazelden Education and Publishing.

Searles, H. (1979). *Countertransference and Related Subjects: Selected Papers*. New York: International Universities Press.

Segal, H. (1975). *An Introduction to the Work of Melanie Klein. Notes on Symbol Formation*. London: Hogarth.

Stoller, R. (1975). *Perversions: the Erotic Form of Hatred*. New York: Pantheon.

Stoller, R. (1991). Eros and polis: What is this thing called love? *Journal of the American Psychoanalytic Association*, *39*: 1065–1102.

The internet porn "epidemic": by the numbers. Retrieved January 10, 2012 from http://theweek.com/article/index/204156/.

Young, K. (1998). *Caught in the Net*. New York: John Wiley and Sons.

Young, K. (2000). *Tangled in the Web: Understanding Cybersex from Fantasy to Addiction*. New York: John Wiley and Sons.

Whitty, M. & Quigley, L. L. (2008). Emotional and sexual infidelity offline and in cyberspace. *Journal of Marital & Family Therapy*, *34*(4): 461–468.

Wood, H. (2006). Compulsive use of internet pornography. In: J. Hiller, H. Wood & W. Bolton (Eds.), *Sex, Mind, and Emotion: Innovation in Psychological Theory and Practice* (pp. 65–86). London: Karnac.

Wood, H. (2011). The internet and its role in the escalation of sexually compulsive behavior. *Psychoanalytic Psychotherapy*, *25*(2): 127–142.

CHAPTER FIVE

Musings on therapy and technology

Sharon Zalusky Blum, PhD

We are living in an ever-changing, highly mobile world where new technologies continue to alter the way people are born, live, relate, and die (Zalusky, 2000). New modes of communication are exploding rapidly, transforming the ways in which people connect across boundaries. As therapists we find ourselves in an unusual position. The seclusion, the privacy of the therapeutic encounter, and removal from everyday life—all have long been considered necessary components for change to occur. Yet privacy as we have conceptualised it no longer exists. The sanctuary, the perfectly constructed cocoon where patient and therapist could create a transformative experience, is constantly being trespassed upon by the ring of cellphones, the notification sounds coming from text messages, emails, and Facebook, all signifying that the outside world has entered the confines of our offices.

The myth of the anonymous analyst has taken its last breath. It is only the most technologically removed or constricted patients who would not first do a Google search of their prospective therapist before beginning treatment. Often, when analysts or therapists have written papers, their publication history if not the papers themselves can be found online, which has a direct implication for confidentiality. This access on Google generally has changed the practice of writing up cases. As a consequence the tenor of our psychoanalytic literature is changing as well.

Many of us who have been practising psychoanalysis and psychotherapy for a considerable period of time have learned that major changes in our personal technique almost always originate directly from the special need (or desire) of a particular patient who pushes us to rethink our past traditions and prejudices (Zalusky, 1998, 2000, 2006). Even the most reticent of our colleagues have to acknowledge that our changing world affects how we ultimately relate to our patients and our peers, and they to us. Technology can and does create expected as well as unexpected possibilities. We have before us an opportunity to expand our understanding of our patients' lives across multiple levels if we open ourselves up to new ways of thinking about old problems. Our younger patients may in fact be our guide to the new, exciting, and sometimes frightening world that is technology.

As therapists we must acknowledge that there is a continuous tension between our desire to maintain the protected intimate practices of our past and our hope to maximise the potential benefits from the ever-changing new modes of communicating today. Technology in many of its permutations has entered our consulting rooms. At times we may be prepared for the changes and adapt to them seamlessly. Other times, like creatures of habit, we may be hesitant to alter our business as usual. In order to be relevant and effective, psychoanalysis needs to engage with the greater implications of technology for the psychoanalytic process. We need to connect with the patient of today.

The ever-changing patient: the ever-changing analyst

In 1998 I published "Telephone Analysis: Out of Sight, but Not Out of Mind" to document my reluctant foray from the traditional analytic frame with its known boundaries into a new mobile, potentially flexible playing field. Over fifteen years much has transpired from my patient's request to continue our work on the telephone (Zalusky, 1998). So much has changed. Telephone analysis is no longer in the closet. I am proud that my articles (Zalusky, 1998, 2003) sparked an international debate that continues today about the effectiveness of telephone analysis. Even my most strident critics (Argentieri & Amati Mehler, 2003) acknowledged that they too at times work on the telephone. Their main objection seemed to be whether or not we can call it analysis. On the most fundamental level, I believe, what we *call* our work has little importance as long as it remains an effective treatment.

In most of the articles I wrote about telephone analysis I continued to refer to it as a therapeutic compromise, which was by nature conflictual. Today, having done many treatments that have shifted over time from the office to the telephone and many times back to the office, I would no longer consider it a compromise, but a continuation of a treatment that is progressing. In every one of these treatments that shifted primarily from my office to the telephone, my patients opted to pursue personal life-altering goals, which increased their productivity and their connection to the world. Our work on the telephone allowed them to make adaptive and meaningful transitions into new phases of life in the least painful manner possible. Rather than using the telephone to express a resistance, they found a way to bring our therapeutic work with them. The ability to maintain a connection with a caring and interested other via the telephone brought about a new type of relating.

For years I concentrated on how telephone analysis affected my patients and what meaning it had for them, but retrospectively I can see that in the process something important happened to me as well. I also made an important life transition from an analyst who accepted without much questioning the received theories of our field to one who adapts our theories to the special needs of individual patients in order to help them progress towards their goals (Hoffman, 1994, 1998; Renik, 2010). Rather than seeing telephone analysis as a transgression, I believe that working on the telephone has allowed me to think more creatively about how I work with my patients.

The most important change in the way I think about how I practise is my conceptualisation of the meaning of the frame for therapeutic purposes. Like almost every other aspect of therapy, I believe the frame (the setting, number of days, the consistency) is co-created by both participants in the therapeutic endeavour. It need not be a one-size-fits-all frame. Some patients may require a firm frame while others may feel the need for the frame to be more fluid, capable of adapting over time as they themselves develop. Some might need flexibility in the beginning and stability as they progress. For others it might be the reverse. In changing my attitude about the frame, I have learned to listen more closely to what my patients believe they need; and when it makes sense, I try to adapt my technique to meet their personal concerns. Often the act of taking their wishes seriously in and of itself becomes a corrective emotional experience (Alexander, 1946).

Not only is our work on the telephone developing, but also the telephone itself is evolving at rapid pace. When Freud in 1912 recommends to physicians practising psychoanalysis that we use our own unconscious "like a receptive organ towards the transmitting unconscious of the patient", he does so by employing the metaphor of the telephone: "He [the analyst] must adjust himself to the patient as a telephone receiver is adjusted to the transmitting microphone" (1912e, pp. 115–116).

Freud was ahead of his time. Few people during Freud's era even had telephones. The first telephone itself was a primitive instrument. There was little privacy, let alone portability. Today almost everyone including ourselves has a mobile phone that is almost always with us. When we leave the office, we have a choice. We can choose to transfer our calls to our home phone or our cellphone. In my case, I permanently transferred my office number to my cellphone. If I leave the country, my number comes with me. Obviously each one of us has to consider how available we want to be and what the degree of our availability and unavailability means to our patients and to others. Paradoxically, I have found the more I am available, the less my patients call me in-between sessions, if ever. That arrangement has had a liberating effect on me. I no longer have to worry about calling in for my messages.

It is also quite interesting to me that in many ways we are returning to the earlier days when the phone lines were not very stable. The new mobile phones, though ever present, are less reliable. Many people, especially young people, only have mobile lines. Phone calls are frequently dropped. Intuitively, one might expect patients would have unconscious reactions to being dropped, but I have found because it happens so frequently with almost everybody, people have grown accustomed to the nuisance without missing a beat.

The phone is not just our telephone any more. It often is our camera, our video camera, our photo books, our secretary, our internet, our message board, our encyclopaedia, our personal movie theatre and entertainment centre, and whatever else we choose to put on it. Young people have a unique relationship with their phone. Often they do not use it in the way we expect a phone to be used. Rarely do they talk on it. They often communicate by texting. If they need to change an appointment time with you, they text you the request. I have grown to appreciate texting as an efficient form of short communication. In many ways it has replaced conventional voice mail.

I have found working with adolescents and young adults that they want you to see their lives concretely. They bring their friends to session via photographs. When they have a crush on someone, they want to show you the other's Facebook page. When someone hurts them, they read the email letter they just sent off. What started off as the way young people interact with me, has reached my older patients who show me their grandchildren from their iPhone, the new home they are thinking of buying, or playing back a piece of music they are writing. I believe the connection with my patients deepens when they allow me to witness their lives. They tend to share more openly and quickly their fantasies, their fears, their desires, and their conflicts.

One young patient, an angelic looking, introspective young woman who came to me because of problems at school, began to open up slowly, showing me (literally) things that intrigued her on the internet. When she would leave Los Angeles to return home during school breaks, we would continue the therapy on Skype (to be discussed below). As time developed, and she became more trusting of me, she began to tell me how she used the internet to invent another persona for herself. As a young teenager she described how she would torment a young immigrant from her school in cyberspace. At school they were good friends, but in the privacy of the internet, on instant message she would show up under a false name and verbally assail and torment her for reasons she could not express or understand in person. The anonymity of the internet increases the ease of acting out fantasies that have real life repercussions both for the victim and tormentor that endure long after the actual events have occurred. Today my patient feels both shame and terrible guilt over the fate of all the young people who have killed themselves presumably because they were victims of cyber-bullying. She does not know how her anonymous assaults affected the ongoing life of her high school schoolmate. When she remembers what she did, she becomes crippled by pain and remorse, which affects her view of herself. But rather than simply listening to my patient talk about her remorse and her ongoing self-destructive behaviour, I have been able to engage her in an exploration of why she may have needed (and at times still needs) to create an alter persona (or possibly more than one) for herself. I believe because I accepted the use of the internet in our sessions, she had more confidence that I could understand her private alter world. Technology in her case was the bridge between fantasy and action which created pain and suffering for both parties. In the past what might have stayed solely in the realm of fantasy, creating conflict and mental anguish, has with the anonymity of the internet a new and destructive tool to overcome internal resistances to action.

Referral then and now

Everything seems to be changing in my practice now that I have opened myself to the world as I find it. I have been seeing patients in private practice since 1985. In the beginning, each new patient invariably would present in the same way. They would call my office and leave a message if I was not there to pick up. During the first few years of practice, I had an answering service. When that went out of vogue, I changed to an answering machine to assure confidentiality. Most recently, like so many others, I replaced the machine with voice mail. If a prospective patient left a message, I would return the call as soon as possible to set up an appointment. It did not occur to me until recently that there could be any exception to this procedure. Here are two examples that took me by surprise, precisely because they did not conform to my established routine.

Example of X

I was out of town away from my office. As usual I checked my messages on my iPhone. But instead of a voice message, when I checked my email I found on an old AOL account (one I rarely use any more) the following email:

> Dear Dr. Zalusky,
>
> I was referred to you by a friend of mine who has relocated to Boston. I am a bit in over my head and need someone to talk to. I have been in therapy before, I was diagnosed and medicated for bi-polar disorder, but I have not taken medication for over a year. If you have time in your schedule to meet me, I would appreciate that. If not, perhaps you have a colleague you can recommend who does. Thank you for your time concerning this matter. Sincerely,
>
> Signed electronically X
> Telephone: (XXX-XXX-XXXX)

There with the signature was the patient's telephone number. I was both perplexed and intrigued. Who is this person who reaches out via email, I wondered? And why email? I had never seen this happen. What did it mean for him to call or not to call? The oddity of the experience overwhelmed me for a moment. I was caught off-guard, not expecting a letter from a stranger. I felt a bit invaded. I was also struck by the fact he used my old name, Dr. Zalusky. Whoever gave him the referral either did so several years ago or did not know I had changed my name to Dr. Blum. I was curious. Doesn't he want to hear my voice? Or is he afraid I might answer and catch him off guard? Maybe he is afraid of human interaction, I thought. On the positive side the email was fairly succinct, full of important information, polite and engaging. I went back and forth in my mind: do I call him back or do I respond in like fashion through email? Or should I phone him as he also left his number? I was struck by the risk he took—whether he even thought about it consciously—sending an email not knowing whether that account still existed. I might not even have known to get back to him, since up until recently it had been years since I checked that account on my computer. Given all the possibilities, I surmised he must be highly ambivalent about contact.

I began to interpret my own anxiety, not so much in anticipation of transgressing a norm, but in reaction to the challenge of not knowing about who this person might be, how best to respond to him, and whether emailing him (or any patient) would be effective as a first form of communication. I looked for precedents. I remembered Hoffman's (1994) discussion of the dialectic between traditional theory and the need at times to throw away the book. I also wondered about how Freud might have received his referrals. As noted earlier, few people had telephones when Freud began to practise. They must have written letters to one another. They would have to wait for responses. And then it struck me, email is the modern version of the old way of doing things only with immediate results. I chose to email him the following email:

Dear X

I'm happy to meet you, but I'm out of town until Monday. Please let me know your availability next week.

Thank you,
Sharon Zalusky Blum PhD

X immediately responded:

OK. I am free next week. I am in school—I'm 30—it's for architecture. But my classes are at night, and I'm not working at the moment. So any time is good for me. Thank you for responding, please let me know what's convenient for you. I look forward to meeting you.

I replied right away, giving him the time we could meet, and then did not hear back. Ten days later I received the following email communication:

Dear Dr. Slusky, [Note: Now he used the wrong name entirely] One of my many major obstacles in my life is that I am extremely obstinate. My family is very intent on my seeing a Dr, to discuss this, among other things, but the more they insist, the more resistant I become—so I wrote you, fully intending on seeing you, but my family became so enthusiastic about my prospective appointment that I lost interest in the whole pursuit. Unfortunately, it's normal, and I do really need some help. I know that. So, if you could still meet me that would be fantastic. I also have to figure out how to extricate myself from a very entangled relationship. It's kind of a priority. Although working through that obstinacy thing would also be top of the list. Thank you for your time.

This time I responded,

Dear X

Of course you can come in. Why don't you call me at 310-826-1281 and we'll schedule an appointment.

Best
Sharon Zalusky Blum PhD

Within an hour of sending my email, X called and left a voice mail. I returned his call within a few minutes, but to no avail. I then left a message stating I knew it was difficult for him communicating on the telephone. I told him I had an opening the next day at 3.00pm and would hope to see him then. Immediately he responded via text messaging thanking me and acknowledging he would be there.

To my surprise, he arrived on time, but more than that I was captivated by his ability to engage in a warm and available way. I had not expected that, imagining someone more overtly ambivalent about relating. He discussed how difficult it was for him to talk on the telephone and how frightened he was to begin therapy with someone new. He was open about his past and present problems and how he self-destructed. He spoke freely about his childhood full of physical ailments and surgeries that both kept him from school and affected his body image. He spoke lovingly of his family, though he was able to recognise their shortcomings and his frustrations with them. He had many long-standing important friendships that seemed to bring him joy.

We talked about the meaning of his introduction to me through email, and the discrepancy between his fear of connecting on the telephone and his ease of engagement in the session. When it was time to end the session, we agreed to meet twice weekly. Clearly I knew that though he was capable of communicating, it would not be smooth sailing. So it was not much of a surprise that he called at the next session to tell me he was having car troubles. I left a message on his phone saying I wondered whether he was not feeling ambivalent and overwhelmed by our first meeting. I told him I hoped he would be able to come to our next scheduled appointment. He then texted me to say he appreciated my message. He said I was right. He was overcome by emotion, but he would be there at our next appointment time. Again, he showed up and dealt openly with his fears of therapy. For the next few months, he would intermittently attend, cancel, email, and text until he disappeared totally. His exit was in keeping with his beginning.

I present X not because he was a success story, but to illustrate how different the world is today. Had I not been open to the "multimedia" approach, I would probably have never engaged as long as I did with him. I will never know what the meaning of our work was to my frightened patient, but I hope he left feeling as if someone had tried to meet him where he was coming from. Had I not engaged, the treatment might have ended before it had a chance to begin. I am hopeful one day he will try again with someone.

As I was drafting this essay about this most unusual method of self-referral via email, I bumped into a friend who works at a talent agency. She asked if she could refer a colleague to me. I said, "Certainly." "Great," she responded. "I'll have her text you tomorrow." Again, a bit taken back by such an approach, I responded, "Why not have her call my office?" Without missing a beat, she told me her friend was out of the country and texting would be much easier. Though unfamiliar for me as analyst or therapist, this approach seems to be common fare for young people living in a busy internet world. There would be plenty of time, if she came to therapy, for us to understand how she functions in the world and the meaning it has both to her internal and external life.

No article on therapy and technology would be complete without mentioning the place of Skype in my practice. While I use Skype infrequently, I have made some anecdotal findings. I have noticed that my young patients who are in their late teens to early twenties seem to prefer Skype to the telephone when they are out of town. My patients in their late twenties and older all seem to prefer the telephone. I have both wondered to myself and analysed with my patients their preferences. I believe my younger patients simply are not as comfortable with telephones for the purpose of talking. They rarely use the phone for long conversations. They Skype, instant message, and use Facebook and other social media to connect with their friends. Forty-five minutes on the telephone may seem like an eternity to them. It appears my younger patients also prefer Skype because it tends to keep them focused. Often they worry they would multi-task if they were only on the telephone with me. And some worry that I, too, would want to read a magazine or work simultaneously on my computer if they were not looking at me, constraining me to look at them. I believe it has something to do with the bombardment of stimuli that they take for granted. Some examples serve to illustrate the preference for Skype in my young patients and a young supervisee:

> One young patient who never travelled away from home found it comforting to be able to connect with Skype when he ventured away for his study year abroad. Certainly, Skype has the advantage that it does not cost anything additional as long as one has the internet. He was able to stay connected while attempting to separate.
>
> Another teenage patient who has always been conflicted over dependency longings would hold her session over Skype when she was out of town. Just the fact that she wanted to Skype while on vacation was itself significant. Often I would notice her leaning so closely into the computer that it would feel like she was almost in my lap. She would at those times appear to look lovingly into my eyes. Our work on the computer has helped me to understand the intensity of her longings, and how in person she tried to suppress them.
>
> A young supervisee explained to me how she much preferred Skype sessions to telephone sessions when her patients requested them. She, too, would feel distracted while on the phone. As many others have indicated, Skype allowed her to continue to notice the non-verbal aspects of her patients. Recently she spoke about a patient of hers who was having difficulty coming to the clinic. She agreed to have a session over Skype to help her young patient deal with her intensifying resistances. Much to the supervisee's surprise as the Skype session began, she realised her patient had brought her laptop into bed. Still dressed in pajamas, hair dishevelled, the patient had very little interest in working therapeutically. The patient refused to talk about her difficulties coming in. When that failed, the therapist tried to explore the possible meaning of literally bringing her therapist into her bed with her, but to no avail. Clearly without the non-verbal cues, the acting out quality of her resistances might have gone unappreciated.

Other patients refuse to use Skype. One patient who prefers to use the telephone when she is away told me she had a boyfriend in another city who would always want to engage in cybersex on Skype. It left a bad association for her. She also worried about her appearance, a fact she had never discussed with me when we were meeting in my office. Many of my patients who debate between telephone sessions and Skype often mention how self-conscious they become when using Skype. They fear they would become obsessed looking at the picture of themselves in the corner of the screen.

In fact, I, too, for other reasons prefer to work on the telephone. As of yet, I find the primitive quality of the Skype video off-putting. My patient's face breaking up into coloured squares, at times the lack of synchronisation between voice and picture creates a less than optimal environment for me. But it seems it is only a matter of time before the technology improves. Here, too, age might make a difference. My young supervisee much prefers Skype sessions to telephone sessions, because it helps her focus on the patient. She also feels that what she gains seeing the patient outweighs the technological glitches. Like almost everything in life, whether one uses the telephone or Skype to conduct a therapy session, there will be the strengths and weaknesses of each approach.

Conclusion

As psychoanalysts and psychotherapists we live in exciting times. Technology is permeating all aspects of our lives, including our patients' lives. It would be foolish to think that technological changes would not affect how we work and think about human interaction. In order to stay relevant, we must be open to the world as we find it. We have an opportunity to grow, to refine our theories of technique and to examine the implication of the changes we are making.

References

Freud, S. (1912e). Recommendations to physicians practising psycho-analysis. *S. E.*, *12* (pp. 111–120). London: Hogarth.

Hoffman, I. Z. (1994). Dialectical thinking and therapeutic action in the psychoanalytic process. *Psychoanalytic Quarterly*, *63*: 187–218.

Hoffman, I. Z. (1998). *Ritual and Spontaneity in the Psychoanalytic Process*. Hillside, NJ: Analytic Press.

Renik, O. (2010). *Practical Psychoanalysis for Therapists and Patients*. New York: Other Press.

Zalusky, S. (1998). Telephone analysis: Out of sight, but not out of mind. *Journal of the American Psychoanalytic Association*, *46*: 1221–1242.

Zalusky, S. (2000). Infertility in the age of technology. *Journal of the American Psychoanalytic Association*, *48*: 1541–1562.

Zalusky, S. (2006). The disappearing (or ghost) mother transference: In search of the available mother within. *Psychoanalytic Inquiry*, *26*: 118–136.

PART II

TELEPHONE AND INTERNET IN TREATMENT

CHAPTER SIX

Clinical issues in analysis over the telephone and the internet

Jill Savege Scharff, MD

Teletherapy, the practice of psychotherapy conducted remotely using the telephone and the internet, is increasing in response to more mobility in the population. In psychoanalysis, more than in psychotherapy, there has been tremendous worry about violating the purity of the classical method when sessions are conducted on the telephone or over the internet. Some have said that any analytic treatment done by an analyst working with an analysand on the telephone may do some good but it cannot be analysis: it must be supportive psychotherapy (Argentieri & Mehler, 2003). I find this remark rather unfair to the practice of psychotherapy, but rather than get distracted by jumping to defend psychotherapy, I want to use this chapter to focus specifically on the value of psychoanalysis conducted over the telephone and the internet. Since teleanalysis occurs three to five times a week, those of us who practise it have an opportunity to study its pros and cons in depth over time. Our findings can be helpful to psychotherapists who do not have the luxury of time, and analysts who have not tried to work with patients at a distance using the telephone or the internet.

There is quite a controversy as to whether the use of technology leads to a dilution of analysis or to adaptive innovation that is clinically effective and true to the tenets of psychoanalysis. I will review the psychoanalytic literature and show the development of analytic thinking about this technology-assisted practice of psychoanalysis. I will summarise analysts' perceptions and experiences of the advantages and disadvantages, and consider the indications and contraindications. Opponents who say that teleanalysis cannot be analysis point to the violation of the frame, ignoring resistance, and the lack of analytic process, but I will counter their arguments with an extended clinical example that shows attention to the frame, respect for resistance, unconscious communication among internal objects, unconscious fantasy, transference and countertransference, and interpretation. Throughout the chapter I will give vignettes from the analysis of a man with trauma-related depression so as to address the concerns raised and to support my argument that analysis using the telephone and the internet is a viable, clinically effective alternative to traditional analysis where necessary. In Chapter Twenty One on advanced training, I will give four vignettes to further discussion of clinical practice on the telephone and the internet in order to set the stage for exploring the use of technology in the training of psychotherapists and psychoanalysts.

The use of technology in psychoanalysis

The development of a global economy in the twenty-first century with increased travel and instant worldwide communication has produced a social and personal transformation of the mind and its concept of the body in space. This governs the mindset and lifestyle of analysands to which psychoanalysts must now adapt their treatment approach. So, psychoanalysis has to find ways of transcending the limits of distance to reach the analysand of the twenty-first century. Possible solutions are to diminish the frequency of sessions (more like psychotherapy), condense them into periods of availability (condensed analysis), or require travel by analyst or analysand (remote condensed shuttle analysis). Another solution is to maintain frequency through the use of communication by voice, using the telephone or the internet, possibly including the use of a one-way or two-way camera. Harnessing technology to the analytic aim may be a creative adaptation to the modern world but it raises many questions concerning the viability of the frame, the emergence of resistance, the maintenance of the therapeutic alliance, the sensitivity of response to unconscious communication of affect and fantasy without access to non-verbal cues, and the development of analytic process (Scharff, 2010).

Technology has been used in conducting psychoanalytic sessions for six decades but its acceptability was limited for years by available equipment, ethical concerns, and paucity of data about its effectiveness. There is no doubt that in-person sound is more comfortable to listen to, but the analyst can adapt to telephone communication for analytic sessions when necessary. In the 1950s the first report of the use of the telephone in psychoanalysis recommended the speaker phone as the closest approximation to in-person sound (Saul, 1951). A cluster of reports appeared in the 1970s (Robertiello, 1972–73) and an edited book on the telephone in intensive psychotherapy at the turn of the century (Aronson, 2000a). The telephone was used as needed for dealing with crises and reaching a reluctant or bedridden patient. It was seen as an extension of the transitional space (Aronson, 2003b). It was used as a substitute for in-person analysis for patients who were phobic of in-person sessions. It was used with patients who had to move so that they could maintain an established analytic relationship and prevent premature termination. Lindon (2000) reported in detail on the analysis of a single case with serious pathology in which he dealt with a transference filled with anger, disgust, contempt, paranoid fantasies, and fears of engulfment. In contrast, Leffert (2003) reported on nine analyses in which he found that telephone sessions were indistinguishable from in-person sessions, but he did not support his findings with detailed process. Even though he had shown the power of telephone analysis, Lindon (2000) thought it second best. Benson, Rowntree, and Singer (2001), who saw its value, and Zalusky (1998), who is an advocate for the appropriate use of the telephone in psychoanalysis, nevertheless regarded it as a therapeutic compromise. Disagreeing with such a modest assessment, Sachs (2003) cautioned that this view of telephone analysis may "over-emphasize being cautious in its use and totally diminish its value" (p. 29). Most writers recommend a trial of telephone sessions before agreeing to switch from in-person sessions, with periodic return to in-person sessions on a flexible schedule.

In 2003, the use of a telephone headset attachment was being recommended as being "operationally transparent" and offering a superior sense of connection (Leffert, 2003, p. 117). In 2011, the headset is commonly in use by analyst and analysand, but now it is connected not only to the telephone landlines but also to the internet, using Voice over Internet Protocol (VoIP) by companies such as Skype, the trade name of the major carrier, Google-talk, Oovoo, and others. The telephone distorts the inflection of the voice, and critics fear that this will interfere with the reception of the communication (Argentieri & Mehler, 2003). Skype, the digital connection most used by psychotherapists and psychoanalysts, has the advantage that it provides high fidelity stereo sound by using more megahertz than telephone lines, and this means that the voice is startlingly vivid. When it enters the head set, the voice of the analysand is delivered inside the analyst's mind in a more total way than in the room where there is more space between them and visual input as well. Varela (personal communication, 2007) holds that the analyst's voice coming straight through the headset into the analysand's ear fosters a sense of connection that supports the containment offered by the analytic process.

Furthermore, Skype now offers analyst and analysand the choice of visual transmission by using a webcam so that analysand and analyst see each other at the beginning and end of the session and the analyst can look at the analysand's body movements as the webcam is trained on the analysand's couch. Some analysts, even those in the United States with analysands as far away as China, find that this degree of physical communication approximates closely to that of the in-person analytic session (Snyder, 2011). Other analysts find the telephone more evocative of the in-person session in which looking and seeing are less important than following and responding to verbal associations with unconscious fantasies and communicable thoughts.

There are legitimate concerns about security and reliability of connection. Cellphones are not secure, and so if the telephone is chosen, analyst and analysand require landlines. If Skype is selected, patient and therapist both need high quality broadband service. Some claim that computer-to-computer Skype is secure because it sends information by dividing it up into packets that do not connect until they reach the destination (packet-switching) and because it does offer encryption. However, Skype is a free social platform with consumer-grade performance, and does not claim to be HIPAA compliant. It is not as secure as using a Videoteleconference service (VTC) that does claim to be HIPAA compliant and offers a medical grade platform. But VTC is more expensive and is not as practical in private practice.

Whether on the telephone or Skype, analyst and analysand may experience technical problems—extraneous noises on the telephone line, tinny sound and fuzzy images when the broadband connection is weak, pixillating, tiling, and freezing of the image on Skype, and dropped calls when the broadband connection is interrupted. These problems are the technical equivalent of an empathic failure, but even technical failure can bring the transference into focus, as the following example shows:

A technological problem and its dynamic meaning

Mr. M, an adult male analysand with trauma-related depression, began analysis in person and moved to telephone analysis while still in the early phase of treatment, because his company sent him to work in an area with no local analyst. He attended four times a week by telephone, and returned in person for a week three times a year. His communication in person and on the phone at this stage of treatment was characterised by quiet speech, many pauses, long silences, and only a few dreams.

Mr. M grew up in an industrial region known for its toxic air, which left him sickly. His father worked long hours at the factory and his mother took care of him on her own, her own family being across the border in Canada. As a child, he felt a nuisance to his mother. Being a quiet boy instead of a lively girl as his mother would have preferred, he felt that she did not love him. His life-threatening failure to thrive, accompanied by recurrent infections, required frequent hospitalisations, which must have exhausted his mother. One time when he had pneumonia, she left him in hospital where he was isolated in an oxygen tent and saw only nurses and doctors. When he tried to call out for her (which was hard because he could not breathe well on that occasion) he felt chastised by the nurses.

A telephone line cut-off happened early in his treatment. After some minutes of telling his analyst hesitantly what was on his mind, Mr. M fell silent. Hearing nothing from him, she began to interpret the persistent use of silence as a resistance, as a denial of the need of the telephone, and for words as the vehicle for the treatment, and as a way of testing her capacity to endure non-connection. Unknown to her, the analysand was speaking but the analyst could not hear him because her headset failed. He was puzzled by her ever more frantic attempts to interpret his non-response as his way of exerting silent control, making the telephone analysis impossible. After they discovered the problem and reconnected, she learned that he had actually been speaking, and had been experiencing irritation in her voice as if she were not satisfied with what he was saying and not responding to him. She was thinking of this as a vivid, concrete example of her "not getting it", not being able to tune in to him, an empathic failure. Feeling embarrassed, she apologised and said, "I must have sounded like a crazy person." This had resonance for him since, unknown to her, he indeed worried about making her crazy. But mainly he felt that he was in trouble for not talking. He felt as he had felt in childhood when his "too quiet" way of being irritated his mother and drove her crazy. He had the sense that talking was pointless, since it seemed to make no impact even though he was desperately trying to communicate. So, this session of telephone analysis brought into focus a transference view of himself as an unsatisfactory child, evoked a countertransference in identification with his irritated mother; and analysis of this transference-countertransference relieved its impact on the treatment alliance.

The development of analytic thinking about teleanalysis

The younger generation of analysands and analysts grew up conducting intimate communication on the phone, emailing, and texting, and to them it is quite natural to call in to a business meeting, job interview, or psychoanalytic session from another location. They live on their cellphones and laptops, and when they travel for work, they cannot maintain the desired level of analytic frequency. Technology is driving their choices, and their lifestyle is driving their need for technology, including the need for technology assisted psychoanalysis to maintain the optimum frequency of analytic sessions for in-depth analytic work. To comprehend their reality, psychoanalysts are developing a sophisticated psychoanalytic understanding of the changing dimensions of time and space in the twenty-first century (Aryan, Berenstain, Carlino, Grinfeld & Lutenberg, 2009; Aryan & Carlino, 2010). They are exploring technology's effects on the social unconscious and on the individual mind whether analysed in person or on the phone. They are balancing the provision of an appropriate analytic stance and an appropriate response to the impact of sociocultural change on the patient, and on the analyst's identity and the nature of his practice (Rodriguez de la Sierra, 2003).

Like traditional analysis in person, teleanalysis values the standard psychoanalytic tenets. Hanly (2008) found in his experience of telephone analysis that responsive holding, witnessing, and interpretive functions can be sustained, free association occurs, and the expression of paternal and maternal transferences are not compromised. Aryan (Aryan, Berenstain, Carlino, Grinfeld & Lutenberg, 2009), Carlino (2012), and Lutenberg (2011a and b) agree that teleanalysis is similar to traditional analysis in using the analyst's suspended attention to free associate, working with the unconscious and its derivatives and repressed childhood sexuality, and in analysing dreams and transference. Mirkin (2011) found that phone analysis, where continuity fosters intensity and distance protects from impulsive action, "allowed intense affects to be expressed, tolerated and reflected upon" and "helped an exploration of defenses unfold" (p. 669). Even though the body is absent, the telephone session is effective because it echoes the "silent-but-holding environment presence of the mother" (Leffert, 2003, p. 10). Just as traditional psychoanalysis can be extended to treat analysands with pathology that is not classically neurotic, teleanalysis can be effective in perversion and psychosis in some cases. Symington, whose analysand had to travel after years of in-person psychoanalysis, found that the dislocation of being away from home and having to connect to him on the telephone revealed a transference delusion previously not brought out in the consulting room (Anderson, Scharff, D., Scharff, J. & Symington, 2009). Richards (2003) reported on an analysis by telephone in which a sexual perversion, hidden in person, emerged only in telephone sessions, and this recalled excited phone calls to the analysand's mother.

Although analysis by telephone or Skype has its proponents, it remains controversial, and like any proposed innovation has stirred lively debate. Conceding that the telephone might occasionally be a useful therapeutic tool, Argentieri and Mehler (2003) nevertheless concluded that it is not compatible with a psychoanalytic process and is traumatic for both analyst and patient. Their concern is that the offer of telephone sessions denies separation and loss, and at the same time creates loss in depriving the patient of the bodily presence of the analyst and therefore of good holding containment. Yamin Habib (2003) found that the stance of the telephone analyst is not properly authentic, neutral, and impartial: instead it is indulgent and paternalistic, privileging action and the exchange of information rather than providing a lived experience. Brainsky (2003) described the analytic relationship on the telephone as "an unusually spectral relationship" resulting from condensations of tone, timbre, and word that render the analyst's voice as a persecutory part object (p. 23). He believed that telephone analysis is more likely than traditional analysis to result in idealised transference and to fail in the task of containing projective identifications.

Therapeutic regression occurs in analysis by telephone and on the internet as it does in traditional analysis. However, it must be admitted that this is more anxiety-provoking for the analyst who may experience increased anxiety about doing harm and being censured. As Chodorow says of telephone analysis, "Regression can be really palpable, and sometimes, to me, scary … something you feel you can control more in the room" (2004, p. 4). More than anything, this anxious and guilty sensation translates into the commonly held view (despite a lack of research data) that in-person sessions are better. But regression is worked through by psychoanalysis on the telephone as it is in person.

Nevertheless, teleanalysis is not the same as analysis with the analysand in the consulting room, and yet it is more alike than different beyond surface characteristics. Leffert (2003) pointed out that "the telephone, like the couch, alters the dimensions of the non-verbal environment: it de-emphasizes or eliminates some of them while emphasizing others" (p. 124). Communication occurs through sound, not sight, an echo of the earliest days of life when communication between mother and baby was perhaps through the whish of blood in the umbilical cord (Benaim, 2009, personal communication). The telephone is like the couch in limiting visual cues and freeing the analyst's attention from the demands of gaze interaction (Richards, 2003). The analyst listens with the third ear to the underlying theme, like the analyst sitting out of sight behind the analysand and listening better with eyes shut (Hanly, 2007). As Freud put it, the analyst "must turn his own unconscious like a receptive organ towards the transmitting unconscious of the patient" (1912e, p. 115) and "must adjust himself to the patient as a telephone receiver is adjusted to the transmitting microphone" (Freud, 1912e, pp. 115–116). Zalusky linked the experience of telephone analysis unbounded by personal presence to "the timelessness of the unconscious" (2000, p. 38). Each participant creates and sustains a mental representation of the other in fantasy, and in this way, a new type of analytic process develops (Zalusky, 2003b).

Adaptation of frame, resistance, and technique in teleanalysis

In teleanalysis, as in traditional analysis, the analyst respects the frame of the treatment and secures a circumscribed, reliable setting with regular frequency of sessions and time boundaries to each session, and an agreed routine for periods of in-person sessions. However, in teleanalysis, in contrast to in-person analysis, with the analyst and analysand in two different locations, there may be a considerable difference in the space, hour, and season of the setting for each of them (Aryan, Berenstain, Carlino, Grinfeld & Lutenberg, 2009). Unlike traditional analysis in which the analyst provides and controls the setting, in analysis using the telephone or the internet, the analyst and analysand think together about how to secure the frame, but analysands alone are responsible for the external arrangements, for securing the confidentiality of the at-home or in-office setting in which analysis occurs, for providing their own tissues, and if they choose to use a webcam, they are responsible for placing the couch suitably in relation to the camera. How they fulfil this responsibility is an expression of their endopsychic structure and their resistance, which can then be analysed as usual. Chodorow (2004) reported that the analysand's creation of a physical surround—the room, the couch, the furniture, the light, the weather, the presence of pets, food, and drink—made her more aware of the analysand's sense of physical space (and of her own sense of her surroundings), than in in-person sessions where aspects of the shared space are taken for granted. Aspects of the analysand's location are evocative objects that become vehicles for understanding the psychological space that they reflect or protect against.

It has been said that in adapting the frame, teleanalysis accommodates to resistance instead of analysing it, but the teleanalyst analyses both the need for the phone and the reluctance to use it when indicated. The request for telephone sessions may be a neurotic need, an enactment, an ego adaptation, or a mixture of defence and adaptation. Some analysands resist using the phone to avoid feeling deprived of the sight of the analyst. They may prefer visual connection to the analyst via a webcam at the beginning and end of each session. Some choose Skype with webcam because they want to imagine the analyst looking at them. Some refuse because they do not want to be looked at when they cannot monitor the looking and the analyst's reactions, the same resistance as they would feel in person on the couch with the analyst out of view. Some do not want to be looked at, because they want to hide their struggle which is evident on the face, as if the face were the only sign of their distress.

On the telephone or on the internet, the analyst deals with resistance expressed in forgetting to call, speaking softly, not using a headset, moving away from the microphone, accepting other calls, and chatting as if on a social call, in addition to silence, hesitation, coughing, lateness, non-payment, displacement, and so on, often seen in in-person analysis when anxieties block the flow of associations. Analysts via telephone or via internet observe the usual technique of maintaining a neutral position conceptualised according to their respective traditions as being equidistant between the generations; and among ego, id, and superego; or among ideal object, rejecting object, exciting object, central ego, antilibidinal ego, and libidinal ego. They work with dreams and free association, sometimes more easily on the phone for those analysands who are inhibited by the bodily presence of the analyst. So although one area of exploration is hidden, another comes to the fore. As the sessions continue over time, the issues are revisited and worked through. Transference flourishes on the telephone as in real life, evokes a countertransference response from the telephone analyst, and the transference-countertransference dialectic is analysed as it would be in in-person sessions.

Clinical example: reflections on telephone and in-person sessions

After telephone analysis had been established for some months, the analyst learned that when Mr. M, the analysand I described earlier, was nine years old, his mother had sent him for a couple of weeks to his aunt's house across the border in Canada. Mr. M perceived this as a punishment for his having witnessed and spoken about his mother's seduction by a powerful person at their synagogue, which resulted in a huge upheaval at home and the departure of her lover. Repeatedly at his aunt's, he was left with a male babysitter who, apparently unknown to the aunt, was sexually abusive. When the boy asked to call his mother to take him home, his aunt would not allow it until he cried and cried. Then it took many tearful calls before his mother accepted him home. He was vulnerable to sexual abuse because of the overstimulation and guilt around his mother's affair, and unable to speak about it because of the fear of causing more trouble. So neither aunt nor mother was told of the reason for his need to leave for home.

Mr. M's worry about calling in terror of the next abuse was re-created in difficulty calling his analyst, which he described as follows: "Perhaps I think my call to you for help will not be met or will be dismissed, or you will not understand that things are as bad as they are, when I actually think you get it. So, the telephone is my way out of my internal trauma, as it was with Arthur [the babysitter]—at least, that is the hope, but it seems to take many, many calls for this to happen. Just like it seemed I was with Arthur forever, it seems like it's taking a very long time to get through all this. I often wonder if you're there on the other end."

Falling silent on the phone reminded Mr. M of being unable to call his mother the time he was left in hospital for pneumonia. As he put it, "I couldn't talk much anyway, because my voice was weak. I feel this same feeling on the phone at times in my silence. Words are in my head, but I can't seem to get them out. While in the hospital, it felt like there was no way to reach my mother, partly because even when she was present, she seemed so absent."

Mr. M said that losing in-person sessions because of his move reminded him of the time he was sent away. "My mother may have had good intentions for my health in sending me to her sister, but I experienced it as being sent away because I wasn't the right child. My mother had a baby on the way by then, a girl, the right child. I felt like I was too much for her, which was part of the reason for being sent away. I was too sick, too quiet, too needy. I feel I am not a good patient—too sick—and not a good phone patient—too quiet, just like I felt with my mom. And I am afraid of being too much for you."

Mr. M was, if anything, even more anxious in person when he came to the analyst's office for a week of analysis approximately three times a year. He attributed that to having spent so much time in a doctor's office, and raising the fear that his analyst, like that doctor, would send him to the hospital, a fear which became intense when she did refer him to a colleague in a large medical building for a medication consultation. "The travel required to your office may re-create those moments of travel to the doctor's office, which I simply dreaded, yet needed to stay alive. I also feel concern about you keeping the door locked. I fear being trapped on the outside (can't get in, like I couldn't with my mother's heart) and trapped on the inside so that I can't escape from harm. Being shut in your office with the double door is like being trapped with Arthur, especially when I feel tormented in your presence. At least on the phone, I feel a bit safer."

Mr. M noted that the analyst seemed more distant to him in person, and was puzzled as to why that was the case. He tried to explain: "It may be my experience of my mother as absent when present. It may be that the phone provides a kind of intimacy, a whispering in my ear, like a mother might do with a child. You just seem closer on the phone." In the office, he found the analyst's physical presence a mixture of reassuring and threatening, especially when talking about traumatic sexual material which nauseated him. He said, "In your office, I find it embarrassing when I feel like I am going to throw up on your rug and we work on the feeling together, but over the phone there have been a couple of times when I actually did have to throw up, and hung up a few minutes early." At moments like these, the frame offered by analysis on the telephone could not fully contain the anxiety felt in the body. On the other hand, the use of the telephone allowed the analysand to reveal more vivid detail about sexual abuse than was possible in person and gave the body freedom to give full expression of fear and disgust. Hanging up the phone a few minutes early gave expression to the wish to remove himself from the analyst as a torturing figure.

Childhood was punctuated by trips to the doctor and the hospital. Similarly, the in–person analysis was interrupted by telephone sessions, and the telephone analysis was interrupted by in-person sessions. For Mr. M, telephoning the analyst has multiple meanings: it is both reminiscent of being in the hospital and at the aunt's far from his mother whom he cannot call, and also reminds him of finally reaching his mother and being listened to. The telephone is both the block to, and the means for recovery, but the telephone analysis goes slowly as did the time the analysand spent as a child feeling frightened in the hospital and at his aunt's. Being in the office is reminiscent of being trapped in a hospital room, especially of the time he was in the oxygen tent, being shut in behind locked doors with a frightening babysitter, and also of being with a mother whose good attention is longed for.

Verbal and non-verbal communication in traditional analysis and teleanalysis

Remote analysis by telephone is different from traditional or shuttle analysis in that the two bodies, analysand and analyst, are not together in the office, and the contact is primarily auditory. However, in both traditional analysis and teleanalysis, the analyst privileges conversation over bodily interaction: The body of the analysand is lying down in a state of reduced mobility so that action is not available as a discharge route but in traditional analysis the body gives out non-verbal clues. The use of the telephone relies upon speech and analytic listening as the primary mode of exchange in psychoanalysis. Continuing in telephone analysis with a woman patient who had to move after a period of in-person analysis, Hanly (2008) learned that erotic elements of her transference were evoked because she could imagine him as a younger man without visual contradiction, and a dependent maternal transference (previously covered by a paternal transference in in-person sessions) was revealed due to hypercathexis of his calming voice. Indeed, without the libidinal presence of the body, the telephone privileges semiology of voice (Aryan, Berenstain, Carlino, Grinfeld & Lutenberg, 2009).

Focusing on only the medium of speech, the analyst becomes more intent on listening. Working with a woman patient, Zalusky found herself "more present to hear the nuances of her associations" (2000, p. 24). Finding that he listened more intently, Leffert said that "[T]he treatment becomes an analysis of words and voice: the verbal comes to carry all the contact and interaction, replacing appearance and visual contact" (2003, p. 117). It is … a "hyperanalytic process" … putting "everything into verbal utterances … a central goal of any analysis" (p. 24). From clinical experience, we know that the unique form of a person's verbal expression signifies a great deal about that person's history, culture, and personality, and specific internal object relationships. From research using the adult attachment interview we have learned that speech patterns predict attachment style. Sensitivity to the voice increases when the visual channel is blocked. The voice provides a substitute channel for understanding, through which the symptom comes alive to be worked with directly. As Freud put it: "While we are working at one of these symptoms we come across the interesting and not undesired phenomenon of 'joining in the conversation'" (1893a, p. 296). Even though we cannot see the analysand in analysis on the telephone, and we must relate through the voice, the body joins in the conversation. This is shown in the following example.

Clinical process: the body joining the conversation in teleanalysis

In the mid-phase of treatment when Mr. M eventually found the words to begin telling what actually happened when shut in the room being terrorised by the male babysitter, he began to cough uncomfortably, and so did the analyst. The analyst thought at first that she was coughing in resonance with the boy's general anxiety about his safety, but then an image of gagging on a penis entered her mind and suggested a more specific source of his anxiety, possibly conveyed to her by projective identification. She felt embarrassed by being unable to speak for the benefit of the analysand, because of trying to suppress the cough, the terror, and the specific image. The analysand continued coughing almost to the point of vomiting, and in response to the analyst's telling him that she had the impression that he was trying to evacuate a traumatic image, he eventually found his words and told of the trauma of being forced to perform fellatio and then being too afraid to tell a parent who would not believe him. The analysand understood the vomiting impulse as a wish to get rid of the ejaculate. The analyst recovered, and work continued, analyst and analysand reviewing what had just happened.

Mr. M said, "I guess it was the only way to convey what happened, which I had blocked from my mind. It only came forward for me at the moment it did for you. When you were incapacitated like that, it reminded me of my illness being too much for my mom. I couldn't orient myself, and it felt as though you couldn't either. I am worried about hurting you, worried that my stuff will get into you (as it did). I felt an absolute sense of desperation in the moment, and I had to struggle to breathe. When Arthur was abusing me, that struggle to breathe took the focus much more than what was happening sexually. I was always worried about surviving with him, like I am at times with you."

Reviewing this sequence together, Mr. M and his analyst joined in understanding the horror of the event, the shame at being taken over by it, the wish to evacuate the sadistic object, and the longing for an empathic response, empathy having been absent not only at the time of the abuse but also for a moment in the session when the analyst was incapacitated. Without visual clues and without words, the anxiety of the moment had been clearly transmitted in eidetic form as a projective identification, received, and put into words.

The interacting unconscious mind in teleanalysis

In in-person sessions, the unconscious minds of analyst and analysand are interacting in the context of bodily presence where desire and abstinence are evoked and, driving the recall of infantile sexuality and early experience, give access to implicit memory behaviours (Sachs, 2003, p. 29). However, in telephone or Skype sessions, the analyst's tone of voice alone produces a bodily response in the analysand and vice versa. True, the analyst cannot see the analysand's bodily response, but uses other observations, such as hesitations, tearfulness, catches in the breath, and changes in tone that reveal so much more than words alone.

Having moved from the in-person experience to the telephone session, the teleanalyst starts listening with an image of the person, sitting in the waiting room, entering the door of the office, lying on the couch, and later, leaving the office. And the analysand has a corresponding image of the analyst in the analytic chair. These images endure in telephone sessions in which there are no non-verbal cues. As the session proceeds, the sound of the voice delivered through headphones or from speakers in the room evokes an image coloured by the relevant affect. The voice of the unconscious conveyed in association, affective tone, hesitation, slip, and silence conjures up a sensation that conveys the analysand's internal situation. This is no different from in-person analysis where although the analyst is looking at an analysand lying on a couch in the present, in the mind's eye the analyst sees that person in many different situations past, present, and future, here in the office and in outside life, as associations flow. We may think we have a single view of ourselves and our patients in space but many different images and spaces are encoded in the brain (Ferrari, personal communication). The past that is forgotten is constructed in the here-and-now of the session to arrive at a more complete narrative of the person's history (Faimberg, 2009).

When one route of communication is blocked by working on the telephone, other routes compensate because of cross-modal channels of communication (Anderson, Scharff, D., Scharff, J. & Symington, 2009). Unconscious communication can occur on auditory, visual, and sensory routes. Language is embodied in the resonating sensorimotor system: words stir emotions. A purely auditory communication on the telephone provokes a visual image in the listener that is then put into words, as it would be in traditional analysis. Comparing process notes from a traditional and a teleanalysis session from the same analysand, Mirkin (2011) could not tell which is which, and neither could my colleagues in a teleanalysis working group (Scharff, 2011).

Teleanalysis: contraindications and indications

Teleanalysis is not possible if the analysand lacks a capacity for maintaining the alliance and sharing responsibility for the management of the setting. It is not possible to do teleanalysis when the analyst or analysand has uncorrected deafness; when either of them speaks too softly or indistinctly, or is too silent to sustain the connection. It is unwise when the analysand has borderline features with suicidal actions; when there is a need for medication unless a local psychiatrist is willing to take medical responsibility for assessing risk, prescribing, and monitoring side-effects; and when there is substance abuse unless sobriety is maintained. Teleanalysis is not a good idea if the analyst is made anxious by lack of in–person sessions, cannot rely on visualising the physically absent analysand, and feels disconnected. But teleanalysis is possible—and may be easier—for trauma-related dissociation, because the analysand is less embarrassed to reveal split off parts of the self since the physical changes when inhabiting a child part are not visible. In analysis of "severely traumatized people, the telephone may allow a necessary space in which they can begin to tackle the fears associated with intimacy" (Zalusky, 2005, p. 111).

Teleanalysis is indicated when analyst and analysand are confronted with a circumstance that impedes the continuation of an ongoing analysis because of travel for work, relocation, illness including phobia, and commitments that interfere with the analysand's commuting to sessions during the analyst's available hours. Teleanalysis is indicated for those living in another country even if there is no already established analytic process, provided the analyst has met the analysand in person to make the assessment, has established the alliance in a preliminary sense, and has received agreement for in-person sessions at suitable intervals. Although the prior establishment of analytic process in person is preferable, Gelman (2001) has reported that analysis has been started before meeting the patient who lives in a remote country, and Carlino (2011) foresees a day when teleanalysis will be preferred by digitally connected young people even though they live near an analytic centre. In any case, the practice of teleanalysis is still experimental, and so the analysand should be told this before consenting to teleanalysis, and should be warned that it is not possible to guarantee absolute privacy because of the possibility of hacking and eavesdropping on the line; and the analyst is advised to consult with a group of colleagues who are gathering experience in this area for further study.

Experience with the clinical effectiveness of psychoanalysis using telephone or internet has implications for expanding training opportunities for candidates in remote locations and for the spread of psychoanalysis. The question that teleanalysis then faces is whether it is functionality equivalent to an in-person analysis in terms of fostering dreaming, free association, resistance, and transference-countertransference experience of sufficient intensity to evoke in candidates having teleanalysis a conviction about the working of the unconscious, the formation of character defences, and the interpretive skill to achieve therapeutic action such that these candidates become effective analysts with their own analysands (Sachs, 2009). Seminars can be held on telephone conference call or Skype with webcam for candidates in the same or various remote locations in a region. Training analysis by telephone or internet may be authorised for candidates in exceptional circumstances. I will address this issue in Chapter Twenty One, but for now let me just say this. When training analysts across regions have accumulated experience in analysis by telephone or internet, and research analysts have published their results on its clinical effectiveness, teleanalysis may some day be offered with confidence as an alternative or a supplement to condensed analysis for disadvantaged candidates, and so bring psychoanalytic training to remote locations. "We must change our way of looking at the use of the telephone if we are to provide truly patient-friendly analytic treatment and trainee-friendly analytic training" (Richards, 2003, p. 32).

Conclusion

Some analysts believe that psychoanalysis, a professional art based on the harmonics of unconscious communication, augmented by technology, cannot possibly transcend the limits of distance. Others note that unconscious communication and analytic process occur in telephone and Skype analysis as they do in traditional in-person analysis. The deficit of losing the actual communication of physical presence when the analysand is on the telephone or Skype with webcam has to be recognised, and the loss acknowledged. "By being sensitive to what we are losing, we help our patients be more open about their own feelings of loss" (Zalusky, 2005, p. 108). Then we and they are free to develop a heightened appreciation for unconscious communication via the transmission of sound. The objection that innovative telephone analysis is a seductive, fashionable, elastic practice that fails to interpret transference (Argentieri &

Mehler, 2003) may reflect the debate about various philosophies of psychoanalysis more than about telephone analysis itself (Zalusky, 2003a).

I support the view that analysis by telephone, Skype, and videotechnology is indicated at the individual level in exceptional circumstances to augment analytic continuity. But I share concerns about the level of privacy the teleanalysand can count on. I recommend discussing this concern with the potential patient and assessing the level of risk so that the patient makes an informed decision about whether to proceed or not. Of necessity, psychoanalysis is pushed to make increasing use of the telephone, videoconference, and Skype in clinical practice and in teaching. Out of that necessity, teleanalysis finds an opportunity for opening up new pathways of understanding and extending the reach of psychoanalysis to new frontiers.

References

Anderson, G., Scharff, D., Scharff, J. & Symington, N. (2009). Telephone analysis. Panel on Telephone Analysis, International Psychoanalytic Congress, Chicago, August.

Argentieri, S. & Mehler, J. A. (2003). Telephone "analysis": "Hello, who's speaking?". *Insight*, 12: 17–19.

Aronson, J. K. (Ed.) (2000a). *The Use of the Telephone in Psychotherapy*. Northvale, NJ: Jason Aronson.

Aronson, J. K. (2000b). Use of the telephone as a transitional space. In: J. Aronson (Ed.), *The Use of the Telephone in Psychotherapy* (pp. 129–149). Northvale, NJ: Jason Aronson.

Aryan, A., Berenstain, S., Carlino, R., Grinfeld, P. & Lutenberg, J. (2009). Psicoanálisis por teléfono. Panel on Telephone Analysis. International Psychoanalytic Congress, Chicago, August.

Aryan, A. & Carlino, R. (2010). Desafíos del y al psicoanálisis contemporáneo. Vicisitudes de lo establecido frente a lo nuevo que va surgiendo. El psicoanálisis telefónico. Unpublished paper, VI APU (6th International Multidisciplinary Congress, Asociación Psicoanalitica de Uruguay), Montevideo, Uruguay, August 20.

Benaim, B. (2009). Personal communication.

Benson, R. M., Rowntree, E. B. & Singer, M. H. (2001). Final report of ad hoc committee on training analysis via telephone. Unpublished report to the Board on Professional Standards of the American Psychoanalytic Association.

Brainsky, S. (2003). Adapting to, or idealizing, technology? *Insight*, 12(1): 22–24.

Carlino, R. (2011). *Distance Psychoanalysis*. London: Karnac.

Chodorow, N. (2004). Creating a physical surround in the absence of physical presence: Clinical observations on phone treatment. Unpublished paper. Vermont Association for Psychoanalytic Psychology, November.

Faimberg, H. (2009). The past as resistance, the past as constructed. Unpublished paper. IPA Congress, Chicago, July.

Freud, S. (1893a). The psychotherapy of hysteria. *S. E.*, 2 (pp. 253–305). London: Hogarth.

Freud, S. (1912e). Recommendations to physicians practising psycho-analysis. *S. E.*, 12 (pp. 109–120). London: Hogarth.

Gelman, M. H. (2001). The use of the telephone in analysis: Therapeutic compromise or primary modality of treatment. Unpublished paper at the Sandor Ferenczi Conference in Budapest, Hungary, February 23.

Hanly, C. (2007). Case material from a telephone analysis. Unpublished panel presentation. Spring Meeting, American Psychoanalytic Association, Seattle, June.

Leffert, M. (2003). Analysis and psychotherapy by telephone. *Journal of the American Psychoanalytic Association, 51*: 101–130.

Lindon, J. (2000). Psychoanalysis by telephone. In: J. Aronson (Ed.), *The Use of the Telephone in Psychotherapy* (pp. 3–13). Northvale, NJ: Jason Aronson.

Lutenberg, J. (2011a). Presentación de material clínico del análisis telefónico. *Tratamiento Psicoanalítico Telefónico* (pp. 113–142). Lima, Peru: Siklos SRL.

Lutenberg, J. (2011b). Reflexiones técnicas a partir de las sesiones con Irene. *Tratamiento Psicoanalítico Telefónico* (pp. 143–186). Lima, Peru: Siklos SRL.

Mirkin, M. (2011). Telephone analysis: Compromised treatment or an interesting opportunity? *Psychoanalytic Quarterly, 80*(3): 643–670.

Richards, A. K. (2003). Fruitful uses of telephone analysis. *Insight, 12*(1): 30–32.

Robertiello, R. C. (1972–73). Telephone sessions. *Psychoanalytic Review, 59*: 633–634.

Rodriguez de la Sierra, L. (2003). "It if helps, why not?" *Insight, 12*: 20–21.

Saul, L. J. (1951). A note on the telephone as a technical aid. *Psychoanalytic Quarterly, 20*: 287–290.

Sachs, D. (2003). Telephone analysis—sometimes the best choice? *Insight, 12*: 28–29.

Sachs, D. (2009). Far away, so close. Unpublished paper. Panel, International Psychoanalytic Congress, Chicago, July.

Scharff, J. S. (2010). Report of panel on telephone analysis. International Psychoanalytical Association Congress, Chicago, August. *International Journal of Psychoanalysis, 91*: 989–992.

Scharff, J. S. (2011). Findings of the International Working Group on teleanalysis. Precongress, International Psychoanalytical Association meeting, Mexico, August. *Bulletin of the International Psychotherapy Institute, 15*(2): 2.

Snyder, E. (2011). The use of Skype in supervision. Panel, Winter Meeting, American Psychoanalytic Association, January.

Varela, Y. (2007). Transference as a playground: two analytic settings. Unpublished paper.

Yamin Habib, L. E. (2003). Physical presence—a sine qua non of analysis? *Insight, 12*: 25–27.

Zalusky, S. (1998). Telephone analysis: out of sight but not out of mind. *Journal of the American Psychoanalytic Association, 46*: 1221–1242.

Zalusky, S. (2000). Telephone analysis. In: J. Aronson (Ed.), *The Use of the Telephone in Psychotherapy* (pp. 15–43). Northvale, NJ: Jason Aronson.

Zalusky, S. (2003a). Adaptation or idealization of theory? *Insight, 12*(2): 34.

Zalusky, S. (2003b). Dialogue: Telephone analysis. *Insight, 12*: 13–16.

Zalusky, S. (2005). Telephone, psychotherapy and the 21st century. In: M. Stadter & D. Scharff (Eds.), *Dimensions of Psychotherapy: Dimensions of Experience: Time, Space, Number, and State of Mind* (pp. 107–114). London: Routledge.

CHAPTER SEVEN

Legal, clinical, and ethical issues in teletherapy

Angela Carter Martin, DNP, APRN

Our society has moved towards the use of technology in most aspects of our lives. It is no surprise that mental health education and treatment are moving in a similar direction. Some research looking at the different therapy modalities of audiovisual, audio, and text communication found that they provide equal benefits when compared to in-person therapy and that they may offer certain advantages (Anthony, Nagel & Goss, 2010). As patients demand access to mental health treatments beyond the clinic or private office, therapists are offering technologically mediated therapies (commonly known as telemental health) as part of their practices. Yet educational programmes often lag behind patients' and therapists' interest in treatment that is not place- or time-bound. A significant number of clinicians who have no preparation for conducting treatments outside the consulting room are not prepared for the multiple issues inherent in the use of technology to deliver services. The purpose of this chapter is to clarify some of the major ethical, legal, and practice issues therapists should consider when preparing to deliver mental health services through the use of technology.

Definition of telemental health

Telemental health is most commonly defined as the provision of mental health and substance abuse services by phone, text, email, video chat, virtual reality (VR), or other digital means, to an individual in a different geographic area (Doherty, Coyle &.Matthews, 2010). These services may include: 1) crisis intervention or other contacts between in-person sessions; 2) conducting videoconferencing or phone sessions with patients who are not able to attend in-person sessions for a period of time; 3) using email, chats, videoconferencing and other digital means between in-person session contact with patients; 4) assessments and/or psychological testing with or without in-person contact; and 5) using email, videoconferencing, VR, or other means to provide online counselling services with no in-person contact (Anthony, Nagel & Goss, 2010).

Advantages of using technology

Despite the increase in the number of people receiving treatment for mental disorders between 1990 and 2005, fewer than half of the people in the United States who need psychological services actually receive them (Kessler et al., 2005). Telemental health can reach underserved populations by offering psychological treatment that is not place- or even time-bound. Services may include more consistent aftercare to patients no longer in need of intensive services and psychotherapy for patients unable or unwilling to attend traditional sessions in the therapist's office because they are physically handicapped, sick, sensory impaired, mentally unable to go outside, or too depressed to get dressed to come to the office. Telemental health brings therapy to people who otherwise might not ever attend an in-office session. However, while these novel approaches have benefits and may hold promise for providing timely, efficient, and creative mental health care, various challenges interfere with or slow down the adoption of technology.

Disadvantages of using technology

We as therapists are educated to use non-verbal behaviour as part of our assessment. If we cannot see a patient, smell alcohol on their breath, or notice a lack of hygiene, we may miss important cues to deterioration in the patient's condition. Moreover, we consider the non-verbal aspects of treatment important in the conveying of unconscious feelings and anxieties. Sometimes these messages are so subtle that we may miss these cues if we see the patient on a screen. Transference and countertransference issues may be affected in telemental health services.

Psychiatric emergencies are difficult to manage in the office and can become even more difficult if encountered during a phone or videoconferencing treatment. No matter how well prepared we are for technology failures, they are inevitable. Furthermore, some patients may not tolerate the lack of in-person contact. Some therapies may fail to progress, especially those concerned with difficulties tolerating intimacy and impairments in creating and sustaining object relationships. Perhaps future research may reassure us that the clinical effectiveness of telemental health outweighs the disadvantages. However, for now, we must at least acknowledge that we do not yet know fully what impact, if any, the compromised transmission of non-verbal data may have on the outcome of the clinical situation.

Initiation of telemental health services

Prior to using telemental health services, we should consider issues related to safety, informed consent, technology access, billing, licensing, data protection, and HIPAA compliance. We need to develop strategies to deal with these challenges. Few professional organisations have established policies guiding this area of mental health treatment. Each of us has to decide if telemental health care meets our standard of practice. Consistent with our ethical model for practice, we should evaluate the benefits and risks involved in telemental health services, focusing on beneficence and non-maleficence. We have a long-standing tradition of best practice applied to the in-person provision of care by a therapist who meets with a patient in a private office. Some licensing boards continue to support this as the standard (Harris & Younggren, 2011). So, we need to be able to justify our choice of telemental health care. We need to know how much personal contact is required for the treatment to be effective. Without adequate research this may be difficult to determine. Harris and Younggren (2011) summarise key points that they believe should be considered when making the decision to see a patient using telemental health technology. They support its use to continue an ongoing treatment when 1) the patient is required to relocate for some life situation (e.g., college or work travel); 2) when in-person treatment is difficult or impossible to access because of the patient's location or health related travel restriction; 3) when it offers some practical advantage over traditional sessions in terms of frequency and duration of session related to patient comfort, and time limitations; and 4) when the patient desires telemental health and the treating therapist has enough knowledge of the patient to consider him or her competent to make the decision. Harris and Younggren also advise therapists to evaluate the risks and ask themselves the question: if there are plenty of mental health providers in the area where the patient resides and the therapist has no ongoing relationship with the patient, why would telemental psychotherapy be preferable to traditional psychotherapy?

Peer consultations can also help us to determine the best course of action when considering telemental health technology for a particular client. Just as in traditional therapy practice, ongoing consultations can help clarify problematic areas in our telemental health practice and either support the decision to go ahead with the client or look at other alternatives that might be better, especially in the long run.

Patient assessment is the key to success. It is never a good idea to skimp on completing an adequate history, assessment, and consideration of the best treatment options. Keep in mind that for some clients, the appeal of telemental health care is to remain anonymous. This wish may turn out to represent a deeper issue around intimacy. Some therapists will not offer phone or videoconferencing therapy unless they have already met and evaluated the patient during the initial consultation. I think there are valid reasons for this approach. For example, even with videoconferencing, we have to be sure the patient is not a minor, otherwise parental consent is required. Some third party payers, if they pay at all for telemental health services, may require some sessions to be conducted in-person.

Even though technology can be useful, it may interfere with treatment. Disruptive transferences can occur whether a patient is present in the office or not. Having a crisis intervention plan is important, especially if the patient lives out of state or the country. What local resources are available? Is there another therapist in town who can see your patient in case of an emergency? What agreements do you have if the patient hangs up the phone or exits the videoconferencing session because of anger, a sudden wish to harm themselves or an other, or an affect that is hard to manage? Most experts agree that telemental health sessions are not for every patient.

If you decide to provide these services, then you should look for ways to be as educated about these practices as you can be. Write out a business plan for the telemental health aspect of your practice. Send it to your malpractice company, your licensing board, and your professional organisation. Inform them of what you are doing, especially if there are no standards or laws concerning the use of telemental health services in your state. Document all communications so as to establish that you made an attempt to obtain clarification before proceeding.

If you have little or no education in the use of technology, attend continuing education seminars where the issues surrounding telemental health are discussed. Look for online resources that provide skill acquisition. One of the best guides for working with the technology and how to get started can be found at the following web site: (http://www.tmhguide.org/clinicians-administrators/). This information includes the Telemental Health Guide as developed by the University of Colorado, Denver, with support from the Center for Mental Health Services (CMHS, a part of the Substance Abuse and Mental Health Services Administration). Information is presented online about what equipment to buy, how to set up the consulting room, and how to deal with technology failures and other technical aspects (Telemental Health Guide, 2012). You may decide that you would like even more education and consultation. The Telemental Health Institute (2012) offers free webinars, certificate education, and consultation as to how to set up, bill, and adapt to the changing mental health care market. Courses are tailored specifically for the mental health professional, detailing ethical and legal issues with suggestions on how best to overcome these challenges.

Issues of safety

Therapists often self-assess and decide there are certain types of patients that they do not have particularly good results with, either because of countertransference issues or because the patient requires more from them than they are able to provide. The same may be true for telemental health. Offering these services is not for all therapists. Figuring that out may be a crucial step in the process. Patients who are unstable, who have Axis II diagnoses, who are at risk of severe depression or suicide, and patients who are unable to form stable interpersonal relationships are unlikely to be effectively treated remotely (Harris & Younggren, 2011). A general rule to remember is that patients who are more high risk in traditional settings are also likely to be high risk in telemental health care too.

As with all patients, you should make sure that you have a plan for emergencies. Since the patient may be located at a distance, you may have to make arrangements for in-town back-up that includes someone who can admit patients for you if the need should arise. Contracts for safety may include the patient agreement to contact this person in emergencies. If you are prescribing medication, may sure the law permits you to prescribe in that state where the patient resides, if it is different from the one in which you are currently licensed. There is at least one case of a psychiatrist who, following the death of a psychiatric patient, was successfully prosecuted for practising across state lines (CBS4 News, 2007). You should make sure that your malpractice insurance plan does not exclude telemental health treatments. Usually, insurers cover what we are authorised to do by state law only. If you are not licensed in a particular state that requires licensing if you are seeing a patient who resides in that state, then your malpractice insurance could deny coverage for your telemental health treatments.

Issues with informed consent

Informed consent is important whenever we see a patient. Since there are so few guidelines in this emerging field, it is important to explain the options to the patient. Describe the types of services that you provide. Discuss openly the options and alternatives available, including traditional therapy. Provide a list of the relative risks and benefits of each type of telemental health service. Be honest about the risks to privacy and limits to confidentiality. It is possible for a breach of data to occur even when the data is thought to be secure and encrypted—you cannot give an absolute guarantee of privacy. Patients should share responsibility if such a breach should occur. Disclose your fees and make sure the financial arrangements are clear. Provide the patient with an outline of what to do in case of an emergency and who they should contact, including addresses and phone numbers. Make sure that providers covering you from a distance are fully licensed and have not had ethical violations in the past. If you have no experience or education in using telemental health care, you should acquire education and/or experience before making this a significant component of your practice. Patients should know of your lack of experience and accept it as a limitation for which they must share the responsibility if you both decide to proceed. Document in writing the extent of the informed consent covering the areas discussed above. Beware that courts usually side with vulnerable patients, and even if they are willing to share responsibility for the decision to use telemental health services, in a given situation it may be determined that the patient was not able to discern the risk.

Issues of technology access

Before beginning a telemental health treatment session, it is a good idea to do a test run, checking the equipment and software with the patient. Several of the resources identified in the Appendix suggest camera angles and equipment. No matter how sophisticated the program you choose may be, all computerised activities are vulnerable to failure. Outline for the patient the procedure to be used when technology is not available. For example, phone therapy can be an alternative for computer inaccessibility. If the patient calls you and you do not answer, specify other means for contacting you. Can a patient text you? What are your financial expectations for failed sessions? Will the patient still be responsible for payment? Can the patient reschedule without incurring a fee?

Reimbursement

Since there is no universal definition of telemental health and no universal reimbursement policy by public and private sector payers, you will have to verify coverage for every telemental health patient prior to treatment. As of this time, Medicare reimburses for real-time, interactive A-V telecommunications only, no email or phone sessions. Restrictions are placed on where the patient may be located during the service. Medicare does not reimburse for telemental health visits that are transmitted to the home of the patient. The provision of these services to a Medicare beneficiary can only occur at an eligible site (rural health shortage area or a county outside a Metropolitan Statistical Area). Applicable mental health CPT codes include individual psychotherapy (CPT codes 90832, 90834, 90837 or appropriate E & M [evaluation and management] code); pharmacologic management (appropriate E & M code); and psychiatric diagnostic interview examination (CPT code 90791 or 90792, effective January 1, 2013) (National Council for Community Behavioral Healthcare, 2012). CMS (Centers for Medicare and Medicaid Services) require that claims submitted use the GT modifier. Private payers do reimburse for telemental health sessions. To date, thirteen states have enacted legislation requiring private sector companies to pay for telemental health services. They include: California, Colorado, Georgia, Hawaii, Kentucky, Louisiana, Maine, Maryland, New Hampshire, Oklahoma, Oregon, Texas and Virginia. Reimbursement rules vary from state to state.

Billing

Money issues are never easy to overcome and in telemental health therapy they are even harder because there may be considerable distance between you and the patient. It may be harder to confront non-payment or discuss money with a patient you do not see in person. Then you may find yourself ignoring the dynamic implications of the fee arrangements. However, it is just as important to be clear about your billing practices in this situation as it is in traditional office based therapy. You should be clear about the fee, what it covers, and whether there is a surcharge for the associated technology costs. How often will you bill? Do you accept credit cards and tele-transfers into your business bank account? If the patient is expecting insurance reimbursement, make sure the patient assumes responsibility for verifying coverage unless you have a direct relationship with the insurance company and participate as a recognised provider. When providing telemental health therapy, you must disclose it to the insurance company by using a GT modifier or making a note on the bill that you supply the patient for self-submitted reimbursement. Otherwise, it may meet the definition of fraud. Some state laws will not permit reimbursement for phone therapy. For example, in California therapy by phone is not considered telemental health care.

Licensure issues

Determining who regulates the practice of therapy across state lines is probably the single most complicated aspect of delivering technology mediated services. Traditionally, licensing boards evolved to protect the citizens living in a given state from unqualified mental health practitioners by regulating the qualifications and the practice of mental health professionals and conducting disciplinary procedures when necessary. States are unable to perform this function when the provider is located in another state because they have no authority beyond state lines, and therefore state boards have decided that where the patient resides determines where the therapist should be licensed, but within that rubric some states have passed laws permitting temporary practice within their state (Harris & Younggren, 2011).

In response to telemental health issues, state legislatures have passed laws that permit temporary practice by a therapist licensed in another state (American Psychological Association Practice Organization, 2010). You must fully investigate the state where your patient resides to determine if you are required to obtain a licence and what the licence will permit. You can call your board where you are located but they have no jurisdiction over practice that occurs in another state. Your professional board in your own state will expect you to be licensed in that state and will advise you to contact the board in the state where your patient lives. However, some of the laws are limited to a case by case basis or have limits as to how many hours you can practise before you must apply for full licence. Familiarise yourself with state rules and regulations, such as mandatory reporting requirements. Note licensing boards' rules and state and national mental health professional association guidelines and codes of ethics. Once you are licensed in another state, you are expected to understand the laws in that jurisdiction and the laws in the state where you are licensed.

Obviously, one potential barrier to practising mental health is licensing. Seeking a licence in multiple states can be burdensome and expensive. Physicians probably have the hardest time obtaining licences in multiple states. There can be quite a variety of requirements to obtain a medical licence. You may have to meet with the board in person. Many states require the current licensing exam to be taken and passed if it has been more than seven to ten years since the applicant passed the then-current exam. The American Psychiatry Association (2012) urges physicians who provide consultation to another physician, supervise a health care professional, or provide direct patient care across state lines to establish with the state medical board in that patient's state whether a medical licence from that state is required to provide telepsychiatric services. Professionals in other disciplines should consider these guidelines when thinking about how best to proceed.

Nursing is recognised as a leader in trying to solve the licensing issue (Harris & Younggren, 2011). A group of state nursing boards has established a compact state licence whereby nurses licensed in one state can practise in another as long as they follow the rules and regulations of the Nurse Practice Act in a participating state. To date, twenty-four states have agreed to this mechanism as a way to allow nurses flexibility to travel or to provide telemental health across state lines (National Council of State Boards of Nursing, 2012).

Telemental health care may also change tax liabilities. Many states have limits on the amount of income you can receive for services in their state without filing an income tax form. Since licensing boards take the position that telemental health treatment is taking place in the state where the patient resides, it is possible that the income received may be subject to that state's income tax. Verify with your tax advisor or the state tax office as to in which state your tax liability exists.

Data protection and HIPAA compliance

It is well documented that cellphone contact is the least secure of all the technologies used. Landlines are more secure than cellphone connections. Email is not secure because it can easily be hacked and is often retained for years by third parties. Internet security is a major concern in general. For instance, websites are not secure unless they are identified "https". The purpose of the "s" in "https" is to inform you that site is encrypted and therefore so secure that you can have confidence in any purchases made there, whereas "http" sites are not encrypted and not safe for handling credit card information. Then there is Skype, probably the most used platform for videoconferencing by therapists. It is easy to learn how to use, readily available, and free.

But is it secure? The Skype website has a disclaimer regarding its use for psychotherapy. At the end of the day you have to decide if Skype is secure enough for you.

Here's what you need to know to make that decision. Although Skype has 256-bit encryption, it does not claim to be HIPAA compliant. Third party payers such as Medicare or Medicaid expect HIPAA compliant software to be used for telemental health services, but uncertainty arises because HIPAA does not certify software as compliant or not. A company can claim HIPAA compliance if it assumes responsibility for the data collected. While Skype does meet the encryption standard, it does not meet HIPAA compliance for two reasons: Skype does not assume responsibility for the data collected, and Skype does not offer "business associate" contracts to therapists or clinics that use it for telemental health purposes (Zur Institute, 2012).

Just what does the term "business associate" mean? By law, the HIPAA Privacy Rule applies only to covered entities, such as health plan mental health care providers. However, many health care providers and health plans do not carry out all of their health care activities and functions by themselves. They often use the services of a variety of other persons or businesses. The Privacy Rule allows covered providers and health plans to disclose protected health information to these "business associates" if the providers or plans obtain assurances that the business associate will use the information only for the purposes for which it was engaged by the covered entity and will safeguard the information from misuse. Health plan mental health care providers may disclose protected health information to covered entities called business associates only to help the covered entities carry out their health care functions. HIPAA mandates that practitioners must engage in a HIPAA "Business Associate Agreement" with such entities or third parties, which makes the third party HIPAA compliant (Zur Institute, 2012).

If you decide that Skype does not provide enough security or if you are required to use a HIPAA compliant company for reimbursement by third party payers, there are a number of other videoconferencing platforms, some of which are HIPAA compliant. The Behavioral Health Innovations website provides a comprehensive side by side comparison of videoconferencing platforms. The major videotechnology companies are listed in the Resources section at the end of this chapter.

Therapists who decide to offer services with the use of technology should inform patients about safety issues related to privacy. Encrypted videoconferencing is safer than either the phone or email because of its encrypted format but only if the connection does not run on phone service lines. In other words, the transmission of data should occur from computer to computer. Conversations on telephones, particularly cellphones, are relatively easy for people to tap or accidentally overhear because the data is not encrypted. While the probability of unauthorised access is relatively low, especially when users use encryption software and passwords, patients should be informed about who else may have access to communications with you, how communications can be directed to you, and if and how you store information. Internet users should also understand that internet service providers can gain access to email messages. Remember to remind patients that if they choose to participate in a session while other people are in the room with them, you cannot be responsible for what other people may do with the information they overhear. Perhaps the most important issue about privacy and security is to make sure we have fully disclosed the risks posed by telemental health care.

Future trends

Telemental health care holds great promise for expanding our services to even more patients. This is especially true for patients for whom participating in therapy might otherwise be impossible. Significant barriers exist especially in the area of licensing. There is some work already being done to make practising across state lines easier. Without federal regulation such as national licensing, states would have to voluntarily agree to work together to create mutual recognition or make a compact agreement similar to that used in nursing, whereby a professional licensed in one state could practise in another state by virtue of the one licence. Eventually mechanisms would have to be developed whereby patients could file complaints that would be expediently and seriously investigated.

Graduate programmes will have to include in their curricula, courses containing knowledge and experience related to technology-mediated therapies. Professional organisations responsible for continuing education (CE) can highlight the importance of knowledge and skills in the area by offering CE programmes geared to reviewing the ethical, legal, and practice issues unique to provision of the technology-mediated therapies.

Professional organisations could also be more proactive by developing policies that licensing boards can use to determine if the standard of care has or has not been met and whether certain practices by the therapists fall within guidelines for reasonable and expectable recognised practice set by their respective mental health professional organisations. Research comparing traditional therapies with technology-mediated therapies would also help establish for the public the effectiveness of such emerging therapies. More information makes it easier for a patient to decide about which type of therapy might be best in any given situation. Times are a-changing. We cannot ignore the impact of technology on contemporary life. We can be in front of it or behind it. The choice is ours to make.

References

American Psychiatric Association (2012). Physician licensure: an update of trends. Retrieved July 12, 2012 from http://www.ama-assn.org/ama/pub/about-ama/our-people/member-groups-sections/young-physicians-section/advocacy-resources/physician-licensure-an-update-trends.page).

American Psychological Association Practice Organization (2010, Summer). *Telehealth: Legal Basics for Psychologists. Good Practice.*

American Telemedicine Organization (2006). Medicare payment of telemedicine and telehealth services. Retrieved November 19, 2012 from http://www.americantelemed.org/files/public/membergroups/businessfinance/reimbursement/BF_MedicarePaymentofTelemedicine.pdf.

Anthony, K., Nagel, D. M. & Gross, S. (Eds.) (2010). *The Use of Technology in Mental Health: Applications, Ethics and Practice.* Springfield, IL: Charles C. Thomas. CBC4 News (2007). Christian Hageseth III Charged With Felony. Retrieved November 19, 2012 from http://www.ect.org/christian-hageseth-iii-charged-with-felony/.

Doherty, G., Coyle, D. & Matthews, M. (2010). Design and evaluation guidelines for mental health technologies. *Interacting With Computers*, 22(4): 243–252.

Harris, E. & Younggren, J. N. (2011). Risk management in the digital world. *Professional Psychology: Research and Practice*, 42(6): 412–418.

Kessler, R. C., Demier, O., Frank, R. G., Olfson, M. D., Pincus, H. A., Walters, E. E., Wang, P. S., Wells, K. B. & Zaslavsky, A. M. (2005). Prevalence and treatment of mental health disorders, 1990 to 2003. *New England Journal of Medicine, 352*: 2515–2523.

National Council of State Boards of Nursing (2012). Nurse licensure compact. Retrieved November 19, 2012 from https://www.ncsbn.org/nlc.htm.

National Council For Community Behavioral Healthcare (NCCBH) (2012). Major changes to CPT Codes for psychiatry and psychotherapy in 2013. Handout published by NCCBH, September 2012.

Telemental Health Guide (2012). Retrieved November 1, 2012 from http://www.tmhguide.org/clinicians-administrators/.

Telemental Health Institute (2012). Retrieved November 19, 2012 from http://telehealth.org/.

Zur Institute (2012). Telehealth services across state lines. Retrieved November 19, 2012 from http://www.zurinstitute.com/telehealth_across_state_lines-zur.html.

CHAPTER EIGHT

Ethical aspects of teletherapy

Ernest Wallwork, PhD

After more than two decades of conducting phone and, more recently, Skype therapy and psychoanalysis with patients in the two distant cities where I practise—Syracuse, NY and Washington, DC—I am convinced by personal experience with a diverse group of patients, as well as by the reports of colleagues, that good-enough psychodynamic therapy and analysis can be conducted with most patients with the help of the new technologies. The benefits of remote treatment are not for everyone, however. Some patients are just not able to engage affectively via telecommunications technologies. But most are, and for these patients, the benefits of continuing and deepening a treatment by phone and Skype can be enormous and, often, life-altering. The same ethical principles apply in both in-person analysis and teletherapy but there are some unique ethical aspects of teletherapy.

An ethically significant issue related to the analyst's psychic presence in teletherapy

Ken had been in analysis with me on the phone for a couple of years before he started calling me "Herr Professor Doktor Jiminy Cricket". He had laughed uproariously when he first renamed me with this comical attribution, which he did to capture and defend against the very significant moral change that was occurring in him as he began to experience me outside our sessions as a voice in his head or, at least, in his ear: as I was during sessions on the headset he wore on his (not my) couch. Like Jiminy Cricket with Pinocchio, I had become an occasional conscience, who advised Ken to consider alternatives to giving in to his impulsive desire to run off to his version of Pleasure Island and to torture himself afterwards with self-inflicted punishments. To Ken, at this juncture in his analysis, my psychic presence as Herr Jiminy when we were apart was consciously experienced as a good thing; he felt he needed help from an admired superior to avoid the dark places he used to go to. "And what better to put in place of my old man than an analyst who is also a professor of ethics," he declared. But it was scary, and infuriating, too, for Ken to need me in this way. For he feared being taken over, manipulated and exploited as he had been by past authority figures, and so by calling me Herr Professor Doktor Jiminy Cricket, Ken diminished me even as he elevated me. Ken defended against repetition of past traumas by conjuring his analyst as Disney's impotent Jiminy with a tiny top hat and tails that served in their pretentiousness to accentuate the complete powerlessness of his analyst's imagined moral counsel.

In Austria, which Ken associated with psychoanalysis, formal titles preserve a hierarchical status system of respect. First names, like Jiminy, are not used in any social situations other than personal, intimate ones. So, if I were Austrian, as Ken imagined, I would feel seriously affronted, and probably insulted, by being called by my first name. So the "Herr Professor Doktor" part of my title conveyed respect for certain idealised attributes Ken attributed to me; but these titles were no sooner uttered than Ken radically demoted me, first to the status of a close friend, and then to that of an insect, who might easily be squashed for making annoying sounds. Ken tried to mask the hostility behind his radical degradation of me with humour, but the psychic truth was that like an Oedipal youngster Ken felt threatened by his idealisation of me in the transference and, in anger, sought to topple me off the pedestal upon which he had himself installed me. But Ken's humorous attributions also hid a desire to get close to me, to have me whispering in his ear, like a buddy or lover. Ken wanted to have me around all the time, as a powerful alterego, who would help him develop into the new moral agent he imagined himself becoming, but another part of him was in revolt against the severity of the moralistic qualities he projected into me. Imagining me as Jiminy Cricket helped Ken try out new, kinder, more humane ways of being moral towards himself and others, but these new structures were not yet well established and he easily reverted to imagining my moral counsel on the model of his scary sadistic father. As Ken shifted back-and-forth in the transference between the new moral possibilities that were emerging and the old rigidities, I found myself shifting from feeling strongly allied with him in a sometimes playful therapeutic alliance to imagining myself as Jiminy, tumbling off the shoulders of Ken as Pinocchio and rolling on my backside in the dust, watching Pinocchio disappear down the road as he ran off to Pleasure Island: that usually involved buying and using drugs in sketchy back alleys, against his better judgment, which he now heard in his mind as my voice—against which he had to rebel.

There is nothing unusual about any of this, other than that as an analyst who was rarely available to Ken except as a voice in his ear, I was in reality more like a creature of Ken's imagination, as Jiminy, than a person in Ken's life. The fact that we were on the phone altered our relationship in subtle ways. For example, the fact that I was only an unseen voice in his ear meant that the therapeutic relationship lacked the grounding in reality that might have strengthened his new moral adaptations, and yet, at the same time, it gave him the experience of me as more intimately a part of him. Ken wanted both—to distance himself from me by thinking of me as only an imaginary figure, and to ally himself with me as a real person—but the phone seemed to contribute to his confusion as to whether or not his "better judgments" were coming from me or from himself.

When "better judgments" were attributed to me, Jiminy Cricket's imaginary status and my diminished presence in the phone sessions made it easier for Ken to play with new moral possibilities, but the mediation of the phone also undercut his seriousness in grappling with moral issues. Ken could more easily distance himself from our discourse about his addiction by attributing it entirely to me and getting irritated by my Jiminy Cricket voice, while enjoying the image of my falling off his shoulder. When he experienced these fragile new judgments as part of himself, Ken tended to take them more seriously. However, this also meant the judgment could easily get assimilated to his persecutory superego, which often increased his resistance. Ken summarised his complex inner struggle with me as Jiminy late one afternoon when the struggle was especially intense:

> "Sometimes I think, when I'm wrestling with my addictions, that I hear you, as if you're on my shoulder, Herr Professor Doktor Jiminy, advising me not to go there. But then I think I don't really know you. How do I know you even care? You've never said you do. You're just a disembodied voice. I kinda know you don't tell me what to do, but at times I'm sure you do. And, then, I can get really mad thinking, 'You son of a bitch, you're trying to control me,' and I refuse to listen. And I think, 'Fuck you, you're just like Dad'—even though I know you're not. In fact that's one of the biggest obstacles preventing me from getting to where I want to go. I'm at war—against you, Dad, myself. Obviously we have a good relationship but there is deep mistrust, fear, and anger. In the end, I'm not going to do what I'm told. I'm going to go to Pleasure Island. But I get confused about what I want and who wants it—you?, me?, my girlfriend?, the old man?—maybe it's good for me, but I don't want it. Are you still there?"

Because we were on the phone, I did not know that, while speaking to me, Ken was silently drawing. I learned later that he was making a cartoon of Jiminy in a top hat looking particularly cross and confused, sitting all alone, with Pinocchio nowhere in sight. I was not able to explore the multiple meanings of this drawing because, since we were not in the same room, I did not know (like Jiminy, I could not see) what Ken was up to. And so I heard Ken's defiant statement—"I'm not going to do what I'm told"—as part of the ambivalence with which he was struggling and doing a good job of articulating, and did not immediately realise that in fact, Ken had shifted affectively into a defiant stance at odds with his seemingly reasoned discourse. I am sure I would have heard what he said differently if we had been in the same room and I had seen what he was drawing. Even though, while listening on the phone in previous sessions, I had a countertransference fantasy of myself as Jiminy sitting in the dust, an image that corresponded to his drawing, on this particular afternoon I did not appreciate fully where Ken was affectively because of the absence of additional non-verbal clues. It turned out that Ken's verbal associations were more superficially compliant than I realised. He was telling me what he thought I wanted to hear, using intellectualisation as a defence, when he was actually determined to go to "Pleasure Island" right after the session and I was not able to know that until he returned.

Ken's final question, "Are you there?" was partly the by-product of our distanced communication in that literally I had been quiet for a while. But his question also evidenced a projection that I had deserted him, even though he was the one deserting me. My point here is not that teletherapy is always at a disadvantage in comparison with in-person work, because there are occasions when communicating on the phone or Skype is better than in person, and the differences between a patient's transferences on the phone and those in the office are often helpful in understanding deeply buried issues. My point is simply that the work is sometimes different when telecommunications are involved in ways that we need to take into account, technically as well as ethically. In the vignette above, ethically, it would have been better if I had been able to help Ken think more about the self-destructive choice he was in the process of making before he carried his conflicting desires into action and risked seriously hurting himself and his loved ones. No lasting damage was done on this occasion, but he took a big risk that might have turned out very badly.

I might not have been able to have had any more of a deterrent effect that afternoon if we had been meeting in person, but the fact that I was unable to see his revolt as it was taking place in the office made sure that our analytic work that day had no immediate effect on Ken's actions. Of course, Ken was acting out an old pattern of pseudo-compliance that I had not seen so clearly recently, and he might not have been as blatant as actually making a drawing of his defiance if we had been meeting in person. But, even so, I might have picked up his defiance with additional non-verbal clues. Ken had an uncanny bent for unwittingly revealing what he was trying to conceal. Eventually, the analysis was advanced by our subsequent work on what transpired between us that day. So, in this case, the problem was not that the long-term success of the analysis was hindered in any way, but that, ethically, an opportunity was missed that might have proved helpful to Ken in deciding whether or not to risk so much harm. He was very lucky, but that does not diminish the fact that he was deciding in my presence to put himself in harm's way, and I was limited in what I could help him think about before he acted.

Some colleagues understand neutrality as precluding the analyst from taking any moral responsibility for discussing the multifaceted dimensions of a patient's choices. For them, no ethical issues, only technical ones, would be raised by my work with Ken that day. But the point of neutrality is not to eschew ethics entirely, but to adopt a moral attitude of respect for the patient's moral autonomy and the value of truthfulness, which is enhanced, not diminished by taking up the complexities of a patient's decision when it is affectively "hot" (Wallwork, 2012). The analyst should avoid pressuring a patient to make a particular decision, but that is best done by exploring what is going on, not leaving a patient like Ken rebelling in the transference against imaginary pressures emanating from his analyst.

The ethical paradigm: rules, virtues, goals, and decision-making

In clinical ethics generally as well as in telecommunications work, we need an ethical paradigm that is broad enough to capture the many subtleties and nuances of our moral interactions with, and responsibilities for, our patients. Unfortunately, many psychodynamic therapists and analysts implicitly confine the range of their ethical concerns to what we might call the professional code paradigm, which restricts the therapist's ethical imagination to the principles and standards of his/her professional code. Within this paradigm, ethical thinking is chiefly about a few basic duties that envisage the therapist's conduct in stark either/or terms, as right or wrong, good or bad. Ethical decisions within this legalistic or deontological (*deon*, in classical Greek, means "rule" or "duty") paradigm are imagined as primarily a matter of subsuming an action under a general principle or rule, like reporting abuse, obtaining informed consent, and avoiding sexual and financial exploitation. If one's conduct conforms to the rule, it is right; if it does not, it is unethical. As a way of thinking about our most essential moral requirements, like the prohibition against having sex or going into business with a patient, this model works well.

The chief problem with the professional code paradigm is that it provides an essential yet minimal set of conceptual tools for thinking ethically about clinical work. It rightly focuses attention on the basic requirements without which clinical work ceases to be therapeutic, as, for example, when the therapist exploits a patient or fails to satisfy the profession's minimal competency requirements. But the professional code paradigm fails to help us think deeply about other moral matters, such as the values and goals that inform our work and the role-specific attitudes and character traits that define how we deal with patients. What we need is a fuller, richer paradigm for thinking ethically that complements the attention paid to basic principles and rules in professional codes with a robust sense of the other moral dimensions of what we do that is also ethical, even though not often identified as such. We need for this purpose an ethic that focuses less on rule-following, and more on "wise judgment" (*phronesis*, in Aristotle), which involves developing the capacity to balance conflicting values and responsibilities in relation to the particular facts and relational dynamics of specific situations. From the perspective of wise judgment, rules and principles are necessary, but insufficient. Because often rules conflict in practice, the good enough moral analyst must creatively adapt the meaning of diverse moral standards to particular circumstances. In short, we need an ethic that is more like good clinical decision-making, that is to say, capable of taking account of multiple considerations, at different levels of consciousness, including incommensurable values, and synthesising these into moral judgments, decisions, and behaviours that work well in context.

There are four conceptually distinct, but practically interconnected, aspects of clinical work that are important to the task of reflecting ethically on various aspects of teletherapy. The first and most familiar involves the basic ethical principles and rules, articulated in codes, that delineate the clinician's most important moral duties, for example, non-maleficence, beneficence, respect for patient autonomy, confidentiality, truthfulness, fairness. The second ethical aspect of clinical work pertains to the role-specific virtues (consisting of affects and dispositions, such as empathy, benign curiosity, openness, humility, emotional honesty, self-restraint) that are essential affective components shaping the therapist's conduct (Wallwork, 2012). The third ethical aspect of clinical work consists of the immediate and long-term goals (values and ideals) that the parties are working towards, individually and together. The final ethical aspect of clinical work is the implicit model of moral decision-making which therapists and patients utilise in resolving the many moral dilemmas that arise for the patient and the analyst during deep psychotherapy. If we think of teletherapy in these ethical terms, most ethical issues remain much the same as they are in other clinical contexts, but there are some differences that need to be attended to by those of us who do this kind of work.

Non-maleficence and beneficence

The principle of non-maleficence, deriving from the Hippocratic maxim *primum non nocere*, "Above all [or first] do no harm", which directs us to avoid hurting others, looms large at the outset of considering teletherapy as a treatment modality. It directs clinicians to explore fully the risks of various harms that might befall patients being treated from afar. For example, non-maleficence would caution against teletherapy with severely disturbed patients who might deteriorate without the psychic security of a therapist near at hand and who, if they did deteriorate, would need immediate attention from a local therapist who knew them and local resources well. Even with less severely disturbed patients, the possibility that deterioration might occur with deep treatment indicates that the ethical clinician should explore mental health resources, and identify particular referrals, in the patient's community, in case unexpected emergencies arise.

The principle of beneficence which directs us to benefit others—for example, by reducing suffering, augmenting autonomy, and increasing sources of satisfaction—requires the therapist to balance the likely benefits and drawbacks of teletherapy versus the desirability of available alternative treatments. The first question regarding teletherapy from the perspective of beneficence is whether therapy at a distance is likely to work with a particular patient-therapist couple, given the nature of the patient's problems, personality configuration, and distinctive idiom (Bollas, 1992), and the therapist's ability to create a therapeutic context that allows both parties to experience primitive affects, to explore them in depth together, and to work through symptoms constructively. As a general matter, other things being equal, working together in person is prima facie preferable to working at a distance, because both parties have fuller access to each other affectively (as my vignette with Ken shows) and thus to the subtle non-verbal aspects of transference-countertransference enactments that are much harder to discern on the phone or Skype.

However, beneficence not only justifies our traditional practice of working in person, it also justifies remote therapy when face-to-face work is impossible (e.g., for patients in areas with poor or limited mental health resources), or when it is too costly in any number of ways (time, money, starting all over again with a new therapist) for the participants to meet in person. Telephone or Skype sessions also enable patients who are travelling to benefit from maintaining the continuity of intense treatment and from getting the immediate help made possible by sessions that would otherwise be missed. For some patients, like those with severe abandonment issues, mixing phone and Skype sessions with in-person office visits comes at a heavy cost of disrupting the safety and security provided by a more consistent, reliable frame. On the other hand, mixing-and-matching near and distant therapeutic experiences also provides valuable opportunities to relate differently that benefit the work in often surprising ways by opening up new lines of enquiry. For example, therapy on the phone or Skype frequently enables patients to retrieve shameful memories, to reveal perverse fantasies, and to engage in primitive enactments that they are too embarrassed to disclose in the therapist's presence.

Therapists contemplating the use of telecommunications for patients at a distance need to be brutally honest with themselves about self-interested and unconscious narcissistic motivations in trying to keep in treatment patients who might be better off, everything considered, seeing another therapist for in-person work. The questions needs to be faced with scrupulous honestly: is it really better for this particular patient to continue therapy or analysis with me on the phone or Skype as compared with beginning again with a new therapist?; and what can be done to help patients understand transferences that may be interfering with realising and/or acting on what is in their best interests in this regard? It is all too easy for the patients' real treatment needs to be ignored or devalued and for transferences to go unexplored in favour of their therapist's arguments and rationalisations, skewed in favour of continuing to work at a distance, when a patient is "special" to the therapist in some narcissistically gratifying way. What therapists find special about their patients depends on the individual therapist's needs and can include the patient's celebrity status, wealth, power, intelligence, strength, talent, unique abilities, creativity, attractiveness, sexiness, youth, rank, or unique set of challenges (Coen, 2007). Therapists need to be sceptical about the hidden role that their narcissistic desires, including the sense that they are indispensable, play in thinking and talking with patients about the appropriateness of using telecommunications.

Informed consent

Because teleanalysis is still an experimental process and not all analytic couples are able to engage in it effectively, it is crucial that an adequate informed consent process should precede its use, especially when it is to be conducted for a considerable period of time. The therapeutic couple should discuss the reasons for choosing to work in this way, the availability of traditional psychotherapy or psychoanalysis with another therapist, the similarities and differences between traditional analysis and teleanalysis, the problems with maintaining confidentiality when using various telecommunication networks, and the experimental nature of doing analysis in this way. Analyst and patient need to assess the risk that the analytic couple will not be able to connect in this way, that the patient's insurance company may not pay, and that an analysis might become psychotherapy by another name.

The chief ethical problems with obtaining genuine informed consent for psychoanalysis under most circumstances are repeated with several new twists when mutually agreeing on teleanalysis. The first is the difficulty new analytic patients have in understanding what they may expect of analysis before experiencing it. With teleanalysis, most patients, even those who have been in analysis, have difficulty understanding what the analytic relationship is likely to be like on the phone or Skype. The voluntary requirement of informed consent to begin an analysis in person is often compromised by the patient's heightened anxiety about beginning such a unique, seemingly dangerous, regressive process. When considering teleanalysis, the patient will experience many additional pressures on the decision regarding consent, such as anxiety about terminating a promising analysis prematurely, say, because of a move, and finding a new analyst at the new location. And, of course, a patient may feel pressured by transferences even when the analyst scrupulously seeks to avoid any overreaching.

It is crucial ethically that the analyst should engage in a forthright and deliberative discussion of the reasons for and against teleanalysis, appealing to the patient's rational decision-making capacities, despite the psychodynamic forces at play that comprise truly informed consent. The fact of having engaged in a frank discussion seeking informed mutual consent serves afterwards to underscore certain key values of psychoanalysis: truthfulness, respect for one's own and the other's autonomy, freedom from coercion and manipulation, deliberative decision-making. John Klauber puts the issue of the less than ideal conditions for informed consent for psychoanalysis well when he writes: "This attempt to give the patient as full a freedom of choice by rational means as possible is in fact the first way in which he glimpses the ethos and method of psychoanalysis" (2012). The initial glimpse of a mature decision-making process provided by an informed discussion prior to beginning teletherapy, however, needs to be revisited by continual monitoring of how the process is working. The initial use of telecommunications is best viewed as a trial that the parties are free subsequently to modify or terminate.

The frame

The construction or, better, co-construction of a therapeutic frame within which a psychotherapeutic process can take hold always raises a variety of ethical issues, though these are not often adequately separated from technical considerations. In addition to creating a safe context that adequately protects both parties from harm, topics like the fee, payment for missed hours and vacations, and the flexibility of the schedule always raise issues of fairness, informed consent and promise-keeping. The ethical principle of procedural justice is also in play regarding the process by which the conditions of the frame are initially established and altered over time. Traditionally, the therapeutic setting was established and maintained only by the therapist acting under the time-honoured ethical principle of paternalism, which permits a superior to override the preferences of an inferior on the grounds that the superior, like a father, is in an authoritative position by virtue of training, knowledge, and experience to determine how best to protect his charge from harm and to advance that person's best interests. During the last several decades, as a consequence of bioethical arguments on behalf of patient autonomy and the development of relational schools of psychoanalysis, the frame has been viewed increasingly under the principle of mutuality, as co-constructed and co-maintained by both parties. Teletherapy has tended to push the concept of mutual construction of the setting even further, because so many unique features of this kind of work require full discussion and mutual agreement.

Consider, for example, the question of how the confidentiality of the frame is to be maintained when the parties are communicating by phone or Skype. Unless the parties reach a mutually satisfactory agreement on how the patient should protect her privacy during sessions, the therapist may be surprised by the patient's surreptitious alterations of the frame in ways that constrain her freedom to talk. For example, I was feeling frustrated at the poverty of communication in therapy sessions with one patient after we shifted to Skype when I saw the shadow of another person, who turned out to be the patient's boyfriend, moving in the doorway behind my patient's head. She claimed to have no secrets from her boyfriend, but it turned out she had reluctantly acquiesced to his insistence on being present, which was seriously impeding our work. If patients change their geographical locations between sessions, as many patients on the phone or Skype do, the confidentiality provided by the frame may have to be regularly re-negotiated.

The limited range of access to the other provided by the phone and Skype creates conditions of anonymity that enable the participants to get away with breaking the frame without being detected. The fixed frame of in-person analysis which makes it easy to identify deviations and to interpret them may be weakened more than the analyst realises. For example, I discovered belatedly, after weeks of frustration trying to follow one analysand's disjointed free associations, that he was not lying down, as we had agreed. Instead, he was wandering around his house doing minor chores that diverted his attention, interrupting the flow of his free associations. Once his wanderings became apparent, we could discuss their meanings, but his violation of our original agreement did not become evident for a long time, in contrast with the classical psychoanalytic assumption.

Anonymity and ethical breaches

The therapist's increased anonymity on the phone and, to a lesser extent, on Skype has given rise to an as yet underappreciated ethical breach that arises from the temptations the new telecommunication tools provide for therapists to conceal unprofessional behaviour from their patients. I first became aware of this problem some years ago when I was trying unsuccessfully to help a supervisee think about the possible transference-countertransference meanings underlying the poverty of her patient's engagement with her on the phone in comparison with how much more present he seemed in the supervisee's office. We were not getting very far when the supervisee confessed that she had not been fully engaged herself during the phone sessions and, as a result, her process notes were not as full, because she had been reading and responding to emails while her patient was talking. Other colleagues have acknowledged getting away with texting, checking their investments online, skimming through magazines, adding to a grocery list, making to-do lists, and preparing bills, while listening with half an ear. Joyce Slochower (2003) refers to these breaches with evenly hovering attention as "delinquencies or misdemeanors" to mark them as ethically "unacceptable", while, at the same time, distinguishing these "small" ways in which analysts deliberately withdraw from patients from more egregious boundary violations. Slochower urges analytic exploration of the transference-countertransference significance of these seemingly self-interested behaviours, but she also views them as morally unacceptable. Jeanne Bernstein (2003) objects to Slochower's use of ethical terms like "delinquencies" and "thefts" for most of these hidden actions, because she fears ethical discourse inevitably invites harsh ineffective censorious judgments, when what is needed is honesty about one's own needs as a therapist as well as exploration of these actions as countertransference responses, say, to a patient's narcissism or lack of engagement. Bernstein is certainly right about exploring fully the countertransference meanings of these withdrawals as enactments, but her efforts to downplay the ethical significance of engaging in behaviours that interfere with understanding one's patient, as if they were like Anna Freud's knitting, misses a critical component of what is going on. Therapists should be able to acknowledge that actions like answering emails are ethically unacceptable departures from acceptable practices that ought not to be explained away as "necessary retreats to which analysts may have to withdraw in order to be fully present with their patients" (Bernstein, 2003, p. 504). Not everything a therapist does is part of an enactment. She may be acting out of a character deficit or she may be having difficulty coping with all her responsibilities and, concomitantly, overconfident of her ability to multitask, unaware of the burgeoning research on how bad people are at multitasking, because our brains are wired for selective perception (Nass, Ophir & Wagner, 2009). We can do automatic tasks that utilise implicit memory, like knitting, while our minds are engaged with our patients, but the multitasking research indicates we will miss significant information if we try to focus our minds on two separate subjects simultaneously. The result is likely to be impairment of the therapist's affective engagement and interpretive capacities, which, if self-induced, is an ethical lapse that ought to be understood as such and changed. One problem with the anonymity that accompanies use of telecommunications technologies is that accountability is reduced because the impact of harmful actions can go on for a long time without being detected.

Conclusion

My goal in this chapter has been to provide a broad conceptual framework for thinking ethically about the myriad moral issues that arise in teletherapy. I have not sought to provide an encyclopaedic overview of the range of issues or even the most important ethical problems in this kind of work. My main point is that those of us who use the telecommunications technologies re-encounter many of the same ethical issues that arise in our in-person work, but there are differences, like the anonymity of the parties and alterations in the frame, that require us to modify our ethical thinking to capture the various ethically significant variations that accompany this kind of work.

References

Bernstein, J. W. (2003). Analytic thefts: commentary on papers by Joyce Slochower and Sue Grand. *Psychoanalytic Dialogues*, I: 501–511.

Bollas, C. (1992). *Being a Character*. New York: Hill and Wang.

Coen, S. J. (2007). Narcissistic temptations to cross boundaries and how to manage them. *Journal of the American Psychoanalytic Association, 55*: 1169–1190.

Klauber, J. (2012). Personal attitudes to psychoanalytic consultation. In: B. Reith, S. Lagerlof, P. Crick, M. Moller & E. Skale, E. (Eds.), *Initiating Psychoanalysis*. London: Routledge.

Nass, C., Ophir, E. & Wagner, A. (2009). Cognitive control in media multitaskers. *Proceedings of the National Academy of Sciences, 109*(17): 1–5.

Slochower, J. (2003). The analyst's secret delinquencies. *Psychoanalytic Dialogues, 13*: 451–469.

Wallwork, E. (2012). Ethics in psychoanalysis. In: G. Gabbard, B. Litowitz & P. Williams (Eds.), *Textbook of Psychoanalysis* (2nd edition) (pp. 349–366). Washington, DC: American Psychiatric Publishing.

CHAPTER NINE

Impact of a single Skype session on an in-person analysis

David E. Scharff, MD

lements of the frame are of primary concern in the conduct of analysis. In an analysis that proceeds well, they often become all but invisible as the context for work. When there is a sudden shift in the frame, our attention may be called unexpectedly to elements of the patient's life and way of adapting that had been obscured behind the mask of the everyday. Such is the case in the following example of a shift in the frame, or perhaps more precisely in the mode of communication for the analysis, which highlights elements of transference and brings insight into the patient's problems. This patient's adaptation to the relational problems in her life consisted primarily of withdrawal from having any positive expectations from the important people in her life and this led to a chronically depressed attitude towards what life might bring. I had known that she was quite adept with computer technology, but had not appreciated how much of an investment she had made in this in a life otherwise devoid of passion or interest.

What happened in a single Skype session shed light both on her major defence of withdrawal from investment in people since all of them defeated her expectations, and on her transference to me in which she minimised her expectations of me at the same time as she depended heavily on me to offer a faint kind of hope for a better life. This unexpected discovery came one day during a shift from the usual four times a week, in-person psychoanalysis to a single session in which we used Skype because the patient had asked for a session while she would be away for an extended weekend.

Sarah

Sarah is a fifty-year-old woman with two young adult children, one closer to her than the other. As a young wife, she worked in a technology-related career before stopping to raise her children. However, she also retreated into domestic life for the additional reason that there had been conflicts with bosses in more than one job. After years of infidelity and denial on her husband's part, which he blamed on her failure to provide him with satisfactory sex, Sarah asked him to leave. Her twenty-five-year marriage ended formally after almost a year of negotiation, approximately a year before the session I will recount. In the aftermath of the divorce agreement, Sarah became suddenly and severely depressed and was in partial hospitalisation for several weeks. There she began to take an antidepressant and was discharged to continue psychotherapy with me, which soon increased to psychoanalysis four times weekly on the couch. Sarah has now been in analysis for two years. Looking back on her life to date, she wants to work on why she put up with her husband's offhand treatment of her, his continual affairs, and his years of sequestering money and making unilateral investments so that at the time of the divorce, everything was in his name.

Sarah's father was hospitalised for depression before she was born, and again when she was too young to remember. Her description of him has led me to think (and to say to her) that he seemed to have a combination of a severe chronic depression (that required electroconvulsive treatment) and perhaps some signs of an organically damaged personality. He frequently shut her out of his life and she felt rebuffed by him. The signature screen memory of her feeling rebuffed is of following him to the basement where he went to work on a variety of electronic projects, asking him to let her participate or at least to talk to her about what he was doing, and being sent away. Nevertheless she remained interested, and longed for more from him. In her adolescence he called her a slut and accused her of promiscuity without cause, and in her young adulthood she finally stopped speaking to him, and had no further relationship with him, and then he died prematurely. Her mother was a more benign, but still distant and unemotional figure. Her older sister was the somewhat favoured child, but Sarah does not feel the sister got any more than she did.

Sarah has now been in analysis for two years, always in person, always on the couch. She attends punctually and rarely misses a session except for the occasional obligation, never for vacation. She planned for a long weekend visit to her sister in Arizona, during which she hoped to explore their shared or different versions of their childhood, but she did not want to miss a session. So she asked if we could meet during her trip at the usual time by phone or Skype. I agreed that I would accept Sarah's request for Skype contact the Friday before her trip, and that she would then call me from Arizona at the usual time of her Monday appointment. I appreciated that she wanted to maintain analytic continuity across the distance, but I had no idea what the session meant to her or what it would reveal in the transference.

The session

Sarah calls me on time. She positions herself reclining in a low chair but with her face towards the screen of her laptop. I suggest that she face sideways so that the session will more closely resemble our in-person sessions in which she lies on the couch. After she adjusts her position, I see only the upper half of her face, but I do not ask for another rearrangement to permit a better view as it seems to me that this would be an undue intrusion on my part. I find myself re-creating the usual appearance of the rest of her face and body anyway, and so I do not want to waste the time with her moving the whole laptop around for a more perfect view that is not necessary for me to feel connected to her physical presence.

Sarah begins by saying that she asked her sister about their childhood together, but her sister said she really did not want to know more than she already did. She would only answer specific questions from Sarah, and would not discuss things in general or at length.

Sarah says, "I've been spending my weekend with my sister and her husband, watching what goes on between the two of them. That's not really very helpful for me. I can see that my sister has solved the problems we grew up with in a very different way than I have. I let my husband walk all over me for fear of his leaving. My sister has simply developed a life in parallel to her husband. They don't spend much time together or make demands on each other. When I'm not sitting around just watching them, I've had a nice time, though. For example, my sister and I went shopping just to go shopping, and we enjoyed the time together.

"Here's a good one you'll be interested in. Last night driving back from supper, I didn't get at all angry when my brother-in-law came to a red light, and started to turn left. I said, without screaming, "I think we have a red light." He pulled out into the intersection anyway, and I didn't shout or get angry. I just calmly said, "You went through a red light." And it was dangerous because there was a car coming. I used to scream at people in these situations, but I'm controlling my anger totally."

It is news to me that, as a passenger, she habitually screamed at the driver, although I knew about other aspects of her angry outbursts.

I ask, "Would you scream at drivers other than your brother-in-law?"

She replies, "Oh, yes. I did it with my husband all the time. Then it just became a part of me. So no matter whose car I was in I would backseat drive. I always felt my brother-in-law did things like that to me on purpose. It got into my way of being. But I would also backseat drive with my kids, which upset them a lot. Now I've stopped backseat driving in this kind of situation. I broke the symptom of telling others how to drive. I feel not doing it now is a change from what I used to do, and this was the first time I noticed I even wanted to control it. I've broken a habit. It's like I've been able to think about it, and therefore I don't have to do it. Now I actually understand better how annoying it is."

I am pleasantly surprised, both that she can tell me something new about her anger, and that she has shown a new kind of self-observation that led to the feeling she could change her behaviour. We knew that her angry outbursts had marred both her relations with her children and with colleagues in her jobs. I don't say anything, however, because she is continuing with her story.

Sarah now tells a story from earlier in the same evening on their way to dinner. She was using her phone to pay for the parking meter. It took quite a lot of time, so her companions were getting annoyed. But then another man in their party said that he admired how she kept at a complicated task and made it work. She said she had managed to do this unfamiliar thing even though her sister kept calling her phone to ask where they were, and the calls would take over the very screen on her phone that she was trying to work with to pay the parking fee.

Sarah says, "I don't understand why I had intolerance for my brother-in-law's driving when I have so much tolerance for using these technologies."

It occurs to me that the story about using technology is an indirect reference to our way of working today, a new technological element in our analytic life.

I say, "You're using technology on Skype today. How does that feel?"

Sarah says, "I was stuck in so many other parts of my life. But I'm not stuck in the past about technology. I'm not about to let advances in technology hamper my life! I've always thought you should use technology. A lot of people try to resist change. I've never been afraid of machines because I was always curious about them, about how they make your life easier. So I think it's important to keep up with the technology. It feels good to be able to cope with it.

"It's interesting, though, isn't it? I can keep up and cope with this, but in my marriage I didn't have the coping skills to maintain my self-esteem. All I did was to try desperately to keep up with my life, which wasn't working. I was in denial. I'm much better at understanding machines than understanding people. Technology! Either it works or it doesn't! It's black and white, whereas a person is complicated and multi-layered. If a person is negative to me, I don't know how to cope. Now I did teach myself not to scream recently, and you know, today, noticing that I could control myself makes me more curious about how to cope in life in general.

"When I was married, I never thought about how Morris [her husband] refused to think about machines. I always kept up to date with the newest thing out there about computers. It was the one area where I really stood my ground. I wanted to keep up, and so every two years I'd buy a new computer to keep up. I wouldn't let Morris stop me. It was the one thing I maintained my own identity in, and didn't let him take over. Whether he liked it or not, I bought a new computer! He didn't object, but he did refuse to learn the new things himself. I was able to keep up and change in that way, but not in other areas in my life. But in that area I had the stronger will."

I sense now that the Skype session has been important to Sarah not only in maintaining our continuity, but also in allowing her to present an area of strength to me.

I say, "You have had a real pride in how you could adapt to using Skype today."

Laughing, Sarah says, "Yeah, I've used it with my kids a lot, but then *they* would call *me,* and so I didn't have to learn how to make the calls. This is the first time I've called somebody else, but I know how it works. Sure I'm willing to try it. But you know, this apartment where we're staying doesn't have Wi-Fi. I actually don't know how I have a connection right at the moment. But I was willing to make it work."

Puzzled, I ask, "So how did you use it today without Wi-Fi in the house?"

Sarah replies, "I have the feeling the connection I'm on is a general Wi-Fi for the whole condo complex. It seems that there's a signal at 100%, even though it wouldn't register on my cellphone. But there is a signal, in spite of the fact that the rest of the time there's hardly a signal. Usually, I try to make things work until they do. Today I wandered all though this apartment, which isn't very large, to find a signal. That's the thing—I don't let obstacles get in my way, whereas when I was married, I let any obstacle get in my way. So it's interesting that I didn't let technological obstacles get in my way, but I let other people interfere all the time. I don't know how to maintain my identity, and so I must have maintained it with technology. But if I could do that with technology, I should have been able to do more with myself generally. I should have defended myself and believed in myself. When it comes to technology, I guess I have always believed I could figure things out, like how to make them work."

Now, just at this point, the signal cuts out. After a moment, Sarah calls back. She thought it was my signal that had disconnected, not hers. But I'm pretty sure it actually was at her end. All through this I'm aware of wondering how she makes the connection work when they don't have Wi-Fi in her sister's apartment, even though I understand that she may be connected on a signal borrowed from another apartment or the apartment complex. After a few minutes, I realize that my wondering about this must be a kind of marvelling that she can make this work while so much else in her life and in her image of herself is so damaged, so disconnected. In retrospect, this is a musing about the strength of her determination to stay connected to me, a contextual transference that is usually hidden in a diffidence that expresses her wariness to expect much from anyone.

Sarah continues: "So anyway, I assume I can figure out the technology. I had to work with technology even when it was less friendly to me, whereas coping with people isn't a part of me. I didn't learn how to cope as a kid. But even then, I wasn't supposed to be able to use the technology. My father was in the basement, trying to make a TV have colour before TVs had colour. I wasn't supposed to be there in the basement to see what he was doing. That just made me more determined to figure out for myself what he was doing, and I've stayed with that."

I had felt welcomed into Sarah's family life when she asked for a Skype session on vacation at her sister's. Now I feel that she is welcoming me in to her "basement" where, like her father, she feels competent with technology but unlike him does not have to rebuff me. I think of this as a reparative identification with her father, and I experience its re-creation in the transference.

"But I haven't been able to do that with people, and therefore I have more confidence in dealing with machines than in coping with people. It seems to me that I should be able to transfer that capacity over to people, and to be more aware of what I do that doesn't work with them, but of course now I have to think about how to make that transfer. I'm not used to thinking about how to deal with people. So I see that it's inherent in me to deal with technology, but not people. It's sort of strange.

"I guess it ties in with my sister's comment that she didn't want to know more about our childhood. She said that what happened in our house wasn't relevant to who she is today. It's her way of coping by denying the existence of things. I've done that too. But now I don't want to deny what happened to me as a kid any more. It seems odd to me that I am curious and my sister isn't. She doesn't want the past to interfere with the present, while I think the past has to be understood so it doesn't interfere. This ability to not care about what's happened to you that my sister has, that's her way of coping. I can see it doesn't work with adapting to technology, and now I can see that I've also tried to use that denial, and it doesn't work in my life. So it's interesting that we lived in the same house but now we have such different views. We weren't much different in age, our experiences were similar, and we spent more or less the same time in the house, so how did we come out of that house with such different views on how to see and deal with our lives?"

I say, "So it's interesting today that you see that using Skype is an example of how you're adaptive technologically, but you feel you haven't been adaptive about emotional coping with people."

She concurs: "That's right. I'm strong on technology, but I couldn't cope with people, which is more important than technology. You need both, but you should have some people skills, especially with the negative aspects of people, like when they attack me, whether purposefully or accidentally. I guess I have to think about it more since neither my sister nor I cope well. It's almost like I waited for situations where I have to cope. My view of others was that things would always come to a fight between me and an authority figure, and I couldn't deal with it. At least I couldn't in the past. I ignored things until they came to blows."

I say, "You are saying that in the past you looked the other way, just like your sister."

She said, "Yes, that's true. Well, it is, and it isn't. I'd fight, but she'd look the other way and let them win and walk over her. She still just goes into her hole. I won't go into my cubbyhole. She takes the opposite approach. She cowers and hides in the corner. She makes herself as small as possible. So there, I'm the opposite. I come out of the corner. I push my way forward and scream. It doesn't get me anywhere, but I fight and she flees. People like it better if you flee. I fight the whole time. Even though I was unaware of doing the fighting. For example, I didn't win with Morris when I'd fight him. He was more and more in control. I fought and he took more control every time. I certainly didn't succeed."

I say, "We have to stop for today."

She sits up and says, "Well, I'm going have to think about all this. OK, see you tomorrow. Thanks!"

And with that unusual enthusiasm, Sarah hung up the Skype connection.

Discussion

In this example, we see the "intrusion" of a new framework for our work—but it turns out to be an opportunity for new communication through the way the frame it introduces puts forward a new aspect of Sarah's personality. Until this session, I had understood that her use of technology, and of her training in a technical area in which she had worked both for a salary and later as a volunteer, had been areas of competence and even of more enthusiasm than she generally showed for most areas of her life. But I had not understood anything of the compensatory role her technological interest had played, or that it expressed almost the sole area of her personality not battered into submission by her way of fighting and surrendering. This shift to using Skype gave us a sudden, unexpected window into this area of her adaptation to life. The new insight subsequently shed continuing light on the way she had surrendered whole aspects of positive investment to the sense of defeat by her father, the lack of support from her mother, and a kind of hunkering down in the enclave of an expertise that secretly retained the quest to understand her father's interests. If she could not get his attention, she could at least come to understand the things that did get his attention, and she could then use these to appeal to people when other means of relating generally failed. However, in doing so, she also identified with him and his withdrawal from relationships.

In her in-person sessions, Sarah had been pursuing the questions that she seems to unlock here for the first time, but with no sense of affective connection. Why did she always fight, when that was so self-defeating? Why was her enthusiasm for things she might have cared about so dampened throughout her life? Even her way of trying to investigate these things in analysis was muted in a way that mirrored her blunting of investment in almost everything. We could agree about that, but nothing really cracked her affective guarding. It was only in this session that we discovered how she had compensated throughout her life. She knew she enjoyed the technology, but neither she nor I knew the role it played in secretly safeguarding her capacity for interest in life, or the way she used it to enable her to keep fighting in a maladaptive way.

Not only did she develop insight in this session, but also, in iterating the new discovery several times within the session, her enthusiasm for it grew, and my sense of excitement in the breakthrough this conveyed also grew with hers. This affective shift lasted through several of the ensuing in-person sessions. When it inevitably subsided, she was left with the now open question concerning why she had been unable to invest in many things that she actually could have liked, for instance in travel.

Until this session, Sarah would take my lead and accept my interpretations about how something had interfered with her capacity to engage in life or about how her smouldering anger had cost her in relationships, but she could only agree to the extent of saying, essentially, "I guess so." There had been other insights, but they were mostly gained when someone other than me, one of her children or a friend, would make an observation and she could take it in as applying to herself.

On the day of the Skype session, Sarah made the essential observation, triggered only by my linking her minor technological triumph over the parking meter to the use of technology in the session. That set off a cascade of her self-observations that took advantage of our previous work and our established working relationship. The observations today had a profoundly different quality, and so did the transference. In comparison to saying to me, "I guess so!" in acknowledgement of comments in previous sessions, in the Skype analytic session, Sarah was saying to herself in effect, "Oh, I see something that has not worked for me. Why did I keep doing that when it didn't work?" She extended the discovery of her retreat into technology to the discussion of her use of angry fighting and compared it to her sister's use of flight. It was the beginning of a new line of enquiry that, for the first time, she pursued on her own initiative.

The debate about whether a telephone or video connection breaks the analytic frame seems to miss the essential point. Many things can change the framework within which analysis can be done. It is the process of analysis that is essential, not the vehicle. The main thing is the shared, in-depth enquiry in the context of a relationship that can itself be contemplated. Once we accept that premise, then the more interesting question becomes, "How does this new vehicle for communication operate within the particular analysis?" In this single Skype session, far from operating as an obstacle, and in spite of the fact that I could only see part of Sarah's face in the screen, the introduction of the Skype video connection allowed us both to see far more in depth than we had until that moment. The technology moved from being part of the frame to becoming the stimulus for new work that formed a turning point in Sarah's analysis.

CHAPTER TEN

Transition from in-person psychotherapy to telephone psychoanalysis

Nancy L. Bakalar, MD

Psychotherapy by telephone allows us to offer treatment to patients who may not otherwise have access to it: those in rural areas; those in high-density population areas in which commuting is excessively time-consuming and onerous; and those for whom, like patients in conservative religious communities, in business or politics, a higher degree of privacy may be required. In the three cases presented here, telephone sessions allowed for continuation of treatment, after I had moved to another state, for patients who had made a hefty investment in their treatments up to that time. Two of the patients are women who transitioned from in-person psychotherapy to telephone psychotherapy, and eventually to four times weekly telephone psychoanalyses, and the third patient is a man who had not been able to attach to the therapeutic process in person but was later able to develop a telephone treatment. Following the transition to telephone psychoanalysis, the two women reacted with intense negative transferences. Using concepts from Klein, object relations theory, and Bion, I hold the frame, follow the affect, and process and interpret the response. I apply the usual analytic functions of holding, containment, and interpretation, just as I would do in in-person analysis.

Why did I engage in telephone therapy?

Retired from an academic and clinical position in the US federal government, I opened a private practice in psychiatry and the psychodynamic therapies in my east coast city. Seven years later, I planned a move back to the mountain state where I grew up, a move planned over the previous ten years, the timing of which hinged on family and other professional commitments. I gave my patients a year's notice prior to my move and referred many of them to local colleagues for follow-on care. However, there were several who had been in twice weekly psychodynamic psychotherapy for over five years and who might prefer to continue with me. I thought of telephone therapy. As a US Navy psychiatrist I had treated patients by telephone and video teleconference in the late 1990s, and so I was comfortable with those media and knew from such personal experience that useful therapeutic gains could be realised. I considered which patients might do well in continued dynamic treatment by telephone. I thought of those who had shown a commitment to treatment, had made progress, and developed transference phenomena that underpinned the dynamic work. Given the offer, they elected to continue with me by telephone because they trusted me, and appreciated the nature of the dynamic work and the progress they had made so far.

Telephone sessions actually facilitated treatments for all the patients who chose to continue with me following my move. My east coast office had been in a metropolitan area known for severe traffic congestion and long commutes which made getting to therapy especially difficult for those who worked regular business hours at some distance from my office. For them commuting times were greatly reduced. Other patients from a plain-dressing religious community in a rural area drove for over an hour each way to my office, and so the telephone sessions allowed them to participate from home. They were referred by church leaders who appreciate that I do not undermine church discipline, religious values, and beliefs, and relationship to the community; even so those patients prefer to keep private the fact that they are in treatment because some in that religious community are frightened about therapy and what the patient may be told or may learn. So, in addition to convenience, treatment by telephone affords patients from that community and other rural settings the possibility of getting needed help in the privacy of their own home.

I was concerned about the problem of the two-hour time difference between my east coast practice and the mountain state I would move to, but this did not prove to be an obstacle. In fact, it facilitated the treatment: in my new location I could "see" patients during late afternoon hours for me, but early evening for them, which allowed them time to get home from work, have a bite to eat, and settle into their selected treatment spot, and it allowed me to end my work day at a reasonable time.

Once we agreed to continue by telephone, I established the frame of the treatment. I agreed to return to the patients' state four or five times a year for in-person sessions. Any of them who required medication would also meet as needed with a local psychiatrist to whom I referred them. The patients agreed that they would always meet in the same place in their home, arrange for complete privacy, and remain seated or lying down during sessions. Most patients chose the seclusion of their bedroom, lying either on their bed or in a chair with their feet up. All of them found times when they would be alone in their home, with occasional exceptions, when a child was home sick or a spouse arrived home early, in which case the patients either cancelled their session or made arrangements to maximise their privacy. Of course, as in in-person therapies and analyses, the parameters of the frame were challenged or broken at times—and then analysed.

Clinical example: Eldon

Eldon was a thirty-two-year-old married man who was referred to me before my move by an elder from a plain-dressing religious community about an hour from my office. Eldon suffered from depression, lacking motivation for his work, finding it difficult to get up in the mornings, unable to feel lovingly towards his wife, and fearing that he did not measure up to his peers in business. Eldon accepted the recommendation for twice weekly in-person psychotherapy. I learned that he was the oldest of six children. His mother suffered a severe depression post-partum up until the time he was five or six, and so was unavailable to him emotionally, as was his father who tried to care for her and the younger siblings in addition to working. When Eldon was thirteen, he and his family were on an outing when a brother and another boy decided to wade out into a lake without knowing how to swim. The boys began to drown when they ventured too far offshore and stepped off an underwater ledge. Eldon and another boy jumped in to rescue the others. One brother and two friends drowned. Only Eldon survived.

I tried to talk to him about his feelings of losing the other boys, and his being the one to survive, but he had no access to any feelings about what had happened. I developed the hypothesis that, having received so little from his parents, he felt relieved that there was one fewer to demand their attention, and had to deny the homicidal wish that preceded the drowning. I also thought that he had internalised a dead mother and father and was left with little energy for attaching to his brother and friends. He had little response to me either. I felt that he experienced me as his depressed, absent, and neglectful mother, even though I was there and tuning in to him. I think he could not bear the loneliness of being alone in the room with me. Eldon stopped and started treatment with me several times before my move, like a drowning man coming up for air, and then finally quit, seemingly because he could not attach to me and could not feel my investment in him.

Two years after my move, Eldon called. He had heard I was still seeing other members of his religious community by telephone and wondered if he could begin his treatment with me once again. On the phone, he deals with me quite impersonally. His discourse is basically a report of his business dealings, irritation with sociopathic competitors, and the nitty-gritty of how he makes profits. He shows what he has done, and I listen, but I still think he relates to me as a deadened mother. But at least he keeps his sessions and sustains the therapy, which he could not do in person. He has now been in twice weekly psychotherapy by telephone for over two years and has made significant progress: he is less critical of himself around costly business decisions he had made in his youth and is able to be dedicated and thoughtful in a current business endeavour that is complex and has become successful financially. He is less worried about measuring up in the eyes of father figures in his religious community and is more compassionate and steadfast with his family and friends. Overt transference feelings have been infrequent and short-lived, and so his therapeutic gains have not been maximised. I think that more frequent sessions are needed to reach the basic fault (Balint, 1979) and work towards its repair. Eldon could not accept working with me intensely in person, but I think he can do so with the analysis on the telephone. Eldon recently accepted my recommendation for telephone analysis.

Clinical example: Mary

Once telephone psychotherapy and especially telephone analysis is established, I find that in-person visits perturb the frame, but not more than absence for illness or vacation usually does for standard in-person analysis. In the case of Mary to be presented here, an upcoming series of in-person sessions stimulated a strong reaction in the form of a verbal attack on me. Mary's outburst and the analytic work on it secured her ability to have empathy for herself and me, to understand her capacity to hurt others, to regret her actions, to mourn for herself and me, and to attempt reparation. She had not been able to move into the depressive state in any great measure before that incident.

Mary was a twenty-eight-year-old married woman on six medications for bipolar disorder when she was referred to me for psychopharmacology consultation. She had seen a variety of therapists and psychiatrists over the previous decade without improvement. She had a history of overdosing on non-lethal quantities of over-the-counter sleep medications and occasionally scratching her wrists with broken pieces of glass. She had a difficult childhood with a father who was overly sexually exciting and a mother who was extremely anxious, frequently agitated to fits of screaming which left Mary in states of helpless anxiety herself. Mary was a shy, awkward youngster who had difficulty making friends, suffered with nightmares, enuresis and nail-biting, but who in the end graduated from high school with good grades and went on to a two-year college where she earned an associate's degree in early childhood development. When she went to college her anxiety and depression re-emerged in full force. She had difficulty separating from her parents and found herself in many abusive relationships with boyfriends.

Despite years in psychiatric treatment with many medications, Mary was still anxious, angry, and frequently given to what sounded like horrendous arguments with her husband, which left her in a miserable, broken mental state. She experienced multiple, rapid thoughts of an obsessive nature, and complained of noises in her head, but she slept well most of the time, and did not wish to kill herself. As her treatment progressed, Mary told me more about her disorganised states in relation to her young charges at the early child development centre where she worked.

Originally Mary came monthly for medication management, but quickly moved into twice weekly psychotherapy. She spoke in a confused way that was difficult to follow. She often grabbed her bowed head, one hand covering each ear. She shook her head from side to side, saying that there were bees buzzing in her head. I thought of these noises as shards of not-yet-describable, raw emotional pain, which Bion (1962a) described as beta elements. She found it difficult to meet with me as she experienced my presence as overwhelmingly intrusive. I did not find it easy to be with her either. She often sat on the edge of the sofa, sobbing, occasionally looking up at me through reddened, swollen eyes. If she caught me shifting in my chair or taking a sip of tea, she became even more agitated and demanded that I stop moving. Even my breathing angered her. My body and mind cringed in response to her attacks. I came to understand that her reaction was related to her experiences with both parents, her mother who was severely emotionally attacking and physically intimidating which had left Mary without a sense of a separate, bounded self, and her father who bathed with her and introduced her to pornography. Mary's agitated response to my ordinary movements demonstrated a porous mental structure, an insufficiently sturdy contact barrier (Bion, 1962a), and a largely absent containment function (Bion, 1963). Mary eventually put words to this: she said that she wished that others would neither move, nor say anything that would agitate further her shaky internal state. During early phases of treatment, she described experiences that indicated that she did indeed turn others into statues in her mind. She was unable to experience them as individuals with their own internal mental life.

Mary's early in-person therapy

Mary's twice weekly, in-person therapy lasted five years. She was distraught and frustrated in dealing with her husband, the children she taught, and the preschool administrators whom she experienced as critical and demanding. It was as if Mary were projecting her angst and disorganisation not into me as her therapist, but into the literal space between us. I felt distant and somewhat numb to her emotional pain, a countertransference response to being treated as a statue. Sometimes Mary criticised me angrily, and then I felt the pressure of her rage. She did not understand how she contributed to problems with others and how to work them out, and so I occasionally gave advice about how to handle difficult problems at work, but most of the time, I bore her agitated emotional states and barbs.

Mary also experienced bodily sensations in sessions in response to interpretations which she considered on target. When under emotional strain, at times she felt sexually aroused, and at other times she directed both inner forearms towards me, saying she had the urge to cut her wrists. I thought of these responses as somatic expressions of the resistance to understanding herself, as attacks on linking and knowing (Bion, 1959). At the same time, they were transference responses: Mary was protecting herself from impingement by me in the present, not wanting to let in my ideas. This transference resistance was driven by the compulsion to repeat her childhood need to repel and relive verbal attacks from her mother and to repel and relive sexual excitement in relation to her father (Freud, 1914g).

It was foreign and frightening for Mary to be asked to think about how her feelings were linked to past experiences. I was working with Bion's idea that it takes two minds to sort out disturbing thoughts but she angrily resisted a partnership, often with an arm outstretched like a traffic cop, signalling me to stop, saying that she couldn't take a single comment from me. After a year or two, Mary became aware of her feelings, and she did not like it. She started many sessions saying, "I hate having feelings! Why do you make me have feelings?" She felt that I caused her feelings and should spare her these overpowering emotional states. Once her anger was targeted towards me as a person, she became able to suffer her emotions and understand the links between her feelings. To do so was much less disorganising for her than to be at the mercy of raw, ill-defined psychosomatic feeling states and beta elements (Bion, 1970).

Once feelings are symbolised with language, there comes a pressure on the patient to think about mental life, self in relation to others, and the integration of thoughts and feelings. This internal experience pushes the patient to work towards understanding by accepting, suffering, and learning from interpersonal and emotional experience. It is an active process of learning, rather than a passive process of living through what is felt to be an attack from without, unaware that it is an attack from within (Klein, 1946). Bion (1962b) believed that thinking was developed to manage thoughts. Once thoughts begin to be generated in the therapeutic process, the patient then feels the pressure to get to work thinking. This was true of Mary. She began to express hatred towards thinking itself, for which she attacked me over many months. Often she reverted to a crying, whining, a not-wanting-to-think self. For Mary, it was as Bion (1967) described it: "The conduct of emotional life ... becomes intolerable. Feelings of hatred are directed against all emotions, including hate itself and against external reality which stimulates them."

When Mary had made gains in therapy, I worked with her to decrease gradually and finally discontinue all her medications. She could not genuinely feel, think, and get to know herself under the mask of so many powerful substances. Taking less medication, she felt better, communicated better, no longer viewed herself as a severely mentally ill person, and her despair and anxiety improved, but she was not yet well.

Transition to telephone psychotherapy

I considered whether to offer Mary the opportunity to continue in twice weekly telephone psychotherapy. I felt that she was suitable for this transition: she had shown a clear dedication to her treatment, coming on time, leaving sessions fairly easily, missing sessions rarely, paying without fail, and tolerating hating and loving me without abruptly discontinuing treatment. She had exchanged powerful medications for the therapeutic relationship and gave up being labelled a seriously sick psychiatric patient. She had moved into a transitional state between feeling under attack by her own internal state and owning and suffering her feelings. She began to think about herself, her own thinking, her enormous distress in relating to her young students, and her tendency to retaliate. She experienced transference feelings towards me and worked with me on analysing them.

When I made the offer of telephone treatment, Mary was stunned. She felt betrayed, abandoned, and in danger of collapse without me. She anticipated missing me as a person, seeing and hearing me in person, and coming to the familiar office. Nevertheless, she decided that she would continue treatment by telephone. Over the year between notification of my move and when it actually occurred, she worked through many reactions to my leaving, which was compounded by her mother's recently diagnosed life-threatening illness. Much of the rest of that year was spent working on the complicated sets of feelings Mary had in relation to her mother dying and my leaving. Mary had difficult conversations with her mother during that period, and was left with the feeling that her mother still misunderstood her and mislabelled her feelings and intentions. Unfortunately, Mary's mother died two weeks before our last in-person session, but, despite this additional stress, Mary made the transition to telephone treatment and continued mourning the loss of her mother and of me in person, and grateful that she still had me available by phone for therapy.

Transition to telephone psychoanalysis

Mary's twice weekly telephone therapy continued for two years. She described problems and complaints about her personal and professional life: she was still cranky and whiney in relation to others and to me, and yet she was gathering insight. She was in a "working through" phase. However, after about two years, Mary stopped making appreciable gains: she still reported fairly serious and frequent arguments with her husband and frustrations with her colleagues. I was especially concerned about stories she told of being enraged by the toddlers she cared for. In response to their childish pranks, Mary sometimes "got into their faces" and yelled in a primitive way. She now suffered for this. She "knew it was 'wrong'", but did not know how to conduct herself differently, or even how to think about it. I believe it was the sorrow I felt for the toddlers, the damage I believed she was doing to them, and therefore to herself, that led me to recommend increasing the intensity of her treatment to psychoanalysis.

Mary was stunned again. She was incensed that I would suggest that she was "that sick". I told her that I thought she had been stuck for a couple of years, and that a more intense treatment would offer her the possibility of understanding herself more fully and feeling better. Without much hesitation, Mary agreed to four times weekly telephone psychoanalysis. Before we began, I told Mary that I would listen more and speak less, and that she should say whatever came to her mind. I requested that she lie down in the same place each time, and ensure that she had complete privacy. These latter instructions are important in setting the frame for telephone analysis because, unlike in in-person analysis, the analyst cannot manage the physical space of the treatment setting.

Early response to the transition to telephone psychoanalysis

Mary was relieved that she could talk to me four times weekly, but the positive feelings lasted only a short time, quickly replaced by anger as soon as she experienced the sessions as intense. She felt my interpretations as criticism, and she reeled in response, angrily rejected what I had said, and conflated me with her internal objects: "You are just like my mother! I could never please her!" Over many sessions, I simply responded, "But I am not your mother or father. We have a different relationship. We are here to help you understand yourself and to help you feel better. I have no reason to want to hurt you." The many repetitions of these statements eventually helped Mary to delineate me from her internalised bad objects based on experience with her parents. Appreciating the distinction between them and me was soothing to her.

Mary reacted to my hurtful comments by wanting to cut herself or by feeling sexually aroused. When Mary responded to me by saying that she wanted to cut herself, I said that she wanted me to know that she felt cut by me, and wanted to cut and attack me back as if I were her hated mother and father. I added that she wanted to make a cut in her skin boundary so as to let out the horrible feelings that she felt had been put into her. When she responded to me by saying that she felt aroused and excited, I said that her body was excitedly longing to hold on to her father, whom she loved, and to me whose work she appreciated and also that the vaginal muscles were clenched to keep out my interpretations and stop them from upsetting her.

So, in summary, over the first year of telephone analysis, Mary and I worked intensely on the negative transference. Mary heard my comments on her aggressive actions and reactions to others and to me as criticism but she gradually realised that she was indeed excessively aggressive with others, and she was trying to bear her guilt and suffer remorse, but with limited success. She was still operating mainly in a paranoid-schizoid position.

The frame of the telephone analysis triggers movement into the depressive position

I will now give extracts from process notes of some of Mary's in-person sessions and the preceding telephone sessions to illustrate a major shift in character structure, a transformation to the depressive position. Mary is now beginning her own business where she is mentoring assistants, but she still feels like a little girl in a world of adults.

Telephone sessions

Mary: Asking for help from my mother or father didn't work. Yeah, it pisses me off I need help from other people. Now I have to delve into the realm of asking for help and that puts me in the little girl position. "Please, sir, may I place my business card on your bulletin board?" Do you know how awful that makes me feel?! [Mary is crying.]

Analyst: You've moved away from thinking about needing help to wanting to be the adult who's helping others. You want to be the grown-up, the mentor. You hate being the one mentored.

Mary: Yes. Just like our relationship. There is a piece of me that hates you because you seem to know what you are doing. I am intensely jealous of you. You seem to have figured it out, and I hate you for that. I think I diminish myself and I don't give myself credit for all I have done. I do hate you for being in the helping role but I need your help, and it is a terrible feeling for me. I feel vulnerable.

In the following Monday's telephone session, three days before we were to meet in person, Mary expressed some anxiety about seeing me, as it had been three months since our last in-person session. She talked about her recent weight loss of approximately forty pounds, about how good she felt, about how trim she appeared. Then she said that she had been struggling with some mean thoughts about me, but felt compelled to say: "When I saw you last time you looked terrible. You looked so old. That was a shock and I didn't like it. I'm worried about seeing you Friday!" Mary had never before criticised me so personally. I felt stunned and stayed quiet as I gathered myself from the attack and worked to understand what was going on.

In the next day's telephone session, I learned that Mary was afraid that I wouldn't answer the phone. She was suffering the full impact of her envious attack on me:

Mary: My stomach hurts. I feel miserable. I'm scared because I feel as though I am a bad person. I feel like I need to hear that you still care about me even if I hurt your feelings. It scares me greatly that I have said something hurtful to someone I love and need … It is OK to be mad, but it is not OK to be mean … I want you to say, "You know, Mary, it's OK." I want to know that you can withstand the hurt. [She pauses.] How do I feel the pain and remorse and let myself mourn how I have hurt our relationship? You answered the phone today! I really want to ask, "Do you hate me?" but if I ask that question, it puts me in the little girl position. I want to ask, "Do you still love me?" I am asking for help from the one person that I hurt! How do I ask you for help now? [Crying and sniffing.] I am in a dangerous place. My fantasy is that you are going to say, "Mary, I can't work with you any more. Our therapy is done! Click!" … I sound so whiney. How could you possibly love me when I feel ugly and mean? You're still there, right? [*She fears she has lost the telephone connection—a transference fear of losing me because of her attack.*] When I say something hurtful, that is the ugly part of me. Then you will hate it because I hate it, and you will take your love away. Again it makes no sense, but that is how it feels. [Pause.] I am incredibly envious. I know very little about you, but you have your own business. You can move out of state, which I am still mad at you for. And I am still having a hard time handing out my business cards, and I am taking it out on you!

Following this session, Mary and I worked on her envious and hurtful attack which was a displacement of her unconscious envious attacks on herself for losing weight in addition to feeling more competent in business and more at ease in relationships, all signs of her progress in analysis.

In-person sessions

Two days later, during the first in-person session following this session, Mary made no direct reference to her attack on me until the very end of the session, instead telling me about a horribly angry and sexualised attack on her husband that erupted the night before the anticipated in-person session. Then Mary said, "I feel guilty that I was mean to you. I have a sexual feeling right now. Last night wasn't good. It was an explosion. I kept you at a distance today." I noted how she moved from her husband to me and back again. I spoke of her feelings of longing, loving and hating me, her husband, and her father and mother originally.

The following day was her last in-person session of the series. Mary was able to integrate what had happened between us, in relation to her husband currently and her parents in the past:

Mary: I want to work on my relationship with you so that I can understand it better. Yesterday I told you a long story about my argument with my husband, and I excluded you. This work is frightening and I don't want to look at it. In my growing up, my father was scary, my mother could be hysterical, and as an adult, I feel anxious around other people. I am charming, gracious, bubbly, but on the inside I feel like a frightened little girl. I know that if I work in here, I'll get better, but I am angry with you and I have no good reason for it. Last week I told you how I felt, how I hated you because I was envious. Tuesday I had the thought that I'm losing weight, and I said to you (I've apologised profusely) that the last time I saw you, you looked old, and I said it with a bite. How am I supposed to talk about it? This is dangerous! [Sighs.] I don't want you to be a statue. I see you, and I don't want to get close.

Mary's dynamic shift was triggered by anxiety in anticipation of seeing me in person again after she had responded to an apparent change in my appearance. Mary was shocked by the visual impact of seeing me in-person "large as life". It may be argued that the shifting frame from telephone to in-person sessions created the perturbation, but I think that this is similar to disruptions in the patient's perceptions of the analyst as gaunt upon return from a long absence, whether for vacation or illness, or as fatigued or distressed on any day, depending on the analysand's projections.

Mary's continued progress in telephone analysis

In doing therapy and analysis, I hold in mind many psychoanalytic theorists, especially those of the Kleinian and object relations schools. I find especially helpful Klein's concept of projective identification and Bion's concepts of beta elements; alpha elements and alpha functioning; containment; the contact barrier; learning from experience; and the interpersonal links of L, H, and K (his symbols for Love, Hate, and Knowing), their opposites -L, -H, and -K (attacks on linking or understanding), and his concepts of T (Truth) (Bion, 1962a, 1962b) and O, the astonishing, ineffable, inexplicable, un-namable aspects of experience (Bion, 1965, 1970).

Over the next year of telephone analysis, I saw the integration of Mary's thinking and the development of her maturing character structure. In italics and parentheses below, I note some of Bion's concepts to mark Mary's progress from anger to empathy.

Mary: Michael who is four years old was in the lunch room today, and I yelled at him. I took away his juice box. It looked like he was messing around ready to spill it. He began to cry. Then I felt sorry, and said, "Oh, you didn't know how to open it?!" (*Mary becomes empathic as she recalls herself as a little girl who couldn't ask for help from grown-ups.*) I went to Michael's aide and suggested she pair Michael with an older buddy who would help him. The next day Michael came running up to me and hugged me. I asked him if he got his buddy, and he smiled and nodded. And I asked him, "Will your buddy help you?" and he smiled and nodded … Michael gave me something—the opportunity for forgiveness (L). You know, he gave me a hug, and I wanted another one. (*Mary acknowledges Truth: she does not need to deny her longing.*) But I didn't ask for one because I am there for him. (*Mary shows Love for him:*) He is not there for me. (*Mary has Knowledge of her role and meaning to Michael*). I told him instead that he made my day! (*She shows Love.*) I expressed my gratitude to him in words. (*Here, L, T, and K, Love, Truth, and Knowledge, come together.*) I made some mistakes today, but I had some beautiful moments with the children. (*Mary speaks from a more integrated ego state in relation to a softened superego.*)

Mary further contemplates this experience and notes feeling sexually aroused, converting alpha elements to beta elements as a defence, a -K, an attack on her learning and integrating what she has just experienced and also an attack on our analytic work together; but then her alpha functioning begins anew as she gathers insight and integration:

Mary: I think I know why I have the sexual feeling. It is a reminder of my parents. I wish my parents could have taught me that it is normal to suffer. It makes me angry that I suffer, that I have emotions, that I have to think about them and that I have a responsibility to myself, to the kids, and to my marriage to think about things. (*Mary is in touch with the reality principle.*) This beautiful moment with Michael sprouted from a painful moment, from a learning experience, but it has a stain on it—like I will get poisoned. (*Mary slips into a paranoid-schizoid moment.*) A beautiful moment gets attacked by pain (*alpha functioning, insight, and truth are evident again, and I note the transformation* (Bion, 1965, 1970)).

Below is a final vignette that shows Mary's growth in understanding herself. Her analytic work is transmuted to a more integrated, effective, compassionate way of relating to the children.

Mary: I am in the world of little children. They teach me more than I teach them. (*Mary shows gratitude, L, K.*) There is a little girl in my class named Katie, a very smart and fussy little girl. She is a diva and a bully in a little-girl way. Her older brother treats her pretty badly and she often comes to school upset and then is mean to other children … Today a little boy was sick and threw up on Katie. He got some vomit on her socks. So, I took the children to the office to clean them up. I got some wipes to clean Katie's legs (*L*). Then I scare myself. (*I note the change in tense to the present: Mary is now reliving the moment in the session.*) I worry that I am going to wipe underneath her skirt (*paranoid-schizoid moment, beta elements attacking L and K*). I felt an immediate fear that I was crossing a boundary because I was wiping her leg. I am aware that I am creating this in my mind (*alpha functioning, restoration of thinking and learning*). I feel like I was taking advantage of Katie like my father did of me in the shower (*identification with her father, continued alpha function and learning*). I have guilt that I am touching a child, even though I'm taking care of her. I have witnesses—I'm in the office! (*Mary is reliving the past in the present in a paranoid-schizoid moment.*) Then I look at her and she has an expression of relief, as if she is thinking "Someone is taking care of me", almost a look of love (*L, K, O*). After that, she had no more behavioural problems for the rest of the day. (*Returning to the appropriate past tense, Mary brought herself back to awareness of being in the session.*)

Summary of case of Mary

Mary came for help with a psychotic style of thinking. Numerous psychotropic medications had not eliminated her symptoms of bees buzzing in her head and her exquisitely painful ways of relating. Near the end of her treatment which moved from in-person psychotherapy, to telephone psychotherapy, and finally telephone psychoanalysis, Mary had developed a thinking mind that could note and integrate experiences, which could then be drawn upon in new situations. It demonstrates psychoanalytic growth and development in each phase in sessions on the telephone as well as in person. In Mary's case, the anxiety in anticipation of seeing me erupted in an envious and hateful attack, followed by remorse and sorrow, catapulting her into the depressive position. Never again did Mary negate me or treat me like a part object, a statue. And it was from that time onward that she was able to fully experience her husband and young charges as separate, other, people who deserve her empathy and, in the case of the children, her help and guidance.

Clinical example: Anne

I wish now to present briefly another patient who, like Mary, began in twice weekly in-person psychotherapy and whose treatment was transitioned to telephone psychoanalysis. Anne was a thirty-five-year-old married woman, the oldest of five siblings, who was referred by her father, a scientist and entrepreneur. He had come to the United States from another country on a scholarship to study engineering. A man of modest means, leaving behind a world of poverty, he founded a manufacturing business which had grown to seven plants across the United States. As the oldest child in the family, Anne was pressed into service as a substitute parent, while her mother kept busy in the family business. Anne's father became well-respected in his community and industry, but at home he was tyrannical, perfectionistic, critical, anxious, and demanding, using his children, especially Anne, to wait on him hand and foot. He could not tolerate the younger children chewing their food loudly, let alone the rowdiness of the large family. It was Anne's job to keep the house neat and clean, to keep the children quiet and orderly, and to keep her father's shoes shined, clothes tidy, and car spotless. Her younger siblings argued with her, mocked her, and learned quickly how to bring her to tears for which her parents then chastised her.

In spite of her father's demanding nature, Anne idolised him. As she grew older, she prided herself on being his "right-hand girl", fetching him coffee and slippers, typing up memos, and waving as he drove out of the driveway because her mother was not there to do it. Anne identified with her father as a revered leader, and eschewed marriage and children at first, instead wanting to follow in her father's footsteps of doing "the important work in the world". However she did marry. She chose a man who also was entrepreneurial but without advanced education. So the young couple set out making a living by numerous small business endeavours for which she again found herself pressed into service. Anne had become exhausted in the process. She had two very difficult births and had been bedridden for three months during her third pregnancy. She was depressed, anxious, angry, and had lost interest in friends and hobbies. She was unable to take care of her home, and barely able to get out of bed to care for her children. Sadly, she had also been diagnosed with two autoimmune diseases, and was on numerous medications including several psychotropic drugs.

Over the years of in-person therapy, Anne made good progress in coming to understand that her unhappiness was related to anger and frustration in relation to her parents, her father especially. Anne had so idolised her father (and herself in identification) that she was shocked to understand that he was not as ideal as she had imagined. Because Anne had made good progress during the in-person phase of treatment and had committed to the process despite a long commute from a rural, industrial area, when I was about to move, I offered, and Anne accepted, twice weekly telephone psychotherapy. The transition was not disturbing to her. I believe the therapy-at-a-distance, by telephone, facilitated her treatment, not only because she did not need to commute which made the treatment more practical, but also because it afforded some privacy from the agitation and shame that she felt when she experienced me as her intrusive, demanding, judgmental father.

As Anne emerged from her depressed state as the ill wife and mother who could not or would not fulfil her role in family life, she erupted in anger and turned it on her spouse whom she had always presented as the steadfast, dutiful, hard-working husband. For months, Anne and her husband suffered vicious arguments that left them confused, distraught, and discouraged. Anne's husband regressed under the strain, and he counterattacked not only Anne but also the children. I was sympathetic to Anne's husband, and angry at Anne for her demands of perfection from him. Anne could not take in nor make use of interpretations that the origin of the anger she levied towards her husband was originally in relation to her parents, especially her father, and she had little overt negative transference in relation to me.

Although Anne had made significant gains in that she was no longer bedridden, frightened, and helpless, I felt pessimistic about her making further progress in understanding herself in the twice weekly telephone psychodynamic psychotherapy. Anne did not seem bothered by the stalemate or lack of progress and gave no indication of wanting to stop treatment. In fact, she seemed satisfied to use me in the sessions as a receptacle for her frustration and other psychic pain. My interpretations seemed not to "sink in", and so were not helpful to her. She resisted self-understanding which would fracture her overly idealised view of herself as the oldest, brightest, most responsible child. My choices were to offer more intensive treatment, telephone psychoanalysis, in order to gather the negative transference, or alternatively to consolidate her moderate gains to that point and terminate therapy.

Like Mary, Anne was shocked at the offer of four times weekly psychoanalysis, but I gave the same explanation of needing intensive treatment to get over the stalemate, and Anne accepted. She became angry about the suggestion, however, but also embraced it as a *Red Badge of Courage* that "proved" to her family, especially her father, towards whom she now felt a lot of anger, how damaged she had been by him.

The negative transference developed rapidly, as Anne came to experience my offer of the analysis as her intrusive father making demands on her. She developed severe anxiety and panic attacks with some agoraphobia, the first one at a weekend get-away with her husband at the beach, where she feared the ocean would rise up and flood them in a third-floor hotel room, a half-mile offshore. At the same time, she feared me and could not get me out of her thoughts. I had flooded her mind. Anne became anorexic, lost thirty pounds, paced for hours, and developed insomnia. At the height of the negative transference and maximal regression, Anne felt impelled to check herself into a rural psychiatric ward as a way to expose and bring shame on herself, her father, and me as the analyst treating her at-a-distance, just as when she was a teenager she had fantasies of embarrassing her father publicly. Fortunately, Anne saw a local psychiatrist for medication management, and had numerous other medical doctors overseeing her care which allowed me to feel contained during the crisis and deal interpretively with the dynamics behind her wishes for hospitalisation. This allowed her to avoid acting out and to continue her analysis.

As with any analysis, there were many interwoven complex dynamics between her inner objects, her current family, and her family of origin, all manifest in the transference. Over time, Anne came to see that our task was one of helping her to understand herself, even though focusing attention on her inner life left her feeling criticised. She labelled her anxiety as a fear of the "boogey-man", or a threatening big, mean dog, popping out from nowhere, teeth bared, ready to attack. This then got linked and understood in terms of her father's severe anxieties and spontaneous tyrannical demands, and to me, as the analyst who "popped" up in her life four times weekly making interpretations which to her felt like "attacks". Eventually she was able to distinguish me as a separate person from her father. She came to understand that in relation to her father she had "set aside" aspects of her self, "downloading" his thinking as her own to quell his and her own anxiety. Taking on his philosophy of life bolstered her sense of a *broken self* (Balint, 1979) by identifying and internalising her idolised view of him. Once she disentangled her sense of self as separate from her father, her anxiety emerged again in the analysis. She was frightened that she was empty and nothing was left of her. For months we worked on her fear of "the wide open spaces" (Balint's "philobat", 1955), manifested in her fear of leaving the house to take her daughter to school or to the grocery shop, as well as her fear of being close to others (Balint's "ocnophil", 1955), eschewing company or visiting others. I handled Anne's challenging regression in the telephone analysis by holding the frame of regular sessions, by interpretation, and allowing for rare extra sessions when she was overwhelmingly distraught.

Currently, Anne is in the early stages of termination. She has raised the issue of what life will be like after her analysis has ended. We have spent arduous months, she experiencing interpretations as attacks, criticism, and demands, and insight as a task to be perfected, and I reminding her that I am not the father who makes demands and that our purpose is to help her understand herself and to feel better. Anne has introjected the analytic process and is largely doing her own analytic work, re-thinking the vignettes from earlier sessions, adding new ones, making new links, garnering new insights, and occasionally expressing worry about "not doing 'it' correctly". Now I track the process and intercede in her dialogue only occasionally to identify the traces of the old dynamics with her parents and siblings. The negative transference is largely resolved and she appreciates me as someone different from her father, someone who has stuck with her despite her petulant attacks. She is anxious about no longer having sessions, but she is also looking forward to getting back to her own life and creative endeavours of writing and volunteering in the community. She sees her medical doctors less frequently, her autoimmune diseases are improved and her medications have been decreased. Her relationship with her husband is loving and supportive most of the time, and the relationships with her daughters and between her daughters and husband is much calmer.

Discussion

A marked, negative transference rapidly developed in both analytic cases when Mary's and Anne's telephone therapies were converted to telephone psychoanalyses. Both patients had done considerable psychodynamic work in the five to six years beforehand, and so the development of the negative transference neurosis was primed. But I believe another factor also was in play: both Mary and Anne suffered from demanding, critical, harsh superegos (internalised bad objects) which led them to attack themselves and me as the analyst, express rage, and then suffer shame and remorse. The medium of the telephone allowed for analysis-at-a-distance, which enabled them to feel safer to express their rage and hatefulness and to bear the shame of their behaviour more easily. In the presence of the analyst, patients may suffer more anxiety and fear, consciously and unconsciously, about attacking the analyst and being attacked by her. The medium of the telephone puts the analyst and patient in two separate physical spaces while maintaining a shared mental space, which I believe allows the patient more leeway to express hate. This arrangement also offers the patient a buffer for the shame she suffers. In contrast to the old adage that "children should be seen and not heard", my two patients preferred that they "be heard and not seen". Anne especially talked about how ashamed she was about the severity of her depression, her inability to function, and her unwarranted hateful feelings towards me. She felt that she might not have been able to bear the shame of all that if she had to face me in person. Both Mary's and Anne's treatments were facilitated by the use of the telephone because it afforded them distance from me as an object representing the intrusiveness that they had endured in relation to parental figures. The modality of the telephone for treatment may allow for earlier and/or more profound regression which could facilitate a quicker and deeper cure.

Some think of analysis by telephone as a parameter (Eissler, 1953) but I think of it as an extension of accepted psychoanalytic method. The technique of classical psychoanalysis occurs without analyst and patient facing each other, but being in the presence of one another. The analyst listens to the patient's verbal and non-verbal productions, pays attention to free associations, notes the tone of voice and mood, slips of the tongue, listens to the patient's responses to interpretations (Faimberg, 1996), and notes the elements in the field of the sessions. All this can be achieved in telephone analysis. One young man said that he thought not being able to see me facilitated his telephone therapy in that it allowed more room for him to fantasise and experience (transference) feelings towards me, feelings that he originally felt towards his grandmother who cared for him after his mother died unexpectedly in a car crash when he was very young. Nevertheless we do miss how the patient appears, smells, and moves during a session, although patients will sometimes spontaneously describe such things to us to help fill in the gaps.

Summary

My clinical experience of telephone treatment with Mary, Anne, and Eldon suggests that in certain cases telephone psychoanalysis may be required and preferable to in-person psychoanalysis—cases in which there are difficulties in attachment, overwhelming shame, physical or sexual abuse, to name but a few. The three patients knew me well before telephone therapy and analysis began. We had already achieved a therapeutic alliance with an optimal level of trust and attachment. Before conducting analytically oriented treatment on the telephone, initial in-person sessions, or at least face-to-face sessions by video-teleconferencing, are necessary in order to develop the working alliance and ground the analytic process in a real experience of two people. Conducting treatment only by telephone might stimulate a paranoid-schizoid state. All the patients I now treat by telephone know me from in-person sessions. All of them have local health care providers. Treating someone who is not known to the analyst is not sufficiently secure either for the patient, or the analyst: analyst and patient each need a containing environment. When there is a proper context for the telephone treatments *and* the analytic work is sufficiently contained that it can proceed, *then* patients can make progress and feel better.

References

Balint, M. (1955). Friendly expanses—horrid empty spaces. *International Journal of Psychoanalysis, 36*: 225–241.
Balint, M. (1979). *The Basic Fault: Therapeutic Aspects of Regression.* London: Tavistock.
Bion, W. R. (1959). Attacks on linking. *International Journal of Psychoanalysis, 40*: 308–315.
Bion, W. R. (1962a). *Learning from Experience.* London: Tavistock.

Bion, W. R. (1962b). The psycho-analytic study of thinking. *International Journal of Psychoanalysis*, 43: 306–310.

Bion, W. R. (1963). *Elements of Psycho-Analysis.* London: Heinemann.

Bion, W. R. (1965). *Transformations: Change from Learning to Growth.* London: Tavistock.

Bion, W. R. (1967). *Second Thoughts: Selected Papers on Psycho-Analysis.* London: Heinemann.

Bion, W. R. (1970). *Attention and Interpretation: A Scientific Approach to Insight in Psycho-Analysis and Groups.* London: Karnac.

Eissler, R. (1953). The effect of structure of the ego on psychoanalytic technique. *Journal of the American Psychoanalytic Association*, 1: 104–143.

Faimberg, H. (1996). Listening to listening. *International Journal of Psychoanalysis*, 77: 667–677.

Freud, S. (1914g). Remembering, repeating and working-through (further recommendations on the technique of psycho-analysis, II). *S. E.*, 12 (pp. 147–156). London: Hogarth.

Klein, M. (1946). Notes on some schizoid mechanisms. *International Journal of Psychoanalysis*, 27: 99–110.

CHAPTER ELEVEN

Setting and transference-countertransference reconsidered on beginning teleanalysis

Asbed Aryan, MD

The ethics of psychoanalysis include an expectation that psychoanalysts will continue to learn about new theory, paradigms, and clinical techniques that extend the applications of psychoanalysis and lead to philosophical, sociocultural, scientific, and economic transformations. We can no longer depend only upon the classic, known practice of psychoanalysis. What were once new developments are now clinical facts. What were once obstacles are now opportunities for research into areas beyond what had so far been seen, known, theorised about, and put into practice. When a new clinical problem arises, before we try to build a new theory to account for it, we think of it as a variant of what we already know. But when this new problem is found in several of our patients, and those of colleagues, and when it defies our current theories and techniques for trying to understand it, we must see this problem as not only the patient's problem, but a problem arising from limitations of our psychoanalytic method.

We can say that analysis comprises a contract and analytical dialogue but that hardly does justice to the characteristics of the link of the analytic couple. The patient seeks analysis and develops an expectation of benefit despite resistance to the emergence of unconscious conflict and despite resistance to the strange method of talking on a couch. The analyst who has experience, skill, and confidence in his practised method, nevertheless deals with some resistance in himself and in the limitations of his method. He wonders if he will succeed in understanding the subjectivity of this patient. He wonders if he will be able to realise the psychoanalytic potential of the analytic couple. Will he be able to foster the joint work of analyst and analysand? What else may be required of him that will take him into unknown territory?

Some general considerations

The psychoanalytic method is the application of a set of rules and standards to investigate the unconscious. It stimulates the universal tendency to transference in which repressed infantile sexual desires, pregenital conflicts, Oedipal anxieties, and defences are displayed in relation to the analyst. The method has now expanded to include awareness that our personal traits and our way of applying the method evoke the patient's transference, which is no longer seen as purely an individual occurrence. Similarly, it is now recognised that the therapeutic setting for the method is jointly constructed.

At times, and under certain circumstances, the traditional setting has to be re-imagined to fit the demands of the modern world. For the patient who has no access to a local analyst, the psychoanalytic method may adapt itself by using the telephone for sessions. The use of the phone must be properly indicated and its effectiveness reviewed, in the same way any innovation is reviewed, as happened when analysts began to extend the psychoanalytic method for use with children and adolescents and people with borderline psychotic states of mind.

The analytic couple will consider both the desire for analysis and the obstacles that may arise in implementing the analysis. Analyst and analysand talk together to see what they can do to fit the method to the needs of the patient. One size does not fit all. To try to fit all patients to an arbitrary standard is to turn psychoanalysis into a Procrustean bed, which does violence to patients. Many patients need frequent sessions but not all can travel to see the analyst so frequently. This is an indication for considering teleanalysis.

Including teleanalytic sessions introduces variables that need to be reckoned with. Some believe that the recommendation for teleanalysis is a resistance to the traditional analytic setting. In concentrating only on resistance as an attack on the setting, they avoid the importance of the link created by analyst and analysand. This link is the main thing to be considered (Berenstein and Puget, 1997). Within this link, repressed material emerges and gets deposited in external objects, including the analyst. Whether the analytic couple works in person or on the telephone, defence and resistance drive increasingly repetitive cycles when narcissistic, non-integrated aspects of the personality empower regressive behaviour. To accommodate the link structure and its possibilities, we need to revise our view of the setting to provide continuity when patients must live elsewhere. The patient on the telephone seems different, being unseen, but retains his previous features and way of relating to the analyst. As he goes on listening to himself talk, we note new components of transference that we had not noticed when meeting in person. They arise because the patient reacts to the new setting, and so do we.

Clinical example

Juan, a businessman in psychoanalysis with me, proposed the use of the telephone to sustain the continuity of his treatment because he started having to travel very often. He was a loose, thoughtless, dispersed, and confused person. He did not take care of his belongings and abused the people in his life. He only took care of his business and analytic schedules. When I agreed to the change in context, he became a person capable of looking after something of his own, namely the relationship with the analyst. What had been seen as resistance and abuse continued to appear in the same manner and these aspects could be analysed in relation to the analytic link and other links in his life.

I will return to the treatment of Juan in detail later. From this and similar clinical experiences, I maintain that the possibility of implementing a change to suit the patient changes the psychoanalytic potential of the patient and the vision of the analyst. Modifying the setting to support the analytic situation encourages the emergence of the unconscious fantasies. When the requested or proposed change can help the patient's analysis, we believe that it is ethical to modify the setting even though it is not in accordance with tradition. Then the ethical psychoanalyst will continue to assess whether the analytic process is established and whether transference interpretation is possible in the new setting. Yet the analyst who proceeds in this responsible way is still working outside accepted policy. Even though the topic has been presented and discussed in panels and working parties in three psychoanalytic association congresses, and even if the analytic process has been demonstrated in these presentations, it has not been enough so far to achieve widespread acceptance of teleanalysis. In fact, some psychoanalysts maintain that teleanalysis is not analysis at all, merely a form of psychotherapy. The exploration of the clinical effectiveness of teleanalysis has been insufficient. What is needed is a more enquiring, truly psychanalytic attitude into its strengths and weaknesses.

Those who present on the topic of teleanalysis in these scientific meetings are all fully qualified psychoanalysts, members of national and international professional organisations, and some of them are approved as training analysts. What I want also to emphasise is that those who present know and can demonstrate in sufficient measure the essence of psychoanalysis in their teleanalysis sessions and course of treatment. These analysts have curiosity and respect for differences. Those who argue against usually have not had direct experience of teleanalysis themselves. We need to provide increasingly detailed studies of clinical sessions and do more to encourage the growing interest of research into the topic of teleanalysis. Beyond raising the scientific profile of teleanalysis, we need to consider the political implications.

Whether treatment by a psychoanalyst on the telephone is truly psychoanalytic or not has already become a political matter. Opening the discussion seeks to redistribute the power of our professional institutions. I believe that we cannot hold an absolutist position stating unilaterally that a particular practice is or is not psychoanalysis. We need to engage in a scientific discussion of the influence of the new temporospatial paradigms on the lives of our patients and ourselves and how psychoanalysis can remain relevant in modern life. Technology-assisted living creates new definitions of reality and personal presence. Audiovisual communication creates a virtual reality that is a real component of everyday life. Distance is now measured in hours not weeks. A person in one location routinely works with a team in another town, state, or country.

We all agree that psychoanalysis depends on concepts of resistance, defence, transference-countertransference, and interpretation as the essential aspects of psychoanalytic dialogue. But it is imperative that we refine our understanding of how psychoanalysis applies in the modern world, in such a way that reflects change in social history and culture. We need to remedy the academic dissociation of a position that excludes the context of worldwide knowledge in order to defend an outdated method of practising psychoanalysis. The defence of psychoanalysis is necessarily linked to the defence of the human being in society. Psychoanalysis is one of the few disciplines that can ensure the humanisation of technology.

We must reconsider fundamental psychoanalytic concepts that until now have been studied only from the Platonian and positivist point of view. The increasing use of the telephone is only the latest in a series of changes in paradigms necessitating a rethinking of the concepts of subject, object, and representation. If psychoanalysis conducted on the telephone is capable of addressing unconscious conflict, splits in the psyche, infantile sexuality, and transference/countertransference, then it can contribute to understanding the dynamics of the human subject in the current culture. Using technology, psychoanalysis pioneers new knowledge refound in old knowledge. Surely that is more productive than sticking with what we already know, limited to that gathered only in the analyst's office. Let us not forget the impressive metaphor of Heraclitus that "No one can bathe in the same river twice." Each time we approach the river, it is the same river, and yet, because it flows, it is no longer the same. We want psychoanalysis to be a free-flowing river with many tributaries, and not a stagnant, swampy lagoon. We cannot continue to bathe wistfully in the same water of psychoanalysis and believe that we can sustain it eternally, divorced from the movement of humanity.

One obstacle to accepting the value of teleanalysis is the economic aspect. Psychoanalysis made more mobile by harnessing itself to technology could create a redistribution effect in the same way as so many social movements have produced in the history of mankind. Since the colonisation of and evangelical outreach to the Americas, Africa, Indonesia and Oceania, cultural adaptation has founded several alternative hegemonies. Psychoanalysis must see itself in relation to other sciences too, but more than other sciences, psychoanalysis must stop to ask about reality. Most sciences just advance accumulating knowledge compulsively in the discipline without questioning why, for what, or for whom, and leaves it in the hands of large agencies for capital funding and implementation. But psychoanalysts cannot be scholars of a single knowledge and a singular mode of practice, but of holistic reflection. Psychoanalysis must therefore think about the culture and historical context in which it operates. Psychoanalysis values erudition but equally values the questioning of absolute authority. We must make the effort to chart our policies guided by scientific, philosophical, and economic considerations. We must be careful that no sector of our profession is guided by principles of hegemony. After Freud, no one holds the trademark of the term psychoanalysis. A claim of being the only way is anti-psychoanalytic. It limits vision, ignoring cultural context, environment, and the temporospatial aspects of contemporary psychoanalytic practice with patients, many of whom live in highly mobile circumstances unknown in the last century. Psychoanalysts working today need an epistemological posture and a pioneering spirit to practise psychoanalysis in situations outside the usual.

Analysis on the telephone or VoIP

An objection arises that the analytical session must surely be unworkable if there is no direct contact between analysand and analyst in a controlled and private office setting. Only this way, it is thought, will the analyst receive the concentrated, fully developed audiovisual perception of his analysand. It must be admitted that he will lose the visual aspects of non-verbal elements of the analytic dialogue. How could a psychoanalyst construct an image of his analysand if non-verbal ingredients are missing? In reply, I ask, "Since when were the exclusively visual, extra-verbal elements such an important part of the material that it was impossible to psychoanalyse without them?" This would mean that the blind cannot be psychoanalysed and should not be psychoanalysts.

The question is raised, "How can the psychoanalyst understand what he has been told when he is alone in an office with a communication device, and not a person? I believe that this question confuses *the channel of communication* with *the link*. When the patient comes to our office, we are using our sight, hearing, touch, and smell but we are communicating not with his senses, but with him. When the channel of communication must be virtual, we train our senses—especially our hearing and our intuition, to be highly sensitive, as if we were blind analysts compensating for a handicap. We admit that working virtually we do not have total access to everything going on in the session. Our narcissism rests not on feeling powerful, but on feeling that we are doing the best for the patient in his circumstances and on recognising when it is possible and when it is not. Analysis conducted in person has been extended to include diagnostic categories previously thought unanalysable—serious borderline personality, drug-addiction, perversion, and psychosis. These categories may not be manageable in analysis by telephone or VoIP. We will have to see. When psychoanalysis was extended for the treatment of adolescents, some analysts refused to treat them because they did not want to deal with disobedient patients. Others specialised in their care with the full approval of colleagues who did not want to do that work themselves. The same could be true for teleanalysis. Whatever the diagnostic category, and whatever the training of the analyst, not all patients will be analysable and not all analysts will feel capable or ethical or willing to analyse using the telephone or VoIP.

We need to do research into the clinical effectiveness of teleanalysis. We need to reconsider the concept of analysability in relation to the syntactic, semantic, and pragmatic distortions of teleanalysis. Perhaps our experiences with teleanalysis will lead us to update Freud's classic recommendations to physicians on beginning treatment. But who will authorise such changes? Can the field of psychoanalysis re-envisage its methodology if we do not have a strong figure like Freud to create a strong and positive transference to the new ideas? Can we learn from our modest experience in teleanalysis, communicate the resulting ideas, and have our colleagues listen and comment? We are aware of a widespread countertransference against teleanalysis, and we will need to attend to it as thoroughly as Freud and the pioneers had to deal with reactions against psychoanalysis in the early twentieth century.

Let us not forget that it is already accepted that the concepts of following the fundamental rule using free association and floating attention is an ideal difficult to attain for many reasons, including the interference of sensory-visual perception that concentrates the analyst's attention. Trying to counter this, Freud conceived of the couch, so that the eyes of patient and analysand do not meet. He recommended listening to the analysand with eyes closed, sitting behind the couch, and not looking closely at the patient. The actual bodily presence of the patient was reduced in its impact by the use of the couch and was then felt symbolically in its absence. This is how the analysand's presence is felt in its absence when sessions occur in the virtual space of the telephone line or VoIP.

We are now at an historic moment in which digital media have ensured that *corporal presence* is no longer essential for holding a confidential business meeting or private personal communication. Parents who communicate by telephone or Skype with a child who resides abroad feel in touch and find that they can share ideas and emotions, feel empathy, express concern, and influence one another. The geographical space between family members or business colleagues is no longer measured in kilometres but in minutes or hours. The difference between East and West is fourteen hours, a key factor in managing globalised markets. The possibilities for privileged encounter are no longer limited to corporal closeness (space factor): it is sufficient that there is concurrency (time factor).

Clinical material

I will now describe in detail my clinical experience with Juan, the businessman I mentioned earlier. Juan has been in analysis for eighteen months: the first ten months were in person twice a week, but only when his travel schedule permitted, and the last eight months have included telephone sessions to maintain frequency.

Three consultation sessions

Since he was seventeen, Juan worked in a major company that was begun by his grandparents and managed by his uncles and his father. As the eldest son, Juan has an important place within his nuclear family. As a successful businessman he can afford beautiful things but he cannot think of them as his belongings. When he was forty-one he proposed selling this company and, with the participation of uncles and grandparents, the sale went through successfully to everyone's benefit. After that, he started a new independent project for which he travels all over the world doing business. But he finds his life too complicated and disorganised. He feels claustrophobic in relationships, especially in intimate relationships where commitment is expected. He has not been able to marry and has no children. He insists that although he is a person who can take decisions and meet his responsibilities, he always feels he is not the real protagonist of his own life.

In our first consultation session Juan said, "I find it quite difficult to free myself from the past to invest fully in new things. I started my own company, opened offices in Europe, bought an apartment, and thought of emigrating, but I don't want to leave everything I have behind and make the leap. The same happens when I am part of a couple. My last relationship was with a very pretty woman. We had a strong relationship and we built a house at the seaside together, but we never lived together, and after ten years we split. We were never a real couple. It's been two years already and I still feel stuck. I say to myself, "You have to turn the page and start a new life, come on! Otherwise, go back to her!" I get stuck between living with her and being unable to be part of a real couple because of the responsibility it represents. I want to break with the past but I can't take the definite step forward." I am always questioning who I really am, and what others think of me. Life is too complicated. Honestly, being forty-four years of age does not help me either.

When I asked Juan what he meant by "complications" he answered he had always been more responsible than fun-loving. "I have a totally ruthless, cynical vision of life," he said. "When I was twenty I got to know existentialism. My readings took me in the direction of finding life hard to accept, and this was reinforced by reality. The concept of happiness in the way human beings live has never convinced me totally. I always feel we have to trick ourselves into happiness, but I cannot cheat myself. And having to be alive makes it worse. Likewise, I cannot tell and stop being an arsehole". This was his usual way of speaking to himself.

Juan had been in treatment previously. As with his romantic relationships, he had a number of treatment relationships. Between the age of twenty and twenty-seven he worked with a Lacanian analyst with whom he felt comfortable, and had returned for two more years. The family company required him to make a three-month trip to Europe, and he could not decide to go because he did not want to leave his responsibilities at home. The analyst told Juan to stop obsessing and simply go and enjoy himself, and without further understanding simply ended the stalemate—and the treatment.

But Juan's problems persisted. He consulted the therapist of a close friend to get a referral and was disappointed in the therapist who tried to keep him as a patient. After that, he chose to see an elderly man, but he found him a little lightweight and not sufficiently challenging. The man talked too much and gave his opinion that Juan's problems were ordinary and he simply had to accept them. Juan felt that this therapist might be right that Juan thinks too much of himself but he did not continue with him because he felt that he did not comprehend the depth of his complaint. Juan told me, "I like being with a woman in a relationship, but I cannot assume the costs of making a choice. If you choose one thing, you have to give up the rest. I am aware of my issues. I think about them. I analyse them, but I find it hard to make a choice and stick to it. I just do not have the guts. I think I am a coward."

I found Juan to be intelligent, competitive, and articulate. I noted that he is highly defended and narcissistic, both omnipotent and fragile in his self-esteem. I began to build a hypothesis about his psychic structure. He has an omniscient superego that commands the impossible—an ideal where there are no losses. But this gives only the illusion of narcissistic fulfilment. Juan operates on the fantasy that he is to please himself, and need not pay for what he has! Then each time he has to give up something he feels he has fallen short of the ideal. But he cannot mourn the loss of the object or the loss of self-respect because of falling short of the omnipotent fantasy. So he falls into melancholy.

Juan's problem is long-standing and one that really calls for psychoanalysis. He has already tried previous therapy relationships. I was clear that he was asking to be able to define his own choices, but I was also well aware that he felt unable to commit to anything, to assume the costs of any choice, to accept any of the hard conditions of life. How could he face an analysis without any ability to commit and assume its costs, especially those of time and of self-esteem wounds? I did not make a recommendation. I asked to meet again in consultation.

The first thing he told me in our second encounter was that he had felt comfortable and understood, and that he had thought more about the things he had told me. He had remembered that when collecting his first important salary he had decided to move out on his own, but he still had no idea why he had done that at the age of twenty-one when he had a good family and a comfortable home. Had he been decisive and daring in doing that? Was it driven by some other motivation, or was it simply impulsive? In contrast to that, walking away from an important person usually takes some time. He had been separating from his girlfriend for two years, and it was making him very sad.

I found this reflection somewhat reassuring about his ability to sustain a therapeutic relationship. And he had found me helpful. Nevertheless his ambivalence was clear to me. He both wanted and did not want to form a therapeutic couple. At the end of the interview I told him his self observations and his analysis of his situation were correct but they were not enough to diminish his suffering because they were too intellectual and too impassioned, in the same way that existential readings enabled him to make conclusions about the reality of the human condition but did not enable him to understand the reality of his feelings. I told him I had decided to offer to be his therapist, and I asked him what his idea of a treatment was. He answered he had a weekly session in mind, not to contain costs for missed sessions but to accommodate his work travel for three days every other week. In addition to that, every six weeks he travelled to Europe for two or three weeks, and the next trip would come up in ten days. As for the weekends, he went to the seaside to the house he had constructed with his ex-girlfriend, for spiritual retreat and meditation.

I found it hard think of a suitable frame for the treatment, due to his real life of being in three different countries. The frame would have to be firm enough to contain his insecurity fantasies, to counteract the defensive discontinuity present in his relations, and yet flexible enough to accommodate his real life business model and his tendency to feel claustrophobic in relationships. It was one thing to understand his psychopathology and a different thing to work with him in psychoanalysis. I told him that due to the complexity of his situation related to his lack of time and experience with commitment it would be better for each of us to think carefully about it together in a final consultation when I would propose a way we could work together. He totally agreed.

At the final meeting of the consultation phase, I told Juan we needed to work on his multiple explanations for the difficulties he faced and the troubling things he went through. I said that the same things kept on happening and the same old explanations kept not helping because they were firmly believed-in answers, but then he came up with very few new questions. I added that he needed to consider his issues in a more flexible way and in relation to a therapist, not only inside his own mind. He had suggested once a week but I felt that I could not do the work at such a low frequency. I preferred three times week, but I suggested twice a week with the option of increasing to three times weekly if we realised this was not enough. So we began twice a week psychoanalytic treatment.

Twice a week treatment in-person

Two months after beginning treatment, Juan went back to his girlfriend to try again but I hear little about his life with her. In fact he shared little of his daily life with me. He preferred to check the solidity of his intellectual concepts, or to describe his guilt and his torment in general, confirmed or underestimated by an ever-present entity called "the voice". I felt that this preoccupation with "the voice" was his defence against building a daily relationship with me so as not to feel emotionally attached and exposed.

One Monday on his return from a trip to Chile, he told me that the previous weekend he had felt very anguished. He had been unable to concentrate on any of the things he enjoyed doing, listening to music, reading the newspaper, writing, and jogging. He admitted that this happened to him frequently in his spare time, but that this time it had been more intense, and he could not see why. He was very annoyed. I reminded him that after his Wednesday session he would be travelling to Europe again, and that maybe the discontinuity in the treatment was bothering him more than before.

When he returned from Europe he said he had thought of proposing three sessions a week whenever he was in Buenos Aires. I welcomed the increased frequency, but I could not guarantee to have an extra hour free. I said that, if he told me in advance, I would look for a third hour for him on those weeks. As was to be expected, he was not careful to inform me of when he would be in town. His schedule for short trips often changed but he did his best to combine his different flights. We went on this way for two more months. He used to say that "the voice" reproached him for imposing his timing on me. I replied he preferred to feel guilty for asking rather than to actually spend more time with me, his girlfriend, and his home. The relationship with me was reconciling him to the necessity of remaining longer at the same place.

I was careful to respect and regulate the distance he needed in our relationship. If I was at a distance, he felt lonely, abandoned, and anguished. If he thought I was too close, the claustrophobia appeared and his dialogues with the voice increased. He saw himself getting involved in a sadomasochistic relationship. All the same, his relationship with me was consolidating day by day, until one Monday after he had postponed a flight to Chile in order to have his session, he surprised me by saying: "I must be growing fond of Dr. Aryan! I don't know if the fact of growing fond of my analyst might cause trouble in the treatment." He would have preferred to think of me as only an analyst, and he did not want to be overloaded with feelings that made him unable to think. He became upset and increasingly sad. The previous night he had been to the theatre with his family and girlfriend. They all felt at ease with one another while he wondered, "What the hell do I want from life if I'm not happy with the one I have?" He reproached himself and at the same time thought, "I really like all this, but I can't be fully here." He felt ill at ease and didn't enjoy it. Crying for the rest of the session, he told me that, as the relationship with his girlfriend got closer, his sexual rejection increased, and he felt guilty and responsible for not providing her with the welfare she deserved, which he thought absolutely unfair and crazy because his girlfriend was "a unique woman, besides being very beautiful". That morning he had hugged her, crying that he didn't know what happened to him. He concluded, "I can't stand this state of mind any more."

I said that, although he was being true to his feelings, he despised himself for having the feelings. Perhaps he thought that it was not masculine to express feelings. He associated to his girlfriend's ninety-year-old father who suffers from Alzheimer's and is in a wheelchair, taken here and there by his seventy-year-old wife, the man accepting his wife's direction in a docile manner. Even though his having Alzheimer's might be the necessary condition for this adjustment, it struck him as a romantic image of two elderly people caring for each other, whereas his parents have been arguing for forty-five years. If his father drinks more than a glass of wine he becomes aggressive, and that weekend he had seven glasses, not one. The father was cursing all the time, and the mother was answering aggressively instead of comforting him.

I then learned that Juan's father looks like his grandfather. Until that moment his grandfather had not come up in our discussions. Like Juan's father he starts shouting if he drinks wine, and his wife is submissive in the face of his yelling. I asked Juan if this grandfather was his father's father. He answered that this grandfather was "the father of his father's wife", a twisted way of referring to his own mother. To my surprise this grandfather so like his father was in fact his father's father-in-law! So far the family company where he and his father and uncles worked so hard had seemed to me to be his father's family company. So his father had joined the company upon marriage to the wife, daughter and sister of the company men. Juan's father had been placed in the books division as he was a reader and better educated than the others, while Juan's uncles attended to the rest of the divisions aggressively. Here was a situation where the mother's line was financially stronger than the father's. Juan did not know who he looked like.

When Juan felt anguished that weekend in Chile or upset at the theatre, he didn't like who he had become but he didn't know how he wanted to be. I said that he was in conflict as to who he should be like—his grandfather, some uncle, his father. Juan felt relieved. He said that he experienced his relatives as a huge audience among whom he could not elect a model. If he were sensitive and a good reader he would be like his father who is sensitive and "from the book division". He didn't know whether he liked this. He really wanted to look like one of his uncles, but he couldn't. I responded that it was hard to know whom to marry—a woman like his submissive grandmother, his angry mother, or some uncle's wife—as this choice would also seal his election of a male model.

Perhaps he wanted to have all of them inside him without giving up anyone, so that each of them would have a part of him, and he would have a part of each of them. By not being like anyone, he could not settle down, and so was rootless. He preferred to remain elusive. I never knew where he was, what he was going to do, whether he was travelling, or when he would want to see me for the third hour. If he stayed in one place and became fond of it, as could be happening with his girlfriend and with me, he would have to resign himself to being only himself.

Not wanting to identify with anyone in his family could be a way of withdrawing from the permanent arguing of his parents. With parents who are constantly fighting there is no room for children. An alcoholic father causes further insecurity. In that large family, there was no one to stop the trouble in that couple. Juan's father may have a loud voice, but his mother is the boss. Perhaps his assignment to "stay with the books" had not been enough for him. It seemed that the family assumption was that to have a loving and loyal wife it was necessary to suffer from Alzheimer's.

What was important to me was that Juan understood that having a place is to take a position, and that this was hard for him because he would lose one of the two parents. He has organised a life where he is everywhere and nowhere and does not have to take a position in favour of anyone. But regardless of his coming and going, Dr. Aryan is always there for him and adapts to his schedule. It is a bond which goes beyond his trips. Thanks to this relationship, Juan could understand how bad he feels when he is not anywhere and not with anybody who matters to him. In spite of the interruptions the relationship with me was reconciling him to the fact of staying in one place and this had an organising effect. If it is possible for him to stay in this place and feel deeply, then he can start to think about his own history clearly and see how it influences him to feel the way he does in his present life.

Juan went to Chile and came back. At the end of a three-session week in person he would be flying to Spain and I would then have my two-week vacation. Apart from the single week of three sessions in Buenos Aires, we would have a break of two and a half months. This time he anticipated the impact of the interruption more acutely because he had become increasingly interested in the analytic work. He was enthusiastic and committed to treatment, and he had de-idealised his philosophy in favour of talking about feelings and everyday life.

The day before he left for Spain, Juan said, "Continuous sessions have been much more productive. I heard about telephone analysis. I would call you from Europe at the time of my sessions in Buenos Aires. Would you ever consider that?" I felt lost, and took my time to think it over. He had telephoned me occasionally for emergencies or to try to engage me in a philosophical argument, but he proposed that he would no longer do that. Now the telephone calls would be regularly scheduled as analytic sessions.

Obviously the patient who hated to need anyone now needed me more than he had seemed to, and now found it hard to leave me and his analytic work. This was the result of our work together. Could I accept that? How could I sustain an analytic dialogue on the phone? What would it be like? What kind of analyst would I be? Then I remembered the advice of one of my supervisors, David Liberman, who consulted to me about my distressed countertransference in reaction to the erotic transference of a hysterical patient who was in a state of anguish on the couch, reproaching me for abandoning her. Liberman said, "Listen to her without looking at her, as if you're listening on the phone" (Liberman, 1974, personal communication). Having got over my surprise, and with that reassurance, I told Juan that I had heard about teleanalysis, but I had no experience of it. I had no opinion for or against it but I thought that we would need to try it out and see how it would affect our work and our relationship. We would need to build the confidence together. If it was manageable and productive we could continue analysis on the telephone, with in-person visits when he was at home in Buenos Aires.

After the session, I was not calm. I wondered if I was contributing to an omnipotent fantasy and manic denial of the effect of distances. I wondered how I would be on the phone, and whether transference and countertransference would still occur. Within a few minutes of our first phone session, Juan interrupted himself to say, "You know what? Calling you makes me feel like a fat lady with nothing to do but chat on the phone, and I feel ashamed." I noticed that already he was responding to the change in the format. Having expressed his negative view of telephone analysis, he went on to use the sessions to talk about what was happening in his everyday life and in his relationships. He was no longer discussing philosophy. Thanks to the accommodation I had agreed to, the everyday life of the actual person had come to the fore.

Transference in teleanalysis

Having agreed to proceed in this totally unforeseen and surprising method, it was clear to me that the analytic contract and the essential frequency can be maintained across variables of distance and time. I do not mean that the use of the telephone makes no difference. For instance, when working in person, I used to take the patient's absence as resistance. I found it quite annoying, and I did not want to be reconciled to it. In fact it triggered in me a countertransference wish to impose my preference on him. But when I agreed to the telephone to maintain continuity, I no longer experienced what I had called resistance. When he returned to see me, I noticed that whereas he used to be scruffy, dispersed, confused, and devaluing of treatment, he now took care of himself and his analytic contract. The new context occasioned by my acceptance of the change in frame created a new character who took care of his relationship with me.

I think that if in this particular case I held to the usual concepts of resistance and insisted on his absence, and his request for teleanalysis as an attack on the frame and a narcissistic lack of consideration for the object, a devaluing transference would have persisted. But with a change in the frame, the focus of the analyst changed, and a new atmosphere was created. We tend to use a model in which countertransference occurs in reaction to the patient: if the patient mistreats the analyst, we feel he is mistreating the analyst as a version of his internal object. In fact, the transference/countertransference dialectic is not simply a repetition, but is a co-construction of analyst and analysand. New aspects of transference and countertransference may show up once teleanalysis offers a new frame that removes the obstacle to continuity and opens a more secure possibility for exploration.

The patient proposed teleanalysis, and I wondered what to do about it. I did not want to decide alone, and so I asked the patient to talk about it. He conveyed his associations and I had my own memories. There was a whole dialogue about it. Patient and analyst were physically together trying to find a way through an obstacle affecting both of them. The space for analysis is constructed between two people. Working on the relation with the internal objects contributes to the evolution of the transference-countertransference. Working on a creative dialogue between analyst and patient also contributes to the development of transference as each engages in free association in relation to internal object relations.

With this way of working the internal family structure appears based on childhood experience with parents, siblings, uncles. The childhood script confronts the present stage. So far, it has emerged in couple relationships, in business attitudes, and in his intellectual approach to life. Instead of having individual preconceptions based on philosophy applied to life, now he lives life and thinks about it afterwards. Now he lives the events, narrates the daily stuff in analysis, associates to it, and contemplates the whole, an identification with my way of thinking over his request for teleanalysis. He created a situation in which we confronted his reality without deducing that his request was determined by his past. He was able to see himself in his present situation for who he is. Before then, he was governed by a representation of his family history applied to his present reality. In that state of mind, he did not try to find out who he is. He did things the voice told him, and he did them alone without regard for others. Since we worked out the teleanalysis contract, he feels the need of the other as an other with independent reality, and not as a repetition of his childhood models. He has understood the value of co-constructing his experience.

Countertransference and the position of the analyst

What patients want is to feel symptomatically better and get rid of their inhibitions. We awaken their curiosity for the method, by introducing them to their inner world and its impact on the present, and by exploring their links to the external world. They come to understand what is happening to them, learn about egosytonic character traits, and keep the useful ones and revise the others. Not candidates in training, they care little what kind of psychoanalysis their analyst practises, whether it is pure or impure, orthodox or heterodox, gold or copper. The analyst works at his office as he pleases and does the best he can in the circumstances presented to him.

But when the patient is a candidate, the analyst is under the watchful eye of the training analysts. What if that candidate has to move, or lives at a distance? What if that candidate requests teleanalysis? Again the analyst does not decide alone, but considers the issue in relation to the training system. The training analysts responsible for standards must make sure that the teleanalysis does not adversely affect the training of candidates who move away from, or live remote from, training centres. Without considering teleanalysis from inside their own experience, they tend to find it inferior to traditional in-person analysis. Such rapid disapproval suggests that their argument is fuelled by worry about loss of hegemony and perhaps income.

For those candidates, the education system has invented shuttle analysis in which the candidate or the training analyst travel to the other's location for condensed analysis of two sessions per day for a period of time such as two weeks. But we must ask ourselves, is shuttle analysis in use to meet the needs of the candidate or the training analyst? Is the expense of time and money worth it? Are the results better than with teleanalysis? In my view, what matters is to maintain continuity and to arrive at an arrangement for ensuring that, in discussion between ananlyst and analysand, rather than imposing a single format. Where the analysis consists of a combination of in-person and telephone sessions, we should not have to worry about the percentage of each type. We should simply concern ourselves with ensuring frequency sufficient to support the analytic process. Then we can review the effectiveness of teleanalysis and compare it to our experience of in-person analysis. What is needed is research funding for an extensive comparison study of telephone analysis, shuttle/condensed analysis, and in-person analysis.

Teleanalysis and the spread of psychoanalysis

In the first part of the twentieth century, Freud invented a new method for arriving at an understanding of the dynamics and function of the human psyche. Beginning with Anna O., he let his patients speak freely, and he listened. He proposed a different kind of contact with a patient and demonstrated its effectiveness. Over the years, this method has benefited many people, including the hospitalised mentally ill. People need to be heard. In Argentina and other countries in Latin America that are not in the cradle of European civilisation and that have suffered repressive government in the twentieth century, people need to be heard, and psychoanalysis is popular there. Latin American analysts have added to the Freudian canon the concept of *el vinculo* (the link) in which the individual (including his symptomatology, desires, and fears) is situated on a vertical axis connecting him to previous and future generations and on a horizontal axis connecting him to his extended family and social world. The concept of the link extends the therapeutic reach of psychoanalysis and applies in the academic study of literature, art, and politics. Using the idea of the link, psychoanalysis has been able to relieve social pain, and so reach well beyond the patient population.

As psychoanalysts and citizens of the world, we are concerned about the negative consequences of globalisation in which market economy and multinational financial activity are prized above all. When mentality is governed by the price of merchandise, then no value is accorded that which is priceless—creativity, the search for truth, solidarity, continuity of experience, responsibility, privacy, honesty, respect for diversity (ethnic, linguistic, religious, social)— all subscribed to by psychoanalysis.

One way of addressing the effects of globalised corporatisation has been the compulsive, even violent, injection of spiritual values by faith-based fundamentalist initiatives. Another way is to reach out to those who are relegated to their own internal and external realities and communicate with them in their own language, listening and responding with analytic insight into causality and unconscious motivation. In my opinion, psychoanalysis has an ethical obligation to share its wisdom indirectly through the media, and directly by offering treatment to individuals. This is where I turn again to the importance of teleanalysis.

Psychoanalysis has been reaching out to remote regions such as Eastern Europe and Central America. Analysts who come from those regions and speak the local language are especially valuable in this endeavour. For this purpose, shuttle/condensed analysis was designed. The immigrant analyst, trained classically in already existing institutes, is enthusiastic about the opportunity to disseminate the analytical activity to patients in his country of origin, and his patients are grateful to be heard and understood in their mother tongue. But the necessary travel becomes burdensome to analyst and patient. Each of them has to make a living and maintain continuity with their patients and families. They can only travel infrequently and that means big gaps in analytic intensity. When candidate and analyst reflect on their reality, it is obvious that telephone analysis is needed to sustain the analytic situation. The power of psychoanalytical reflection multiplied by many individuals reached individually becomes an antidote to the dangers of political fanaticism and religious fundamentalism.

Some analysts say that we must accept the grief of being unable to psychoanalyse patients who move, or travel, or live outside analytic centres, and that we must not encourage the manic illusion of offering treatment by resorting to long-distance communication. To me it is not manic: it is pioneering. As we develop ways of reaching people in regions far away and poor, we will be involved in limitations and imperfections, but we will be polishing gradually the methodologies of remote analysis. Early analyses of Dora, Anna Freud (Freud's daughter), Fritz (his grandson), or Melita Schmideberg (Klein's daughter) would not be regarded as legitimate by the standards of traditional analysis today. Yet all contributed to the creation of the psychoanalytic method that is regarded as legitimate today. Where teleanalysis is carried out in good faith by responsible, well-trained psychoanalysts, convinced of the value of the analytic process and sound analytic technique, teleanalysis will enrich psychoanalysis in general.

This will require a revision of the institutional functions of the central power. First and foremost it is important to promote research and discourage authoritarian attitudes that decide what is and what is not psychoanalysis. These attitudes not only aspire to ensure the purity of the method, but protect the institution. Pioneering initiatives such as teleanalysis challenge the psychoanalytic establishment to undergo revisions and changes, which may be felt as threatening to its integrity.

I propose an outreach process of combined shuttle and teleanalysis on a large scale with a view to creating psychoanalytic education as "a refuge in adversity" (Diogenes Laercio, circa 340 BC). I do not mean to suggest a colonialist approach, but a generous international outreach to share our psychoanalytic way of thinking about national and local reality and history. I would like to think that, fifty years from now, psychoanalytical thinking will continue to promote personal and social growth and generate a more advanced culture.

Reference

Liberman, D. (1974). Personal communication.

CHAPTER TWELVE

Case material from a telephone analysis

Charles Hanly, PhD

K was a striking, highly intelligent married professional woman in her late twenties. Despite her attractive appearance, her intellectual and professional achievements and her marriage, she remained narcissistically vulnerable and subject to panic attacks.

K had telephone analysis at four times per week for three years after one year of analysis on the couch preceded by more than a year of psychotherapy. When her husband was offered an excellent career opportunity in a city at a great distance from Toronto we both knew that she had more work to do, especially in working through dependent ties to her parents and their surrogates. I recommended that she should continue her analysis with a colleague in the province to which she was moving. However, the distance between her new home and the city in which analysts were located ruled out this possibility. K did not want to change analysts: she was feeling understood and she no longer had panic attacks, although fear of them persisted. When K asked me for analysis by phone, I agreed with trepidation.

I had three immediate concerns about the telephone. First, I had no experience with telephone analysis. Second, when I make the slight withdrawal of perceptual attention involved in reflective thought, I sometimes involuntarily close my eyes. During the psychotherapy, whenever this happened, K believed that I was dozing because I found her boringly uninteresting. She felt rejected, humiliated, and abandoned. One of her strengths in the therapy was her ability to forthrightly voice these apprehensions about me and thus open up opportunities to explore and test them. This anxiety had provided transferential access to long-standing difficulties in her relation to her father. Even though these reactions had diminished as had her anxiety attacks, I worried that any residual element of transference cure could cause a resurgence of the anxiety attacks with the loss of the holding function of the transference as a result of not being present with each other in the same room.

Third, K often preferred to talk to people on the phone rather than face to face. The phone provided a protective "distance". Might not telephone analysis collude with this anxiety about feelings aroused by physical presence, weaken the transference by turning the telephone into an unanalysable resistance authorised by me? How could the necessary transferences develop bereft of physical presence? How could interpretations have their effect without affect-stimulating proximity?

What follows is a radically abbreviated "before and after the telephone" account of K's analysis to let you judge for yourselves. Her transference was primarily positive and idealising, although the idealisations were punctured by an anxious attention to my age, and the unconscious narcissistic anger of the transference symptom described above. Her parental relations left her feeling emotionally impoverished. Both her father and mother transferences were ambivalent. She longed to create a happy, close, family life with her husband and the children they would have.

The aggressive side of her ambivalent transference found expression in a dream, during her psychotherapy. She was wearing a very long, flowing, perhaps matrimonial, dress with many folds and layers of cloth. The dress was voluptuously beautiful but disturbing to the dreamer because of its power to entrap and destroy, akin to a spider's web. From the image, two sequences of associations followed over the next weeks involving the idea of entrapping and destroying men and the idea of female rivalry.

In her professional life, K's ambivalence to men was manifest in two ways: she feared that men whom she did not admire or actively disliked would be left humiliated, damaged, and vindictive if they adopted her ideas even when her ideas were realistic and useful. She idealised men she admired or liked, had difficulty acknowledging their shortcomings, and became too easily accommodating for her own good.

There was evidence in her symptoms and memories that her father had not been an adequate object for her childhood sexual and romantic feelings, nor sufficiently responsive, supportive, and accommodating later on. He had not been able to ease her envious feelings towards her mother with appropriate responsiveness. He left her feeling unloved, unlovable, unattractive, ill-formed, and dangerously angry. Despite her high intelligence and professional success, she felt herself to be so intellectually deficient that she dared not attempt reading classical literature. K's panic attacks consisted of a feeling that she had stepped through a transparent barrier into a desolate world that forever isolated her from human contact. In the transference, she was struggling to find a way to give up her longing for her father's love and the aggression its chronic loss aroused and sustained.

Unfortunately, from early on the mother exacerbated K's difficulty by jealously controlling her relation to her father under the guise of being helpful and solicitous: "Yes, I know that Daddy is busy and does not want to be disturbed but don't worry, I will speak to him about it." This unconscious cruelty, coating with sweet, protective condescension the mother's claim to exclusive influence with the father, consolidated K's affective alienation from her Olympian father, her lack of confidence in herself, and her dependent bondage to her mother—a bondage that had contributed to the school phobia that had been the childhood precursor of K's adult panic attacks.

Analysis on the telephone

K made an excellent adaptation to her new neighbourhood and career. The gains she had already made remained steadily in place. My concern that the telephone might detrimentally exacerbate her anxiety about my abandoning inattention was laid to rest. If anything, the telephone facilitated the useful development of an erotic transference which made me younger without visual contradiction. The analysis of her wish to be sensually attractive to me released in her a deeper realisation of her rivalry with her mother, for example, in a dream in which a menacing witch-like figure, associated to my wife, was barring her way. The analysis of this rivalry began to release her from her fear of being physically attractive to men and to take a legitimate satisfaction in her physical appearance.

The circumstance in which she now found herself also allowed for a further working through of her father transference. The idea of telephone analysis had come from her. I had accepted it. But my acceptance had neither damaged me nor made me vindictive. This realisation allowed her to usefully undergo some de-idealisation, growth of confidence in herself, and trust in her appropriate aggression on behalf of her own needs.

Along with these gains, there was a "countertransference enactment" on my part. My acceptance of her account of the ways in which her father failed her nourished a maternal transference that denied both K's rivalry with her mother and her mother's failure to help her with it. Her idealising, compliant, dependent maternal transference came to the fore during the period of telephone analysis, whereas her paternal transference had been relatively more dominant in the pre-telephone period.

This transference was at once positive and resistive. It made itself known in a hyper-cathexis of the sound of my voice, from the calmness of which K drew gratifying, soothing reassurance. This transference, during the telephone analysis, was deeper, in the sense of evoking trauma and conflicts from earlier developmental stages, than the previously dominant paternal transference. Her transference fear of being left alone by my disinterest had dissipated and had been replaced by a feeling of being with me and wishing to be like me. This transference was probably reparative of very early trauma at the price of prolonging resistance to dealing with her maternal rivalry. In this sense, the transference was both positive and negative. If the telephone neither helped nor enabled this transference, and the work that this transference made possible, then it did not impede it either.

The interpretation of this resistance and its historical and developmental sources both in and out of the transference was helpful. I shall conclude by describing one important facet of K's improvement in her capacity to mobilise aggression on behalf of her own needs and aspirations. Her husband had adamantly refused to have a second child. At the end of her second year of analysis by phone, despite her husband's grudging acceptance and amid his accusations of trickery, she was again pregnant and, in the following year, presented the by now proud father with a son. K looked forward to her parents' visit at the time of the birth, happily complaining about putting them up. She discovered that she had nothing to worry about and little to be happy about. Her parents had dropped in as part of a prearranged sightseeing tour that was all too evidently the primary purpose of their trip. When she tried to express her disappointment to her parents, her father repeated a familiar reaction, "Well, isn't she something else!" to a passively, acquiescent mother. K's mourning was no doubt facilitated by the timely arrival of her infant son, her husband's now ungrudging pride in her and him, and the potential they offered her for the realisation of her dream of a family more closely knit by bonds of love than her own had been. The outcome of K's mourning was a bond to her parents that tolerated the distance from her they seemed to need. When, a few months later, her father suffered a serious illness, she responded with generosity and caring affection.

Conclusion

The telephone analysis of K indicates that the essential processes of free association and transference need not be compromised by the telephone for the patient. And the basic interpretive, responsive, holding, and witnessing functions can be sustained by the analyst. Modifications need not be introduced. The analysis of K does not show that an analysis can begin and end successfully by telephone. However, the manner of the continuation and termination of K's analysis suggests that possibility.

CHAPTER THIRTEEN

The screen as catalyst for psychic transformation

Caroline M. Sehon, MD

Is intensive psychoanalytic psychotherapy via Skype indicated or contraindicated for patients with an intense internet life? Can therapy by Skype foster the growth of patients who have a long-established preference to socialise in cyberspace? In this context, would the patient's comfort with communication technology leverage the work so that patient and therapist can work more analytically? How can we understand the mechanisms for therapeutic action for such patients?

As a participant of the international working group on teleanalysis at the International Psychoanalytical Association, I pondered these questions before and after I agreed to continue therapy via Skype with a college-bound adolescent patient who needed to work in this way to stay in therapy with me. We were both surprised when his therapy and life took quantum leaps forward to a degree that could not simply be accounted for by other factors. I would like to discuss major signs of progress in my patient, and data to suggest the critical role that Skype served in deepening our work. In conclusion, I will offer some hypotheses for how his significant transformation might be understood as directly attributable to our work via the screen.

How our journey began

When I first met Donald, he was a fifteen-year-old second-year student in high school. For as long as he could remember, he had struggled with depression and anxiety. At his young age, he had already endured many years of being teased and bullied. His social awkwardness, cystic acne, nail biting, and red hair and freckles drew negative attention to him and made him a ready target of attack. Deeply traumatised by these experiences, he felt terribly ambivalent about making new friends, and felt frightened that each new encounter would only result in further rejection. To meet his attachment needs and entertain himself, he retreated into his private fantasy world and into social opportunities that cyberspace provided.

Listening to Donald and his parents, I gathered a sense of his unrelenting pain, his experience of traumatic encounters with his school peers, and his retreat into a self-made world. He and his parents concluded that years of behavioural therapy and countless medications had failed him. Donald's symptomatic difficulties were consistent with features of atypical autism, anxiety, and depression, but I found it more meaningful to think psychoanalytically about the structure of his mind and how a dynamic therapy could help him to heal from his trauma, to refind his self, and to support his growth and development.

Donald is a remarkably gifted young man with a keen intellect, an avid curiosity, a wonderful imagination, and a sharp wit. He is a talented violinist who taught himself to play through YouTube videos and other online courses. He has a penchant for memorising and reciting long passages from TV shows, movies, plays, songs, and fictional narratives. He cultivated an interest in reading, journal writing, videogames, online games, graphic novels, web comics, podcasts, role-playing games (like *World of War Craft*), fan fiction, Facebook, Twitter, and eventually online chat rooms. Looking back, he felt that he coped with his painful interpersonal experiences by investing more and more of his creative energy in solitary pursuits, or in social networks online. From my first encounter with Donald, I was very impressed by his curiosity, and his desire to find adaptive ways to create social engagements that protected him from threat and attack. Although he was very ambivalent about socialising, it has always been clear to me that there was a part of him that longed for meaningful, interpersonal connections with others, and with me in his therapy.

In session therapy: initial phase

Donald was fortunate that his parents supported him having an intensive psychoanalytic psychotherapy. His mother worked as an executive administrator to a large PR firm, and his father was a commercial real estate broker. He had an older sister and a younger brother. Donald and I met in the office in face-to-face sessions, twice weekly for the first year, and three times weekly for his final two years of high school. This individual work was combined with periodic parent guidance and family sessions.

Slowly and surely, Donald developed a positive contextual transference to me. Gradually he came to experience me as someone he could trust and who wanted to listen to him. Initially he filled the sessions with his worries about his school and home life, and his constant fears of rejection. I sensed his urgent longings for understanding and support. He was extremely anxious, sometimes quite depressed, and usually inattentive. He had a tendency to dissociate at times, but he has never presented with a severe dissociative disturbance. Although he wanted to talk about various school and family encounters, I gradually came to recognise that his more pressing need was to acquaint me with the fictive characters that he had "befriended" online, and with the superhero characters and animated cartoons that fascinated and excited him so much.

As if he had been kept waiting to talk to me for a long time, he filled the sessions with his worries and his stories, his podcasts, TV shows, and graphic novels. He freely associated with remarkable ease from the word go. In rapid fire, he jumped from one story to another, then to a song, then to a poem, then to a movie, and then to a daydream. I felt as if he were spinning on board a carnival ride at an amusement park, and it was as if he were challenging me to take the leap onto the ride that was circling round and round in front of me. In my countertransference during the early phase of our work, I felt dizzy and confused at times, unable to find the apparently tenuous links between his associations. I wondered if he was communicating unconsciously to me something of his disorganised state of mind, and his own inability to form links among the separate elements of his thinking. Sometimes Donald would come to a screeching halt in his monologue, saying, "I don't have the foggiest idea why I'm talking about this." Typically, he would tell me a few lines of various narratives without providing the context. He did not show any apparent awareness or concern that I would not have the history of that particular podcast or narrative to allow me to track him and gather the meaning of his communication. Although he struggled to understand his associations, he never manifested psychotic thinking in the conventional sense.

For the first year of therapy, his communication seemed to be aimed at evacuating his anxiety, and talking *at* me rather than *with* me. Eye contact was intolerably intense for Donald, so he usually averted his gaze from me to numerous objects around the office that caught his attention. We worked at helping him to become more aware of feelings that frightened him, and to find words to communicate his angst to me. He had trouble reflecting upon his experience, or mentalising what others might be thinking or feeling. During this initial phase of the therapy, he seemed more interested in tagging me along on his carnival rides, as if to acquaint me with the characters of his world, and with the part objects of his mind. He could not interact with me as a whole object, or play with ideas in a generative context that could support his growth. However, a secure foundation was being laid for deeper work to come later.

In session therapy: deepening the work

As the therapy progressed, he was able to let me in to aspects of his experiences within his family. There he felt like a midget compared to his parents and his siblings, all of whom he idealised and envied for their accomplishments and social graces. In his mind, they were perfect, whereas he was floundering and failing in his parents' eyes, academically and socially.

In reality, his parents praised him for his accomplishments, which became considerable over the years to come. He began to show early signs that he was developing a more secure sense of himself, and he was enjoying some relief from his crippling anxiety and depression. With a strengthening of his ego capacities, he was more able to resist his impulses to retreat into the private wanderings of his mind or to surf the web. In his sessions with me, I noticed that he still dissociated but to a much lesser degree than in the past. He seemed more aware of my presence as another human being with a mind of my own with whom he could interact, rather than primarily as a sounding board that he could talk at. Gradually, his speech became much more organised, and the links between his associations were much easier to discern. He enjoyed more academic success as he became capable of focusing more on his school work.

In the social sphere of his life, he continued to feel stymied, however. He could not keep up with the dialogue of various cliques at school, and continually encountered the all too familiar experience of feeling as if he were a social outcast. He complained of feeling inept at drawing others into the recreational activities that he relished so much. In a concordant identification with him, I had often had a similar experience of feeling as if I were on the edge of his fantasy life, or his online world, just as he experienced being on the periphery of a conventional social life.

With his passage into Facebook, he came to dwell in the illusion that he had hundreds of "friends", whose lives he quietly observed on screen, protected from the threat of intimate interactions, and to some degree, from tormenting bullies. Over time, he gravitated more thoroughly away from face-to-face, social experiences, and hibernated into what he came to feel was a much more intense preoccupation with all the exciting and compelling pleasures that he could reap from his fantasy life and the internet. He became immersed in online fan fiction websites, in which authors post their stories online, as they are being written, to invite feedback and suggestions for other character ideas to enrich the storyline. He particularly enjoyed responding to the requests of authors for new character ideas, proposing to them that they include his many characters in their stories. These writing activities steadily grew in intensity over the years. Bereft of a social group in his daily life, he found others online who shared a similar preoccupation with fan fiction websites, and with whom he felt gratified.

When his parents structured social gatherings for him or encouraged him to make plans with classmates, he felt frightened of his maladroit entrée into that social world, anxious about the frequent emotional collapse that would accompany these experiences, and angry and resentful at his parents for trying to help him in these ways. He felt overshadowed by his siblings, whom he portrayed as navigating the social world with comparative ease, and spoiled by having more social invitations and dates than they could possibly accept. He would either begrudgingly comply with his parents' wishes for him, or retreat into video games hidden in his room. As he experienced much anger towards his parents, he would typically disown and project his aggressive feelings into them, and then fear their retaliation.

He struggled with an extremely rigid and punitive superego, revealed in his barrage of self-criticism were he to slip up in relatively minor ways. In his transference to me, he would seize up with anxiety at times, anticipating that I was about to indict him for eating a bag of popcorn or failing to study longer for a school test. We worked on his transference to me and to his parents, so as to help him understand and work through the effect of this berating, internalised object relationship. Considerable work was done to help him reclaim anger projected onto them, and sometimes onto me in the transference, and to slowly develop a more realistic view of them as whole objects rather than as a system of internalised, bad, part objects.

Preparing for college

By the time Donald had applied for college midway through his senior year of high school, he was faring much better and aspiring to more independent, adult-like roles and responsibilities. He had formed one friendship, graduated from high school with honours, and had satisfactorily held down a summer job at a small camera shop. He felt proud of his considerable progress in therapy. Nevertheless we both recognised that much unfinished work remained. He hoped that college life would give him a new lease on his social life, with new opportunities to make friends in his real life without as much reliance on Facebook, Twitter, and fan fiction websites.

During family meetings, we debated about his taking a gap year or attending college at various commuting distances from home. Donald had longed to attend college on the West Coast, which was a long plane ride away, but he wanted to continue working with me in psychotherapy using communication technology in the form of computer-to-computer Skype with a webcam. We considered this possibility over several months. We tried out Skype sessions while he was still at home, and discussed his comparative experiences of meeting in-person versus online. I considered the situation very carefully, assessing the potential risks and side effects of appearing on the computer screen to conduct therapy with someone with such an intense internet life. I secured the necessary legal provisions to ensure my observance of the laws and guidelines required of clinicians practising in both jurisdictions, including the licensing requirements from my state medical board and the state where my patient would be attending college.

I was impressed by the sturdiness of this three-year therapy relationship, during which Donald had made remarkable progress, and by the strength of my alliance with his parents. It seemed reasonable to try to preserve our work rather than expose Donald to the risks of severing this therapeutic link, and as long as everyone could agree to a new set of clinical parameters as a condition for our continuing to work together. Donald agreed to meet with me in person during school recesses, like Thanksgiving or summer, and at any time that a crisis required him to return home for more family support and for a higher level of service. They would find a private, soundproofed office setting on the college campus that could be reserved for Donald's regularly scheduled therapy sessions. We identified local treatment resources, should an emergency necessitate more immediate care. We were prepared for technology failures: we were ready to use the phone as back-up if our internet connection were interrupted, and Donald agreed to repair his laptop in a timely way, were it to malfunction. Donald and his parents gave informed consent to this revised treatment contract. After careful consideration of these clinical, legal, and ethical matters, I decided to provide this new trial of therapy using Skype with sufficient conditions in place for me to feel confident that I could continue to deliver good clinical work and meet the standard of care.

Therapy via Skype: initial phase

Somewhat to my surprise, Donald quickly adjusted to living away from home, and felt at ease as he transitioned into his new college environment. Unlike the more typical response of college freshmen, he did not have the experience of missing his friends back home, since he was not actually leaving a social group, and his cyberspace milieu remained constant, after all. Like many a college freshman, he enjoyed feeling less accountable to his parents and not constantly in the shadow of his siblings. Since there was a time in the not-too-distant past when it was unclear whether he would even be ready to attend college, he felt proud at having made it this far. He attended his sessions on time, under the conditions of our new agreement for meeting by Skype, and therapy resumed without a glitch.

His crisis came after a three-month honeymoon period, near the end of his first term. Suddenly, he felt he had taken a sharp fall. He descended into an abyss of severe depression and panic, with despairing though not frankly suicidal thoughts. After making some new friends, he began to feel rejected and alienated, and felt as if he were reliving once again those painful social experiences that were all too common during his school career. At the time, he could not tell me what he thought might have precipitated his conviction that others disliked him or why they may have thought he was acting strangely. Nor could he articulate what was actually accounting for his social withdrawal. He lost ground academically. The acute nature of this crisis caught me somewhat off guard, since he appeared to have been adjusting very well to this transition. To increase the possibility of understanding the cause of his breakdown and support his recovery, we met more intensively as an immediate measure to help him manage these extreme difficulties, and to mitigate the risk of his losing time at college or of having to withdraw entirely.

The unveiling of imaginary characters

This crisis heralded a veritable breakthrough in his therapy. Donald found himself unable any longer to hide the existence of Xavier, Dylan, and Adrian, three private, internal characters that he had invented step-by-step in his imagination over many years. It took everything in him to disclose to me the fact of their secret existence, and the massive energy he deployed to conceal his attachment to these imaginary characters over all these years. He recalled, "I spent a lot of time pouring energy into them. Part of that energy was making sure that nobody saw. I guess it is something so private. I didn't think I could tell anyone. I know it is an irrational fear. I know I'm not going to get judged by you. I know I'm not going to get punished, but there is still a wall blocking me."

Donald meticulously designed his imaginary persona to be ideal in many respects, but also to carry selective flaws, such as a disfigured face, a violent temper, or a uninhibited sex life. Annoyed by the many perfect "Gary Stu" characters online, he transformed a typically idealised Gary Stu figure into his very own fictive personality that had extraordinary abilities along with basic human needs, desires, and foibles. Fictive characters succeeded socially where Donald had failed. They carried themselves with a confident stride, and dressed fashionably. Xavier, Dylan, and Adrian evolved over the years from being same-aged peers to adult men. In ways that echoed his describing his envy of his peers and his siblings, he spoke of his longing to live the lives of these dreamt-up characters. He reflected, "I'm pretty sure that if they were real characters in my life, I'd detest them, and I'd be so jealous,'cause they have so much going for them. They have friends, they're smart, they're not at all socially awkward, they have romantic partners, they've had sex. I'd much rather have their lives than live mine."

Plagued by enormous guilt for this all-engrossing, secret life that he had maintained, and that had contributed so much to his withdrawing from others, Donald felt he had to confess to me how he spent countless hours each day involved with his characters, but mainly with Xavier. Most commonly, he would enact imaginary scenarios in the voice of this character, as if he had transformed himself from Donald into Xavier. He would pretend that he was enacting Xavier's life and he narrated various monologues in his mind as if he embodied Xavier's persona. He did not create conversations among his characters, and his retreats into the voice of Dylan and Adrian were relatively rare. He would suggest that fan fiction authors insert his characters' profiles into their narratives when they were seeking a twist in their plots, or release from their writers' block. These stories would then be posted online, for the World Wide Web community to see and imagine.

Until he brought himself to tell me about these characters, no one but Donald had known the extent to which they figured in his daily fantasy life, or the many functions they had come to serve for him. The characters served much like imaginary friends who gave him companionship when he was alone, a sense of self-efficacy, and the hope that maybe he too could feel confident about having friendships or a romantic relationship one day. When Donald needed an antidote to the intensity of deeply painful or pleasurable experiences, he called up Xavier in particular. At times, I wondered whether Donald might be constructing me as a character on screen, or whether he might be conflating aspects of my personality into his imaginary characters. But I never detected any evidence to support these theoretical possibilities. Initially, his construction served adaptive purposes, but tragically, Donald was consumed by the intensity of his retreat into this private world. Speaking of the time he "spent" with Xavier, Donald said, "He's in my head 24–7." He became frightened by the unprecedented extent of his fantasy life: it threatened to hijack his mind and his life. He experienced his link to me via Skype as a lifeline to a world and relationship that protected him from further slippage into his fantasy life. Donald came to see his attachment to Xavier as an addiction. He became so self-absorbed in his imaginings of Xavier that he thought he may have sometimes blurted out these monologues when his peers were in sight. Looking back, he suspected that being unable to resist the compulsion to engage in his role-playing out loud likely contributed to some of the rejection that he experienced by his new friends, just as he was laying roots anew at college. Now I wonder whether, unconsciously, he wanted and needed to let Xavier out, to be rescued from a private fantasy life that had gone bad.

As a little boy Donald had hidden his video games from his parents. As an adolescent he concealed his intense fantasy life from everyone, and from me. His mind had become co-opted by Xavier, as this internal object had come to feel invasive and insistent for all his time and mental energy. His fear of judgment by me seemed to pale in contrast to his fear of the power of this part of his mind. The delivery of this secret into our work brought him tremendous relief. Within a few weeks of its disclosure, he felt emboldened with the hope that he could regain his balance that had been hanging in the breeze. He and his parents gladly agreed to my recommendation for us to maintain this higher intensity of our work, now at four times weekly. During this entire crisis period, he was able, remarkably, to hold steady with his academic work, to re-establish some beginning friendships, and to recover his emotional equilibrium.

Therapy via Skype: deepening the work

Donald's reasons for disclosing this underground life to me at this time seemed plausible, but it appeared to me that our working together via the internet was the central factor in facilitating these developments. Donald said, "The screen is safe … it is familiar … I think I'm much less awkward on the internet. I'm so much cooler online, as the country song goes. It's not as difficult to look at your eyes … it feels a lot safer … probably what makes it easier is there is kind of a digital screen between us, and I feel I'm a lot more comfortable when I've got a screen in front of me."

A startling effect of working via Skype was the appearance of a profusion of dreams, which had been relatively absent before then. Frequently Donald dreamt that various instruments of technology would fail him, like his Kindle Fire cracking. He exclaimed "Oh, my God! I need to get it fixed. Maybe there are also cracks in my sanity. I need to actually go out and meet some people for more than two seconds." He often dreamt of his computer crashing, usually because his malware protection had failed him, or infections from content downloaded from unsafe websites threatened the link he had to me. For example, he said, "I dreamt that an infection came on my iPad. I dreamt that I got these multiple emails from people I didn't know, and when I opened them, they were nonsense. I wouldn't be getting my computer back in a very long time. Suddenly, my iPad stopped working. I realised my malware protection didn't detect the virus. I couldn't get rid of the infection. When I got the infection, it was way past the store closing, so I knew I had to wait a long time, then I woke up." His associations to this dream were to his valued experience of seeing me on his screen, his anxiety about an upcoming separation, and his wish to ensure that his computer was protected from all infections given that the screen linked us together in cyberspace.

Working with dreams and transference-countertransference revealed robust and enduring signs of the treatment's progress. Donald said, "The dream where my computer is being infected is happening every night again. Only I'm a lot calmer about it now." Although occasionally he still reports a nightmare, they are few and far between these days, and when they occur, he feels relieved that the story line has evolved away from a primary focus on computer viruses or technology malfunctioning, to what he describes as "… cliché dreams instead of insane dreams: like it's the day of a final exam, and you realise that you forgot you were taking the course and hadn't done any of the readings." After a session following a terribly lonely day, he dreamt: "I still get infections, but at least I can catch them now … I got this new Symantec anti-virus program that looked different …. It was an S-secure anti-virus program. It could detect my viruses and deal with them, whereas the initial program always used to miss them." He elaborated how this new anti-virus program functioned, unlike those that had always failed him in previous dreams. He associated to a capable and effective friend whom he admired, feelings of love in the transference, and gratitude for learning to manage his emotions better. I thought that the "S-secure antivirus program" referred to me as my surname begins with S, and that through it he conveyed his capacity to transform toxic emotional experiences via alpha function and containment that he identified in me and internalised. At the same time, he acknowledged how difficult it was to work in the affectively charged realm with me. From this perspective, the computer viruses could also be seen to suggest dormant and yet unconscious connections to me in the negative transference, as fear of someone who was exposing him to such an intense, intimate, personal world of relating, albeit across a screen, in contrast to the relatively distant impersonal world of cyberspace.

The entry of Xavier, Dylan, and Adrian onto the therapy stage has given Donald new understanding for the genesis and evolution of these imaginary characters, and has relieved him of the tremendous hold that his fantasy life was having upon him. Gradually, he has succeeded in limiting his time on the internet and his retreat into stories about Xavier in his mind. He has felt excited to recognise that others have been finding him to be quite likeable and enjoyable to spend time with. Reflecting on his desires, he said, "I want the best of both worlds. I want to preserve the connection with fan fiction authors, but not in an obsessional way, where my emotional state hangs in the balance. I also want real friends that I can touch. I want physical friends that have corporeal bodies. I know Thomas (a fan fiction author who welcomed Donald into his narratives) has it, but I've never seen it. I know that you have a corporeal body. I've seen it. I want the best of both worlds."

Increasingly, Donald's sessions are packed with stories of new friends, excitement to join others at a movie or a dance, feeling much happier generally, and succeeding socially in ways he never dreamt possible. He would speak at times about his newfound pleasure in his body, which he had disliked for so long, and his joy at feeling that more of his mind is available to engage with the world, and not just with his "friends" in cyberspace. Recently, he described his therapy via the screen as a hybrid experience, where we are working at the same time "in reality" and "cyberspace". Then, he joked, "Oh, maybe one day, you and I will be able to enter an augmented reality where we could have a session amongst the super heroes and other fantasised creatures in cyberspace. Just kidding. I like the way we work as it is right now."

Now back from college, he meets me in face-to-face sessions at the same frequency of four-times weekly. I have been impressed by his comparative ease at managing the intensity of this in-person contact, and meeting my gaze without difficulty. From his first day back, he had already enjoyed the pleasure of socialising with a friend offline. During his sessions, he has been expressing his preference to develop *"grown up interests"* in *real time* rather than chatting online, or divesting his energy into Xavier or his other fictive characters. Looking back on how he recently dealt with his final exam anxiety, he stated, *"I noticed that when I pulled up Xavier, nothing happened! I guess that means I'm able to handle things better. I don't need Xavier as a shield anymore. I decided that I don't want to give him my confidence anymore. I want to own my own voice."* Beaming with pride about the leaps and bounds in his progress, he exclaimed, *"I'm growing. I'm growing!"*

Reflections

I would like to advance some hypotheses to account for these positive findings, and to consider the constellation of therapeutic factors that seem to have contributed to a deepening of the analytic process during the Skype phase of Donald's therapy.

Shortly after we embarked on this therapeutic journey by Skype, I noticed how much more Donald could sink into the work, and how much more freely he associated across the digital screen. When we met in cyberspace, he was revisiting what had become his safe territory where he already felt so much at home, and where he expected to feel reliably protected from bullying and other attacks. In essence, he trusted the internet as a playground where he could unleash his creativity and cultivate a sense of community. For many years, he had led a secluded social life, behind closed doors and amid an anonymous, virtual universe where no one could see him or mock him. By surfing the web, he could sidestep the dangerous territory of *real time* relationships. In contrast to that anonymity, he could no longer be invisible when conversing with me. He was faced with our seeing each other face-to-face on screen across our internet connection. He noticed that it was much easier to make eye contact with me when we met online. Remarkably, this treatment effect was sustained during his in-person sessions when he returned home from college, possibly representing an internal change attributable to our work via Skype.

In this new online environment, he established a secure contextual transference that enabled him to bring more of himself into the therapy. He unlocked the secret rooms of his pretend world, no longer feeling as frightened that I might judge him or enforce an embargo on his internet activities. Before he could bring his imaginary characters onto the therapy stage, he had been living out his wishes for a relational life online without an understanding about what these activities meant, or what was motivating his compulsive behaviour. Once he could trust me to know more about his fantasy life, we could analyse the transferential meaning of these figures. We could also discuss what his imaginings revealed about his longings to be in real time relationship to others, and what they might say about split off aspects of his self that he had not yet integrated. With this breakthrough in the therapy, he felt happier, and he had more available mental space to focus on his social and academic life. When he returned to my office for in-person therapy sessions from time to time, he continued to feel much more focused when conversing with me. I noticed that the links between his associations were much more readily accessible to understanding and interpretation than had been the case prior to the introduction of therapy via Skype.

We discovered how the digital screen represented a concrete transitional space that bridged his online and real time social worlds. In turn, his therapeutic environment became a more playful and generative arena for analytic work. As he described the therapy hour via Skype, "This is real time. Even if we're interacting across a screen, it's still real time 'cause there's no fantasy medium. When I'm talking to fan fiction authors, or when I'm in my head, there's no real time. It's pure fantasy time." Gradually he became more interested in finding a way to make his real time interactions more important than socialising in cyberspace, and he secured a new circle of friends among his college peers.

This successful outcome is multi-determined, but I often wonder if Donald's treatment gains are disproportionately attributable to the very fact that we were working analytically via Skype. Many factors contributed— his having initially secured a solid foundation of intensive in-person therapy over a few years, his enjoying his newfound freedom as a college freshman, his early academic successes at the start of his college career, and his excitement upon making a new circle of friends probably for the first time in his life. Of course I cannot prove that the Skype phase of his therapy yielded superior results to what might have been achievable in person, if we had worked face-to-face in the office for the entire duration of his therapy. I do not assert unequivocally that the digital screen was the single most influential factor in accounting for his transformation following his relocation to college. I cannot generalise these results to other persons who prefer to socialise in person rather than over the web, or to other individuals who have a different complement of vulnerabilities and strengths than Donald. All these questions and many others await systematic and well-designed research studies.

As Donald's analyst, I feel privileged to have borne witness to the leaps and bounds in his growth and development over the past few years, and to be able to continue working with him in these separate contexts. As his treatment progresses and as he becomes more integrated in his real time social world, it has become harder to discern the differences between the effects of therapy by Skype and therapy in-person. It remains to be established whether Skype or in-person psychotherapy lead to equally effective clinical outcomes, or whether one will be demonstrated as superior.

CHAPTER FOURTEEN

Clinical and technical perspectives on telephone analysis

Jaime Marcos Lutenberg, MD

Telephone analysis should enable analyst and patient to comply with two of the fundamental conditions of analytical technique: the analysand must be able to engage in free association, and the analyst must be able to use suspended attention. Is it possible to conduct a psychoanalytical treatment using the telephone as the means of contact between the patient and the psychoanalyst? What technical and clinical issues arise?

To address these questions I will give passages from two consecutive teleanalysis sessions with commentary in italics to show my work style and way of thinking. I will then review my application of theory of psychoanalytical technique to my work as an analyst. In summary, my ideas are based on Freud who gave us an epistemological, ethical, technical, and theoretical path to follow in doing psychoanalysis. He also guided our research work along new lines of investigation. My ideas are also based on Bion's theory and the influence it has on psychoanalytical technique. The psychoanalytical process that I believe is possible in session on the telephone conforms to the standard analytical process described in their writing and in Etchegoyen's *Los Fundamentos de la Técnica Psicoanalitica* (1986).

Clinical material from a telephone analysis

I shall call the patient Irene. Irene is forty-five years old, a very successful lawyer with her own firm of which she is the principal partner. She lives where she was born in Mendoza, the capital city of the province of the same name in Argentina. Irene is from a traditional family of considerable financial means in this province. She is the youngest of three children. Her eldest brother, Juan, an industrial engineer is six years older, and her sister Ana, a physician, is four years older. Her brother is the administrator and manager of the family company and also works as a consultant for a multinational business.

Her father was a well-regarded lawyer in his province. He died five years ago in 2004. Her mother, who is seventy-five, is a housewife with a busy social life. She receives a pension which is supplemented by family income that includes what she inherited from her husband. Irene and her brother and sister receive monthly payments from the family business set up by the father. Irene had a very good relationship with her father, bordering on the idealising, in my opinion, but understandable in terms of the family history and the image both she and others had of him. The relationship she has with her mother is good, though somewhat distant.

Irene got married at twenty-one, graduated as a lawyer at twenty-three, and separated from her husband fifteen years ago. She has three children who live with her: Alberto, twenty, Eduardo, eighteen, and Maria, sixteen. Her elder son is studying economics in Buenos Aires at a private university, Eduardo is finishing high school and plans to go to university next year (possibly in Buenos Aires as well), and Maria is a secondary school student in Mendoza. The children's father lives in Santiago, Chile and seldom sees his children. He has taken very little part in the upbringing of his children and is reluctant to contribute to the maintenance of them. In order to avoid an ongoing dispute, which at one point went to court, Irene decided to undertake the financial support of her children herself. Her relationship with her ex-husband is distant.

Twice before, Irene underwent psychoanalytic treatment. She sought the first treatment when she was nineteen, because she was afraid of sitting for exams and because of two panic attacks. This treatment was at a frequency of twice a week over three years and was not successful. She sought treatment again fifteen years ago for personal problems caused by her separation. This treatment was at a frequency of three sessions a week and again was not successful. She said that she gave up because "… nothing was happening: it was like a chat between friends."

Irene consulted me four and a half years ago for problems she was having with her partner and because of her grief over the death of her father. We agreed on a series of assessment interviews spread over a period of three months. She would come to Buenos Aires every other weekend for three to four interviews per weekend. After these two months of work, I recommended that Irene should return to analysis. I referred her to a well-qualified analyst in her home town of Mendoza. In spite of my confidence in this suitable local analyst, she told me she wished to continue being analysed by me even if it meant continuing with the programme of fortnightly weekend sessions in Buenos Aires. She maintained that these sessions had been most revealing for her and she had become aware of personal issues which she had not previously noticed. She was quite insistent about the value of a therapeutic relationship with me, and so I decided to offer her sessions in Buenos Aires for one weekend every two or three months, supplementing these face-to-face sessions with a telephone analysis twice a week—on a trial basis. This trial period would last for six months, after which we would each evaluate the experience.

Irene accepted with much pleasure, and we began. After six months, we concluded the trial period, agreed to continue the combined in-person and telephone analysis, and increased the number of telephone sessions to three a week. After a year and a half we added a fourth weekly telephone session. From that time until the present, we have continued the arrangement with four telephone sessions from Tuesday to Friday each week, and three or four face-to-face sessions every two or three months when Irene comes to Buenos Aires.

Here are summaries of two sessions conducted on the telephone with my commentary in italics. I have numbered analyst and patient contributions for ease of referring to them when my thought process and technique are discussed later.

Wednesday, the second session in the week

Irene calls punctually.

Analyst 1:   Hello, how are you?

Patient 1:   Fine. I wanted to tell you about a dream from last night, but first I wanted to tell you that I have been sleeping very well lately. I don't ever remember having slept so peacefully and having got up feeling so refreshed.

I thought of how for a long time she used to wake up several times a night in a state of panic and would not be able to get back to sleep.

Patient 1
(continued):   (Brief silence.) Well, I want to tell you about a dream I had last night. I don't understand why I dreamt it. In the dream I met a very nice, very handsome boy like the athletes I knew when I was a teenager, the kind who evoked feelings of nervousness in me. This boy whose name was Joaquin was a member of the same club as me. He is the type of boy I could easily fall for and who I could like too. As I told you I used to avoid that kind of boy. In the dream I learnt that this boy was going out with Carolina X.

This detail catches my attention. I recognise "Carolina" as the name of a team-mate from her teenage hockey team. This connects to Irene's adolescent fears, which led her to avoid events in which there were "a lot of people" present, and to a recent fear of presenting in front of her colleagues.

Patient 1
(continued):   The boy and Carolina were together sitting on a kind of desk. The three of us, Carolina, Joaquin, and me were there with some other people. The place was very nice and I said to Carolina X., "Do you remember that you had a very nice body when we were young and played hockey together?" She smiled but she looked at me as if she was not really listening or paying attention to me because she didn't believe what I was saying.

Analyst 2:   This Carolina X.—was she really pretty? Were you jealous of her looks? You told me that you were better than she was at sports.

Patient 2:   In fact Carolina X., was not very beautiful. She was quite short and average looking. I don't know how she turned out looking like that in the dream. In the second part of the dream, I seem to be holding some money, which belongs to Carolina, but not to Carolina X., but rather to Carolina Y., my friend who has her office near mine in Mendoza. Well, in the dream, Carolina Y., gave me some money, and I kept it in a sort of box which was installed in a hole in the wall like a safety deposit box. That's the dream.

Analyst 3: I'd like you to help me understand your personal life from images in the dream, especially from your adolescence.

Patient 3: I have no idea where Carolina X., comes from. She was from another club, and I met her playing hockey. I know I was a much better player than her. My game was much better than hers.

Analyst 4: What you are telling me suggests that you were a much "prettier" player or at least a much "prettier" player than her.

Here I am referencing the different qualities of self in her associations—from beauty, to teenage and adult muscular strength, to being the favourite daughter, to competing with her peers and team-mates.

Patient 4: Yes, I stood out much more than her. My name was more widely known than hers and I had much more presence. In the dream she appeared prettier than me. I think I really was prettier than her, but I couldn't think like that at that time. In my dream, the two of them appeared as a couple—that boy, Joaquin, who was very good-looking and Carolina X. Together they made a very pretty pair. What happened in the dream has to do with my feelings as a teenager. In the dream Carolina X., could seduce all the men that she wanted to, as she used to do when we were teenagers. So my prevailing self-concept was always that the men I liked chose other girls.

Analyst 5: This issue which appears in your dream is one we have analysed together.

Patient 5: What kind of issues did we analyse? You mean, that she had a partner?

I am surprised that she doesn't understand what I am speaking about.

Analyst 6: I am referring to the fact that you had a lot of difficulty in admitting that the man you like and is attractive to you, is exactly the man you would never choose. More than two years ago, I indicated to you that, to my surprise, the condition for your rejecting a man was that you liked him. This was a discovery that surprised us both.

Patient 6: Yes, and this is what I felt when I met Mario in Spain. I saw that when he approached me and began to talk to me with great interest, I kept thinking all the time that his wife was going to turn up. I was afraid of that, and I expected her to appear at any moment and that, when she saw me with him, she would get very angry with me. (Pause.) Yes, I remember very well talking about the fear that a man I like produces in me.

On the trip to Spain, Mario came up to me and began to talk. I thought it would last only for a short while, and then he would go away, but no. He stayed beside me, and he looked at me all the time, and I was always wondering when his wife would appear.

Analyst 7:   I remember that in yesterday's session you told me you couldn't talk about anything and that you were very anxious. You also told me that you had spent a complicated weekend, and that it was hard for you to talk about all that. Therefore, we were not able to discuss anything about what Mario's visit that weekend meant for you. The topic that was left floating in the air between us seems to have come up in the dream you just told me. Your dream expresses everything you couldn't tell me directly. The dream offers to show us much more than you could say.

Patient 7:   Yes, I thought exactly the same a few moments ago. Only good things happened to me with Mario and for that reason I couldn't tell you. (Brief silence.) But I still can't talk about all this.

Analyst 8:   But the point is that you can't speak with me about it now, because to tell me what you have experienced, you would have to put your memories into words, and therefore also your feelings.

Patient 8:   You could be right … I'm not sure if it's like that.

Analyst 9:   Yesterday you wanted to stop our phone session so as not to tell me any of this. When I asked you about your presentation last weekend, you said that everything had been smooth and right. You also told me that Eduardo Pérez had said that when he looked at you, he was disrupted by your beauty, and that all this was very disturbing for you to put into words.

I remind her of what happened yesterday when she tried to cut short our telephone dialogue. I remind her of what she said, using her own words. I usually find that this will yield more information when I link it to transference interpretation, as I now do.

Analyst 9
(continued):   I am wondering therefore who I represent for you that you cannot tell me these things.

Here I address her paranoid fantasy and ask her to think about the transference resistance.

Patient 9:   (Pause.) I suppose that the first thing that occurs to me is that this used to happen to me with my mother and my brother and sister. I don't know. Something else I never told you is that I need to drink a bit of alcohol before having sexual intercourse, just to relax. Generally I have a glass of wine. I notice that I have a strange feeling talking about all this, and in particular to talk to you about Mario. I'm afraid of getting trapped if I tell you this.

Irene is feeling claustrophobic in the relationship with me as her transference to Mario threatens to return to the analytic space. I speak to her about its origin in the analytic relationship.

Analyst 10:   This improved relationship that you now have with men, both in the inner world and in the outside world, is connected with the experience we have been sharing in our analytical work.

Patient 10:   Yes, that improvement is happening, but at the same time I can't allow a man to be too close to me. It makes me anxious.

Thursday, one day later, third telephone session of the week

After saying hello to each other as usual, there was a brief silence.

The session begins with a silence which carried over the silence from the end of the previous session. It does not seem necessary to identify what kind of resistance this is. I am considering the possibility of it being the threat of nameless terror. I choose to pose the transference issue in the form of a guess in which I introduce an element of play in my interpretation of her use of silence as a way of hooking into me.

Analyst 11:   Let's try and guess what is going on in Irene's mind now, as she is busy building up a connection with me via this silence.

Patient 11:   (Laughs.) It's amazing. I am feeling anxious, and I was fully expecting not to have the session today. It occurs to me that this is because of all that we talked about and could continue discussing or all that I didn't say about the experience I shared with Mario. No. But I don't know … what … how …. I don't understand. (Silence for four minutes.)

Patient 11
(continued):   At times I am afraid of believing that Mario is something … I don't know … a nice image … (She speaks in faltering speech as if expressing confusion). (Brief silence.) I'm afraid that he might turn out to be something else, not like that.

I notice many hesitations and uncertainties, and then little by little she regains her ability to make complete sentences.

When I spoke to Mario about the times it was convenient for him to ring me, he replied that there was no problem and to forget about it. His response was a relief and a surprise to me. (Silence.)

Analyst 12:   But what you said to Mario could apply also to me in this very session, at this particular moment. You might feel it is not convenient for us to try to talk.

My interpretation includes her transference fantasies of persecution in the here and now with me. I say this because, even though she is afraid of the transference emerging, I feel that she is open to listening to me and able to understand my remarks.

Patient 12:   But I can't say that I don't really want to have the session. I don't know what is happening. I'm lost for words. (Brief silence.)

Irene wants to work with me but she is terrified of the intimacy.

Analyst 13:   When you try to speak to me about Mario you become anxious. It's an inner feeling based on what he represents for you in your internal world. The mental image of him makes you emotionally closer to him and as a consequence when you speak to me about him, closer to me also.

Patient 13:   Yes, he is gentle and doesn't bother me; he doesn't usually say anything because he is almost as shy as me. (Silence for three minutes.)

I now interrupt the silence with an interpretation, using specific words that refer to all our shared history and many of the memories she has shared with me.

Analyst 14:   Notwithstanding your silence, I am convinced that the "supermarket shelves" of our link are full of what we are talking about and of all that you left unfinished last Tuesday. So, although we interrupted our dialogue, you took them up again yesterday through the virtual contents included in the dream you told me.

Patient 14:   I don't understand.

Irene receives the impact of my comments and connects to me by a lack of understanding that replaces her silence. I am surprised that she does not understand. I immediately offer a construction in which I explain to her all the elements that we can use to continue with our analytic work, again using specific words, this time drawn from the virtual content of her dreams.

Analyst 15:   Your dream yesterday was full of references to your teenage problems that are still relevant today. But regardless of these problems with men, there is a link between us. These problems have been present in a latent state during the entire history of our link. These are the "supermarket shelves" I am referring to. We can use these ingredients to make the dishes that can feed us in today's session. You are having a lot of feelings which you can't put into words. That's why these feelings don't come into our conversation. They are related to profound changes that are happening concerning your internal image of yourself. I have the intuition that these feelings appear in your dreams and when we are together, but they quickly vanish. In these last few weeks we have been talking about your relationship with men who are attractive both in their inner personality and in their outlook, men you used to think were never meant for you. You are recalling your teenage years through the relationship you build in your dream with this character that represents your friend Carolina X.

Working at the preconscious level, I hope to create a semantic bridge to connect the different preconscious sections of the split ego, and pave the way for interpretation of psychotic elements. I give a hypothetical construction to draw her attention towards her own mental contents.

Patient 15:   (Mumbles.)

Analyst 16:   It's incredible how the volume of your voice dropped, so much so that I couldn't hear.

Irene did not realise the dimension of her resistance, functioning in the intimacy of the telephone dialogue interface. I focused on the para-verbal components of her speech—pitch, volume, and timbre—to respond to her attack on linking through cutting off our conversation by speaking so that I could not hear. My comment releases her to share some of what she has been hiding.

Patient 16:   Let's see what happens … if anything happens … (Pause.) I've been intending to tell you something for the last few days that is quite difficult … but I hope we can start now. (Pause.)

The second day I met Mario in Spain, we went out together for dinner. Then we went our separate ways and I thought I would never see him again. Each of us will go our separate ways. Then we met up again later and we went to have a drink. Then we went to bed together. It was then that I felt something I'd never felt before. Later I realised that in fact Mario was having a few initial problems getting an erection and putting on the condom. Then the sex was more relaxed between us and it was perfect. I didn't have to say anything to him, everything was in the right order and the right place at the right time. I was really very surprised at how well everything had gone in that respect. The second time we met up was similar; although that time I was very tense at the beginning. Last week, when Mario came to Mendoza we went to the farm together and we were alone the whole of Saturday and Sunday and it was great, much better than in Spain. But something special happened this time, because I felt a great deal of pleasure in a way I have never felt before. On Sunday we slept together again, and I automatically became moist, and I have never had that happen. The experiences of sexual intercourse with Mario are very long, in fact we seem to go on and on, endlessly, and sometimes I feel bad and want to get out of there.

When she recounts her news about her sexuality Irene is producing a positive new stance in the battle against her resistance. With this statement, she shows me how she is putting herself into a better position for working together. The experience has produced feelings of a mental transformation in her that need her elaboration but without my verbal participation. My analytical function is fulfilled by my capacity for reverie and by my container function. This container function ranges from my simple acceptance to wait for her until the moment that she internally feels ready to share her experiences with me, to my willingness to be the excluded third party (a role that she herself felt she had played all her life within her family). Irene moves from being the person who passively accepts being excluded from the primal scene in her family to that of the person who can be included in her own primal scene. I welcome this shift in her internal world but I understand that for her these psychic changes produce a sensation of confusion.

After she speaks so freely, I ask Irene to help me understand what was stopping her from talking until now. I am trying to place the resistance in a problem of the analytic link which has passed unnoticed by me but not perhaps by Irene.

Analyst 17:   Could you help me to understand why is it that you were not able to talk with me about all this before? There is some sort of blockage with me that I can't quite see.

Patient 17:   No, it's me. I don't talk to myself either, but at times I think about it, and I quickly try to put it out of my mind. I try to set aside the thought, and I try to forget it. (Silence.) I never thought that feeling such good things would be so hard. (Silence of five minutes.)

Analyst 18:   I infer that a lot of feelings and thoughts must be arising in your inner world, and you are acknowledging them.

Patient 18:   Yes, something is happening to me now. I'm feeling like the times I have to give a talk in public. I am waiting for the time to pass and for it all to be over. I want to leave the session. It's a big effort for me to continue talking about all this.

Immediately, Irene takes the place of the third included in the primal scene, according to her Oedipal fantasy. This produces confused anxiety which subsequently becomes secondary claustrophobic anguish. She recognises that we are facing a problem which she thinks has no solution. She is waiting for the session to be over.

In her reluctance to tell me about what was happening, Irene put me in the role of the child excluded from the primal scene. This brought to mind a joke about Jaimito. Jokes with sexual overtones in the Spanish speaking world usually involve a boy called Jaimito. Jaime is my name. In telling the joke, I attempt to take the place of the child who is left out of the sexual action.

Analyst 19:   What you are telling me reminds me of a joke about Jaimito. One night, Jaimito decides to go to sleep under the bed of his parents. He is sleeping and is woken by the noise of his parents' intercourse and suddenly his mother screams, "I'm coming, I'm coming, I'm coming!" At this moment we hear Jaimito, shouting from beneath the bed, "Take me with you! Don't leave me alone!"

Taking advantage of our popular culture in Argentina in which there are many jokes featuring a boy called "Jaimito" that revolve around his curiosity and ignorance of sexual matters, I imagine that telling this joke could free up the verbal circulation of forbidden emotions, which had been repressed (neurotic part) or split (psychotic part).

Patient 19:   But Mario isn't included, because to include him is to accept the demands he places on me, to accept that he loves me, and through this take … possession of me. Then later I will feel that I must only be with him, and not with anybody else.

Analyst 20:   This problem relates more to me than to Mario.

Patient 20:   Why?

Analyst 21:   Because if we work together well, we will be able to separate, there being no need to continue working together. The more our relationship evolves, the more certain you become that we can reach an appropriate separation. This is what happens naturally between parents and children if everything goes well.

Patient 21:   I understand that. If I understand you correctly, then I feel much better about the problem that Mario could represent.

Technical and theoretical considerations

The essential components of my technical model depend on a few ideas:

a. The formulation of the interpretation should bring semantic elements which facilitate the path between the conscious and the preconscious.
b. Thinking fulfils the function of anticipating an action in the outside world (Freud, 1915e).
c. Mental activity may produce "alpha elements" requisite for conscious, preconscious, and unconscious thought, or "beta elements" apt for projected identification but not for thinking (Bion, 1962, 1963).

The contents of my interpretation # 9 are designed to reduce Irene's paranoid anxiety, exaggerated by her fantasies of intrusion and penetration. Her fantasies derive from different aspects of the personality, neurotic and psychotic:

a. Neurotic level: fear of intrusion of developmental origin is based on fantasies of penetration by the father and claustrophobic and agoraphobic fantasies.
b. Psychotic part: fantasies of oral incorporation and desire for defensive symbiotic fusion with the mother.

When Irene again said (Patient 14), "I don't understand", I started my intervention (Analyst 15) at the synchronic level and moved to the diachronic level, by referring to both the history of the analytic link and her personal history. To overcome the obstacle of Irene's resistance, my interpretation follows Freud's model of constructions. Freud (1937d) proposed that a construction opens access to the unconscious contents of the patient, and he established a guideline that still applies today. He held that it is possible that our own knowledge, and as I understand it, our own ability to understand at the particular moment, is not always ready to take on the intimacy of the structure of the patient's unconscious. Therefore, he created the concept of construction that prepares the ground for future interpretations of the patient's unconscious. "No harm is done if, for once in a way, we make a mistake and offer the patient a wrong construction as the probable historical truth" (Freud, 1937d, p. 261).

Bion (1962, 1963, 1977a) developed this perspective further. Any interpretation may be the product of an analytical concept that once formulated immediately moves into a state of preconception. That means that we have to consider any interpretation as one variable of the elements that Bion proposes in his grid. For Bion, not only is the semantic content of an interpretation valid, but also the relationship between all the elements in the link (container-contained, PS ⇔ D).

My construction opens the preconscious contents of Irene's mind. Freud's proposal is aimed at resolving repression. My proposal is designed to resolve the splitting of the ego into different parts. For Freud it was not possible to conceive of psychotic transference. My concept of construction includes that possibility. At the unconscious level of apparently conscious discourse, and at the unconscious level of dreaming, transformation in the psychotic part of the personality occurs. Sleep and dreaming facilitates the process of beta elements turning into alpha elements. Through the nature of our analytic interventions, we can foster or hinder the process of transforming the patient's emotions into words. This is what happens in my intervention (Analyst 15). While it summarises succinctly the contents of her speech, it extends to encourage this transformation.

When Irene had excluded me by her silences (Patient 11, 12, 13) and finally by her wish to leave the session (Patient 18) I chose to use humour to construct my interpretation of her dynamics and her transference (Analyst 19). I am speaking not about the humorous joke as such, but about the use of humour in the Freudian sense (Freud, 1927d), humour to reach the unconscious and engage the ego in a creative cooperation with the superego. Irene responded (Patient 19) by overcoming her resistance and finding her own words to confront her fear that intimacy with Mario will lead to a feeling of entrapment.

The positive effects of humour go beyond softening resistance. In my Jaimito joke, I introduce the transference-countertransference dimension. Humour also acts on one of the most complex defences, namely the split in the ego and the superego (Lutenberg, 2007). Humorous interventions promote a potential alpha transformation of a concealed, unthinkable, traumatic story. Humour fits with Freud's use of construction in psychoanalysis at the individual level, and occupies a place similar to that of myths at the societal level. According to Bion (1962), myths form collective alpha transformations which create a matrix of alpha elements so that the society can express unthinkable thoughts.

Irene's unconscious fantasy of always being the excluded third party gives rise to emotions which are rapidly eliminated from her mind by means of a massive projective identification (thereby producing beta elements that could not be thought and communicated). When this defence is activated, Irene cannot put into words what she feels (Patient 12). I also understand that her position as excluded may derive from her proto-fantasies concerning the primal scene from the oral stage, unmetabolised in the course of her development; and not only arising from later Oedipal stage fantasies.

Summary

I have offered a replay of two telephone sessions as an illustration of my technique based on my elaboration of the psychoanalytic theories of Freud, Bion, and Etchegoyen to show the reader that telephone analysis can sustain an authentic psychoanalytical process, in terms of current traditional psychoanalytical technique.

References

Bion, W. R. (1962). *Learning from Experience*. London: Heinemann. Reprinted London: Karnac, 1984.

Bion, W. R. (1963). *Elements of Psycho-Analysis.* London: Heinemann. Reprinted London: Karnac, 1984.

Bion, W. R. (1977). *Two Papers: The Grid and the Caesura* (originally presented as talks to the Los Angeles Psycho-analytic Society, in 1971 and 1975, respectively). Rio de Janeiro: Imago Ed., 1977.

Bleger, J. (1967). *Simbiosis y Ambigüedad*. Buenos Aires: Ed. Paidós.

Etchegoyen, H. (1986). *Los Fundamentos de la Técnica Psicoanalítica* (pp. 459–753). Buenos Aires: Ed. Amorrortu.

Freud, S. (1915e). The unconscious. *S. E., 14* (pp. 161–204). London: Hogarth.

Freud, S. (1927d). Humour. *S. E., 21* (pp. 159–172). London: Hogarth.

Freud, S. (1937d). Constructions in analysis. *S. E., 23* (pp. 255–269). London: Hogarth.

Lutenberg, J. (2007). *El Vacío Mental*. Lima, Peru: Siklos SRL.

Lutenberg, J. (2010). *Tratamiento Psicoanalítico Telefónico*. Lima Peru: Siklos SRL.

PART III

IMPLICATIONS FOR TRAINING OF
PSYCHOTHERAPISTS AND PSYCHOANALYSTS

The power of the establishment in the face of change: psychoanalysis by telephone

Asbed Aryan, MD and Ricardo Carlino, MD

P sychoanalytic thinking which departs from traditional doctrine sometimes encounters difficulty in being conceptualised and developed within the framework of the institution for psychoanalytic education. We will consider the obstacles that arise with the arrival of psychoanalysis practised by telephone.

Power and the vicissitudes of a new idea

We base our argument on some of Foucault's ideas regarding power (Diaz, 1995). In an institution, the intertwined synergy of power by agreement among the participants operates, devoid of antagonistic rivalry or subjugation, in a way that supports leadership and the orderly exchange of ideas among them, and also allows for the dynamic reconfiguration of their changing and emerging relationships. If this consensus on the quality of power in the institution breaks down, power may be used individually to intimidate, dominate, or commit an act of violence against another participant's point of view. The field of ideas is a territory throughout which thinking constantly moves. From time to time, a new idea emerges to meet changing needs or provide a better explanation than we have currently. New responses are called for when a new complexity is appreciated in the subject under study, or when an error is detected, or a gap in understanding must be filled in. We need to rethink, modify, or elaborate on established ideas in the light of new information and trends. As we look at the impact of telephone analysis on the institution of psychoanalysis, we consider the members as individuals (intra-subjective level) operating with colleagues (inter-subjective level) and as part of a community (trans-subjective level).

The intra-subjective standpoint

When a person is faced with a new idea, he may have a number of reactions. He may be happy to find a rich extension to that which is already established. His mind may be shaken and his comfort in conformity lost. He may anticipate a crisis in acceptance of old axioms and worry about the disruptive effect on the ideology of his institution.

The inter-subjective viewpoint

Colleagues respond individually to new ideas, each in their own way. Some people keep an open mind and are attentive to the changes. Some might want to do so, but they are thrown into conflict because as children they have learned to comply with standards and behaviours that will ensure their inclusion as worthy members of society. Analysts work with the ideological map acquired in the institution in which they were trained. Their institutional belonging is strengthened when it agrees with their way of thinking and destabilises them when it does not. So, for some analysts, the new idea works in such a way that the mere fact of having to consider it may threaten some stratum of their identity. They may reject that which is new in order to avoid the loss of narcissistic harmony.

In short, colleagues may discuss the idea amicably, debate hotly, or argue viciously. The new idea may usefully stimulate scientific exchange or destructively create rivalries that stop development. When colleagues respond with an open mind, put the ideas into play, and test them empirically the idea grows and develops and disrupts the coherence of that which had previously been established and promote a reorganisation and updating of outmoded ideas.

The trans-subjective level

The psychoanalytic institution has the mission of providing essential academic information and professional training in accordance with the prevailing ideology within it, so that its candidates can also become worthy members of the institution. When the prevailing ideology is accepted blindly without testing, is used defensively as a pillar of strength, or is the standard that defines what is "normal" or "abnormal", prejudice and unscientific convictions inhibit the development of ideas (M. & W. Baranger, 1961; Pujet, 2004).

If that which is set and established is put upon a throne and considered to be indisputable, the development of ideas is restricted. That which is new is considered *a priori* as bold, disruptive, or even subversive. We may remember that even Freud's ideas were regarded as subversive at one time. On the other hand, new ideas may be received with an attitude of open-mindedness towards their arrival. We may remember that Freud developed, affirmed, added to, and corrected his own ideas about instinctual duality, the theory of anxiety, sexuality, and the evolution of the ego in relation to reality; he discarded the topographic theory in favour of structural theory, and he made a conceptual shift when he ceased to consider transference as an obstacle and began to value it as his main instrument. He is a model for open-mindedness.

From the trans-subjective point of view, when the established ideas in an institution are the only way to conceive of something within a discipline, they exercise a dictatorial role. They issue orders without listening, given that their only intention is to pontificate and protect that which has already been established. This inhibitory process only works if there is agreement among its participants. Any dogmatic idea is only fertile among its loyal followers. The structural configuration of power puts one person in the role of he who has the knowledge and the other he who it is hoped will take on the role of apprentice. When this institutional power operates on an individual's mind, the dictatorial aspect becomes intimidating. It paralyses creativity and blocks the development of new ideas.

When such a sectarian way of functioning prevails, ideological exchange will find itself in a Procrustean bed where only pre-established ideas can enter. Giving these ideas the status of being unique and legitimate, the institution dismisses other ideas that do not resemble them and do not fit into the existing scheme. The individual or the institution impervious to new ideas remains attached to a kind of knowledge whose only objective is to dominate others. Members then renounce thinking about new ideas out of fear of being treated as outcasts, just like the bearers of those ideas were treated for inventing them. The ambience of the institution is infused with the threat of exclusion or even of banishment. The institution may then attempt to drown out the new idea, keep silent about it, and dissociate from it, while continuing to insist on tradition. The institution may excommunicate dissidents; the dissidents may banish themselves voluntarily to preserve their ideas; or the dissidents may identify with the institution's attitude of certainty and consider themselves to be the bearers of messianic ideas.

When a new idea produces unease within the institution, we can imagine a prevailing ideal of conceptual uniformity that promotes an attitude of self-repression that wastes libidinal energy and hinders any possibility of thinking differently. The established ideology is wielded as a weapon to defeat rival ideas out of fear of the narcissistic loss of an organisation with which to identify. A defensive entrenchment of the "already established" prevents contact and consideration of the "new" and exercises power over the "other", due to fear that the "new idea" will somehow transform that which was immutable into something disposable.

When the new idea calls for a shift in technique, more unease develops. It is a fallacy to think that standard clinical technique is essential, when in fact it is merely a formality. Not all patients can fit the standard form of implementation of psychoanalytic theory. Eissler (1953) created the concept of *technical parameter* to accommodate patients who had no chance of complying with all the formal requirements of clinical implementation, but who with this modification could benefit from psychoanalysis. Psychoanalytic theory and technique have to be subject to evolution.

Destiny of the assessment of psychoanalysis by telephone

New ideas cannot demonstrate their true potential if they are asphyxiated by the institution. However, when there is tolerance and the promotion of debate, as opposed to a duel, the exchange with the "new" promises a fertile evolution and transformation of both new and already-established ideas. Between the moment of the announcement of a new idea and its desired institutional legitimacy, there is always a lapse of time in which conflict between the "established" and the "new" can occur. This is where our field is in relation to the arrival of psychoanalysis conducted by telephone.

The impact of psychoanalysis by telephone

In *Insight*, the news magazine of the International Psychoanalytical Association (IPA, 2003) various authors addressed the topic of analysis by telephone as a new idea and a new way of practice. Analysts in support based their agreement on the experience of having personally practised it. Other analysts who had not practised telephone analysis were nevertheless open to considering it. Analysts against made their arguments on principle, not based on their own clinical experience. At the Chicago Congress of 2009, urgent consideration was given by the Board of Representatives to analytic training conducted by telephone for countries or regions where there is no other possibility. The arguments in opposition to the proposal focused not on what the method provides but on what it does not do. Any conclusion about analysis conducted on the telephone, if based in prejudice not reason, does not justify dismissing teleanalysis as inadequate.

Responses to positions which are critical of or in opposition to telephone analysis

Nowadays, analysis by telephone is ceasing to be such a new idea and practice, but it is still controversial. We will present our conceptual stance against criticism of telephone analysis as psychoanalytic treatment. We will focus on some concepts expressed by three analysts, Brainsky (2003), and Argentieri and Amati Mehler (2003) almost a decade ago. It would be appropriate to ask whether they continue to stand by the statements made then. However, for the conceptual purposes of this chapter, it is advantageous that their remarks were written at the early stages of telephone use in psychoanalysis. There we can take stock of the first reactions to telephone analysis, which, at that time, was considered a new idea. Brainsky considers any new idea from the perspective that psychoanalysis as implemented in the analyst's office should be considered as the most genuine of psychoanalytic "being". However, we can not conceive of it as something that is immutable, but rather as something in a state of permanent "becoming". Has that not been happening in psychoanalysis from its very beginning?

Klein's (1928) dating of the early Oedipus complex and Heimann's (1950) and Racker's (1948) elaboration of countertransference were not intended to destroy previous concepts but rather to enrich that which was already established. The analysis of children, adolescents, groups, families, relational psychoanalysis, self psychology, and object relations were once radical ideas that have all contributed to psychoanalysis. For this to continue to be so, it is necessary to maintain a permanently open and reflective attitude within the institutions of the International Psychoanalytical Association (IPA). Although all that is new should not be accepted simply because it is new, neither should it be rejected for being new. New discoveries from telephone analysis need not detract from that which is already known, but rather expand its horizons. When analysts work with a psychoanalytic instrument that does not accommodate socio-cultural transformations, they restrict the range of people and problems they can work with. On the other hand, one can observe in many conferences that take place in three regions of the IPA the repeated interest in the impact that socio-cultural changes are having on the practice of analysis, and concern about the reception of psychoanalysis by patients and the general population.

Psychoanalysis is and has always been in a constant state of change. Freud makes reference to this when he defines psychoanalysis as an empirical science: "Psycho-analysis is not, like philosophies, a system starting out from a few sharply defined basic concepts, seeking to grasp the whole universe with the help of these and, once it is completed, having *no room for fresh discoveries or better understanding*" (1923a, p. 253, our italics). Brainsky rests his case on the premise that psychoanalysis is complete and consolidated and should not be altered. Any addition or innovation should be reviewed very carefully and accepted only as a sort of *ad hoc* aid that should disappear as soon as possible, so that the structure of psychoanalysis will stay the same as it was when passed on to us. Guarding the purity of established psychoanalysis, Argentieri and Amati Mehler state that "Not everything a psychoanalyst does is analysis merely because he or she is a psychoanalyst … One of the difficult achievements in our profession is that of being and remaining analysts while still knowing when and why we are doing something other than an analysis" (2003, p. 18). A psychoanalytic treatment should be considered genuine if it allows the analytic process to be established.

One of the main obstacles that Argentieri and Amati Mehler have found in telephone analysis is the lack of visual access to the patient's body. They partly base this on Rizutto's observation that many experiences from early times are "hard to articulate in words" and that "the human voice produces total body responses" (2002, p. 1338). These early experiences may reappear in telephone communication within the session, not only through the semantic content of the words themselves, but also in their rhythm, cadence, intonation, pauses, silences, lapses, associations, and degree of relevance or deviation from understanding. All these responses give information about the patient's libidinal body.

In disagreement with the telephone method, Argentieri and Amati Mehler emphasise that acceding to patients who, due to a new situation that obliges them to move far away from the analyst's office, ask to continue their analysis by telephone, impedes the analysis of the anguish of the current separation and the reliving of old separations. Furthermore, it also avoids the termination of that particular analysis. They think that an analyst's clinical work on the telephone can be no more than supportive psychotherapy or cognitive behaviour therapy, not psychoanalysis, as if psychoanalysis can only be done in the office of the analyst.

Over the past two decades, technological advances, especially in the field of communication, have permeated everyday life and shaken some of the bases of our logic. These movements, which at times have seemed seismic, have at times disrupted the calm and comfort of our established *modus vivendi*. On the other hand, change is part of the evolution of our civilisation. At this point in our experience we believe that a forced prescription of classical analysis, when it is not the most appropriate, is tantamount to committing iatrogenic suicide. There is a difference between being unwilling or unable to modify the classic setting and declaring it wrong or impossible.

It is common to see the weight of the power of the establishment decoupling the new from the established, thereby blocking development. Brainsky (2003) states: "While the psychoanalytic interchange is predominantly verbal, it is seen as a gestalt between the patient and the analyst that, as far as possible, includes the apprehension of wholes. It involves all kinds of pre-verbal attitudes, such as momentary visualisations, coughs, smells, tactile sensations, facial expressions, visceral projective identifications and counter-identifications, eidetic fantasies, and so on. Telephone analysis entails a whole relationship with the part object represented by the analyst's voice, and is more liable than conventional analysis to result in an idealised and persecutory condensation of the tone, timbre, and expression of the spoken word" (p. 23).

We object to Brainsky's assertion that in telephone analysis there is a part object relationship: "... the voice of the analyst, as if telephone analysis takes place on a pre-genital level" (p. 23). What counts is not only the voice of the patient, but also what the patient says and how she says it and how the analyst listens. The analyst makes a semiological decoding of the multiple messages coming from the voice. He listens with free-floating attention, analyses his own process, formulates an interpretation, and listens to how it is received. This complex communication and personal interaction puts the libidinal body of one partner of the analysis in contact with that of the other, just as would be the case of a session taken in the analyst's office.

The analytic process is something that occurs in the minds of its protagonists and in the dialogue taking place throughout the sessions. In order for this to occur, the analyst must be open to accepting a way of thinking that is somewhat different from that which is already established. Refuting any possibility that telephone dialogue could be considered to be psychoanalytic, Argentieri and Amati Mehler stated: "It is difficult to accept the argument that psychoanalysis, or we psychoanalysts, have to chase after the changing times and society. Our task is to understand and interpret change" (p. 19). On the contrary, we believe that the concept of society encompasses and includes psychoanalysis (Carlino, 2011). Although the analyst must maintain an attitude of technical neutrality, she is not extraterrestrial and cannot be aloof from the transforming phenomena of society as defined by the prevailing values and paradigms in which she operates. The mutations taking place in social habits will influence their psychoanalytic understanding. This is not intended to be a truth in itself but rather an understanding of individuals in their environment, influenced by their personal history and the transferential bond with their analyst. Our idea of psychoanalysis is characterised by the development of a unique link between analyst and patient shaped by their own personal histories in a social and anthropological environment, as well as that provided in the "here and now" of transference and countertransference. We do not take a position on symmetry of roles or unconditional acceptance. Encouraged by the confidence that comes from knowing that we are operating according to our principles and with an attitude of enriching freedom and not of submission to static rules, we can take advantage of technological advances in communication to enhance our practice of psychoanalysis.

We must continue insisting that every act of judgment by an opponent of teleanalysis be based on premises that provide a rationale and an orientation to their base logic. Brainsky ends his presentation with an accurate definition of his own point of view: "... even small changes in the ways in which we communicate with each other may have profound meaning. This is of course very true, but once again we must pause for thought. We are conservative, as it were by definition. That is the thesis. The antithesis is the enthusiastic espousal of everything new simply because it is new" (p. 23). With an implicit logic like that, it is impossible to accept new ideas.

Various positions on teleanalysis are expressed by the Board of Representatives of the IPA. One reaction to teleanalysis in training is unease, seen especially among training analysts in European societies who perform shuttle or condensed analysis. A second position is serenely in favour. The third position places emphasis on maintaining the role of the IPA as opposed to seriously addressing the concerns of a new problem.

In discussion of long distance analysis or remote analysis, a proposal was made to keep shuttle and condensed analysis out of the deliberations with the rationale that we should not be "discussing methodologies that are already accepted" (IPA, 2010). Naming it as "accepted" does not allow review of the value of shuttle analysis and condensed analysis and their comparison to telephone analysis. If telepsychoanalysis were found to achieve the same clinical goals as condensed or shuttle analysis, the practice of shuttle or condensed analysis would be called into question. The appearance of telepsychoanalysis as a new option and its increasingly widespread incidence make it necessary for us to discuss this topic within our institutions and foster and support research so that the results of telepsychoanalysis can be evaluated.

Admittedly the telephone has been in use for many years and psychoanalysis has not needed to make use of it, but that is not an argument to forgo its use now. What is seen today as logical and required was not necessarily a matter of concern in the past. A new proposal like telepsychoanalysis arises in reaction to a limitation in existing methods and in response to demand. For instance, since the fall of the Berlin Wall, the countries of Eastern Europe came into contact with the West and appeared on the horizon of the IPA. The need for psychoanalysis of a group of applicants who resided far from centres where psychoanalytic treatment was available could be met with shuttle or condensed analysis which until then had only been used for exceptional individual situations. Another element of condensed or shuttle analysis is that it affords the ability to be analysed in one's native language which provides for in-depth dialogue. The IPA now comes out to Eastern bloc countries to provide resources for analytic training. These resources should be made more accessible to patients as well as potential candidates.

Science advances because it considers a paradigm as a model for thinking until such time that another becomes more comprehensive, explaining more phenomena and experiences. The ethics of science do not permit us to say: "Do not discuss already accepted methods." Sigmund Freud, Albert Einstein, Umberto Eco and many others have said in different ways and in different scientific contexts that instruments are only useful until such time that they cease to be so. It is dangerous to the health and the future of psychoanalysis to propose that one should never rethink anything simply because it has already been thought. For centuries the Vatican held that the Earth was flat. As a result of this, Giordano Bruno was lost and Galileo Galilei was only narrowly spared by appearing to agree with the ruling establishment in time.

Some analysts object that the term *remote analysis* is improper and confusing. We answer that this is because we have not given ourselves the opportunity to discuss this matter metapsychologically with the seriousness it requires. In the IPA report, the descriptor of analysis by telephone calls or via Skype is used disparagingly. This implies a total ignorance due to bias (Puget, 2006) and lack of knowledge about the seriousness with which the analysts conducting telepsychoanalysis contemplate their work. Should one suppose that the beneficial analytic effect depends on the sofa or the computer and not on the analyst's mind operating with the Freudian legacy?

The IPA maintains that psychoanalysis is based on the meeting by two persons in the same room following the rules of the analytic frame about frequency, timing, and duration of sessions and treatment. We argue that psychoanalysis is based primarily on psychoanalytic thinking and the search for unconscious causality in the transference, not on the formal aspects of the frame. We need to work with the meta-psychological differences between classic analysis and telephone analysis, and do the same for remote analysis, shuttle analysis, and condensed analysis. The only difference between shuttle and condensed analysis and telepsychoanalysis is the concrete presence of two people in a room instead of two people present in cybernetic communication. The rest remains unchanged.

Now that new paradigms have diversified our means of communication, it is high time that we ask ourselves whether a means of communication is really more important than what is communicated through it. Thus far, it has not been necessary to think about this, given that, although the telephone existed, its use in analytic sessions was not deemed necessary. Saul introduced the idea that psychoanalysis could be carried out by telephone as early as 1951. He predicted that it would be met with much resistance and opposition based in prejudice. In 1964, Lindon began to offer treatment via the telephone and had already accumulated twenty-four years of experience by the time he wrote his paper in 1988. Now there are many more voices and other technological realities that are screaming that it is possible to conduct analysis in a more effective and accessible way.

Conclusion

We think that there might be some relationship between resistance to teleanalysis and the lack of candidates and patients for analysis (IPA, 2012). We wonder why young people today do not have the same enthusiasm for studying psychoanalysis, unlike their precursors decades ago. Additionally, we ask ourselves why psychoanalysis as transmitted by the IPA is failing to capture the interest of the younger generation? How can those doctors and psychologists who live far away from an IPA institution hope to develop as analysts when they are offered training seminars and training analysis only within the area of an analyst's office and in a language that is not their own? If young professionals live far from urban centres and/or require much travel time in order to arrive, will they still want to undergo their training in IPA institutions? If new ideas are not considered by our institution, interest in psychoanalysis will wane. We must engage in debate and act urgently on to consider the practicality and clinical effectiveness of telepsychoanalysis.

References

Anderson, G. (2009). Telephone analysis. Panel at 46th IPA Congress. Chicago, July 29–August 1.

Argentieri, S. & Amati Mehler, J. (2003). Telephone "analysis": Hello, who's speaking? *Insight*, 12(1): 17–19. Available: www.ipa.org.uk/Files/media/PrevSite/Docs/NewsMagazines/IPA_ENG_12.1.pdf.

Aryan, A. (2003). ¿Cambios o transformaciones? Reconsideración del encuadre y de la transferencia-contratransferencia a la luz de las modificaciones tecnológicas. Panel sobre Análisis por teléfono, APdeBA, abril 2009. Panel sobre Comunicación y Nuevas tecnologías. VI APU Congreso Internacional y Multidisciplinario. Montevideo, Uruguay, 2010. Originalmente escrito para el 43° IPA Congress. Toronto, Canada, Julio 2003, suspendido.

(Change or transformation? Reconsidering the frame and the transference-countertransference in the light of technical modifications. Panel on telephone analysis. Buenos Aires Psychoanalytic

Association, April 2009. Panel on new communication technology, 6th international Multidisciplinary Congress of the Uruguayan Psychoanalytic Association. Originally written for the 43rd Congress of the International Psychoanalytical Association, July 2003 (which was cancelled)).

Aryan, A. & Carlino, R. (2009). Análisis por teléfono. (Telephone analysis.) Panel at 46th IPA Congress. Chicago, August 1.

Aryan, A. & Carlino, R. (2010). Desafíos del y al psicoanálisis contemporáneo. Vicisitudes de lo establecido frente a lo nuevo que va surgiendo. El psicoanálisis telefónico. (Challenges to and by contemporary psychoanalysis. Vicissitudes of emerging new ideas. Telephone analysis.) Paper at VI APU Congreso Internacional y Multidisciplinario (the 6th international Multidisciplinary Congress of the Uruguayan Psychoanalytic Association), Montevideo, Uruguay, August 20.

Baranger, M. & Baranger, W. (1961). La situación analítica como campo dinámico. *Revista Uruguaya de Psicoanálisis*, 4(1): 3–54.

Berenstein, S. P. de & Grinfeld, P. (2009). Análisis por teléfono, análisis por Skype. (Telephone and Skype analysis.) Panel at 46th IPA Congress. Chicago, August 1.

Brainsky, S. (2003). Adapting to, or idealizing technology? *Insight*, 12(1): 22–24. www.ipa.org.uk/Files/media/PrevSite/Docs/NewsMagazines/IPA_ENG_12.1.pdf, last accessed May 2009.

Carlino, R. (2006). ¿Psicoanálisis por teléfono? (Telephone analysis?) Paper at XXVI FEPAL Congress (the 26th Congress of the Latin-American Psychoanalytic Federation), Lima, Peru, October 3.

Carlino, R. (2008). Radiografía del psicoanálisis telefónico. (X-raying telephone analysis.) Paper at XXVII FEPAL Congress. Santiago, Chile, September.

Carlino, R. (2010). *Psicoanálisis a Distancia*. Buenos Aires: Editorial Lumen.

Carlino, R. (2011). *Distance Psychoanalysis*. London: Karnac.

Díaz, E. (1995). *La Filosofía de Michel Foucault* (2ª edición). Buenos Aires: Editorial Biblos, 2003.

Eissler, K. R. (1953). The effect of the structure of the ego on psychoanalytic technique. *Journal of the American Psychoanalytic Association*, 1: 104–143.

Freud, S. (1923a). Two encyclopaedia articles. Psychoanalysis and libido theory. *S. E.*, 18 (p. 235). London: Hogarth.

IPA (2003). En Esapgnol, En Profundidad. Suplemento de "Newsletter" Publicación de la Asoci-ación Psicoanalítica Internacional: "ANÁLISIS POR TELÉFONO": Siete Psicoanalistas expresan su opinión". *Insight*, 12, June.

IPA (2009). Panel (LDG) on Telephone Analysis. Chair: Hanly, C. (Canada); panelists: Anderson, G., Scharff, D., Savege Scharff, J. (EEUU); Symington, N. (UK/Australia); Aryan, A., Berenstein, S. P. de, Carlino, R., Grinfeld, P. & Lutenberg, J. (Argentina). Congress of the International Psychoana-lytical Association. Chicago, August 1.

IPA (2010). Report of Board of Representatives.

IPA (2012). Report of Board of Representatives *Bulletin*. February, 2012.

Klein, M. (1928). Early stages of the Oedipus complex. In: *Love, Guilt and Reparation and Other Works: 1921–1945* (pp. 186–198). London: Hogarth, 1975.

Kohut, H. (1977). *The Restoration of the Self*. New York: International Universities Press, 1979.

Lutenberg, J. (2009). Diálogo psicoanalítico telefónico. (Telephone analysis dialogue.) Paper at 46th IPA Congress. Chicago, August 1.

Lutenberg, J. (2010). *Tratamiento Psicoanalítico Telefónico*. Lima, Peru: Editorial Siklos.

Mantykow de Sola, B. (2007). En torno a la situación analítica y su construcción en la "situación" actual. *Psicoanálisis*, 29(2): 313–340.

Migone, P. (2003). La psicoterapia con Internet. *Psicoterapia e Scienza Umane, 37*(4): 57–73. http://www.psychomedia.it/pm/modther/probpsiter/pst-rete.htm.

Puget, J. (2006). Los prejuicios como instrumento discriminatorio. (Prejudice as an instrument of discrimination.) Paper read at the 5th Congress of Mental Health and Human Rights at the University of the Madres, Plaza de Mayo, Buenos Aires, November, 2006.

Rizzuto, A. M. (2002). Speech events, language development, and the clinical situation, *International Journal of Psycho-Analysis 83*: 1325–1343. (Referenced by Argentieri, S. & Amati Mehler, J.)

Zalusky, S. (1998). Telephone analysis: Out of sight, but not out of mind. *American Journal of Psychoanalysis, 46*(4): 1221–1242.

Zalusky, S. (2003). Dialogue: Telephone analysis. *Insight Newsletter IPA 12*(1): 13–16.

CHAPTER SIXTEEN

The frame for psychoanalysis in cyberspace

Debra A. Neumann, PhD

The internet is playing an ever increasing role in society, and not surprisingly in psychoanalytic practice as well. Yet it remains a controversial endeavour. In this chapter, I examine some issues that emerge for patient and analyst when using internet videoconferencing for treatment. My main focus is on establishing and maintaining a psychoanalytic frame within which an analytic process can develop. Then I examine some objections to psychoanalysis in cyberspace, pose questions raised for current psychoanalytic understandings of time and space, and suggest areas for future exploration.

In spite of practical, theoretical, and political disputes regarding its merit, teleanalysis on the internet is currently emerging as a prominent feature of contemporary analytic practice. In fact, Gabbard (2001) has drawn a parallel between the frontier of the American West and the position of cyberspace in analytic practice. But the frontier reaches beyond the United States. The China American Psychoanalytic Alliance (CAPA), a non-profit organisation incorporated in 2006 to develop and promote mental health services in China by training Chinese mental health professionals in psychoanalytically oriented psychotherapy, uses the internet extensively for instruction and supervision. CAPA strongly encourages its students in China (all of whom are mental health professionals) to undergo psychoanalytically oriented psychotherapy or psychoanalysis during their training by means of computer to computer video technology using the commercial service Skype. The rationale for this unorthodox practice of psychoanalysis is that, while many Chinese mental health providers are interested in learning about psychoanalytic theory and treatment, there are very few analysts in China who can provide them with training or treatment.

The notion of using computers to conduct psychotherapeutic treatment is not new (Neumann, 1985). In one unsuccessful early attempt, a computer program called Eliza provided Rogerian responses when a client typed in a statement concerning a problem the client was having. Although the intention of making psychotherapy more accessible to the American public by means of computer applications was laudable, its actualisation left much to be desired. However, the immense changes in computer technology since the 1980s and the development of the internet has offered new possibilities for applying internet videoconferencing technology to educational and therapeutic endeavours.

When, as a second year candidate in psychoanalytic training who was eager to gain experience practising psychoanalysis, I learned that there was a waiting list of Chinese students requesting internet psychoanalytic treatment, I volunteered to treat a patient. In consultation with a supervisor, in August, 2008 I began seeing a Chinese patient three times a week using Skype internet computer to computer video technology. After one year, this treatment increased in frequency and depth and now entails a five times weekly analysis using the couch. My journey has enlightened me as to the possibilities and also some of the difficulties posed by this type of psychoanalytic treatment. Of the many things I have learned, I refer particularly to the need for a secure psychoanalytic frame in cyberspace. I have chosen to focus on the design and maintenance of the psychoanalytic frame because that is fundamental to establishing and sustaining an analytic process.

Prerequisites to beginning internet treatment

Several essential prerequisites must be met before undertaking internet psychoanalysis. First, each member of the dyad, patient and analyst, must have at their disposal sufficiently powerful technology to support this type of treatment. The memory available on one's hard drive must be sufficient (at least 2GB) and one's broadband connection must be as fast as possible (a fibre-optic or high speed DSL connection is required). If memory and connection speed is not adequate on either side of the connection, the video feedback is apt to degenerate into pixels, the audio to become indecipherable, and the likelihood of dropped calls is high. When the call quality is poor, the too frequent queries by analyst or patient, "Could you please repeat that?", "Can you see me?", "Can you hear me?", are highly disruptive to both patient and analyst. The quality of internet connection directly correlates with the therapist's sense that a significant analytic process can develop in treatment conducted by Skype.

Second, when treatment is provided in a language that is non-native for at least one of the participants, both analyst and patient must have adequate fluency in the language in which the analysis is conducted. When fluency is absent, much time is spent searching for words either in one's mind or in a dictionary. This can result in a choppiness to the flow of sessions which hinders the development of an adequate interior space for unconscious processing. On the other hand, a colleague found that her patient's lack of fluency in English served to slow the process down in a way she found helpful, as it focused both her and her patient on clarifying what is intended, rather than proceeding on the assumption that what is intended is known and shared (McGaffin, 2011, personal communication).

Third the treatment must meet ethical standards. The criteria for effective and ethical treatment have been articulated by the IPA (March, 2007). The analyst must be capable of fostering and sustaining an analytic process over time. An analytic process is defined as one in which unconscious activity, mechanisms and motivations including the transference, countertransference, unconscious affects, and latent unconscious themes can be recognised and followed and formulations can be made to guide interventions. Progress and impasses and developmental aspects can be monitored. The analyst must follow ethical principles related to the practice of psychoanalysis, and conduct the analysis in accordance with the regulations of the professional discipline in which the analyst is licensed and with the laws related to the particular locale of both analyst and patient. Ways of meeting the requirement to provide ethical treatment vary by profession and by location (see Chapter Six and the resource appendix). Those who are interested in treating a patient in China may find it helpful to consult the Ethics and Confidentiality Statement and Handbook prepared for CAPA members (Buckner, 2011). Others may care to join online list-serve forums or in-person discussion groups at meetings of the American and International Psychoanalytic(al) Associations.

In addition to meeting the mandates of the professional associations of the analyst, the licensing laws regarding internet practice of the jurisdictions in which both patient and analyst live, and provisions for patient confidentiality, the analyst must meet mandated reporting requirements, provide local backup and emergency coverage, and reduce the potential for harm. Among the issues to be considered is Sabin's (2010) view that psychoanalysis itself is subversive and that providing it to individuals living in countries governed by totalitarian political regimes may bring increased and unwarranted risk to the patients.

Safeguarding patient confidentiality is a paramount ethical consideration. Much work has been done to ensure that Skype computer to computer video connection protects the confidentiality of patients. Many who raise concerns about technical security fail to consider that there are three types of Skype—Skype phone, Skype Voice over Internet Protocol (VoIP), and Skype computer to computer connections. Of these, only Skype computer to computer is secure (Snyder, 2011a).

The psychoanalytic frame—past to present

Many factors are involved in the creation of an external and internal treatment setting in which psychoanalytic data can emerge, be detected, and responded to. There are multiple conceptualisations of what constitutes an appropriate analytic frame. In general, the various viewpoints are tied to corresponding theoretical orientations. To begin, I will provide a brief historical overview of psychoanalytic thought related to the concept of frame.

Freud (1913c) in "On Beginning the Treatment" made recommendations about the opening phase of treatment and the need to establish rules for its conduct, using chess as an analogy. Freud's recommendations included arrangements about time and money, for example, his practice of leasing frequent and regular hours (six appointments per week) to his patients and expecting payment for these hours whether or not the patient attended, the need to establish a fair fee schedule, the use of the couch, the use of free association, and following the lead of the patient as to content.

Over the course of time, these recommendations solidified into the traditional or classical conception of "the frame", which comprises fixed conditions that purport to create a therapeutic structure with clear boundaries. In discussing the somewhat arbitrary nature of many elements of the classical frame, Wallerstein (2009) describes several ways that the frame has changed in response to sociocultural factors. For example, Freud's original recommended frequency of six visits per week was appropriate to the culture of nineteenth century Vienna, where the typical work week was six days. When psychoanalysis was imported to England and the US, the recommended frequency was reduced to five days to adapt to the five-day work week of these cultures. After World War II, there was a huge demand for training analyses by returning wartime psychiatrists in the United States. Training analysts had insufficient hours available to meet this demand, but by reducing the frequency for analytic treatment from five to four sessions weekly, the demand could be met. Currently, in many countries, frequency requirements for analytic treatment have been reduced further to three sessions per week.

In the classical model of treatment, the analyst outlines the nature of the psychoanalytic frame in the first session or sessions by providing the patient with a series of clearly articulated policies or rules. Typical elements of the classical frame include regularly scheduled appointments of a fixed length (the forty-five to fifty minute "hour") and frequent sessions that are held at a permanent place. The patient is to lie on a couch with the analyst sitting behind the patient. Sessions are to be paid for on a regular basis, communication is limited to the verbal level, the patient's role is to say whatever comes to mind, and the analyst's role is to listen, formulate and interpret the resistance and transference. It is the analyst's responsibility to maintain the frame and hold it as constant as possible. The analyst's role is to set the frame, the patient's role is to adapt to it.

The rationale offered for holding firmly to these types of rules is that they provide a clear and constant structure within which patients can become absorbed in their internal reality and the analytic process can emerge. For example, Bleger (1967) demarcates two components of psychoanalytic treatment: the first is the process, which is studied, analysed, and interpreted and the second is the frame, by which Bleger refers to "everything else", namely the constants within which the process takes place. From a classical viewpoint, the frame is usually in the background and must be kept stable so that the analytic process can be studied and the transference-countertransference and resistance can emerge fully and in clear relief. Prospective analysands must be able to tolerate the conditions of the classical frame.

Winnicott suggested a modification to this notion of the frame. At the 19th International Congress of Psychoanalysis in Geneva in 1955, he spoke of the analyst's need to adapt the frame to the developmental needs of the patient. Winnicott (1955) referred to the frame as the psychoanalytic setting, and included in it all aspects of the management of the treatment carried out by the analyst. He pointed out that with patients who have deficits in ego development, as well as with regressed patients, management of the setting moves to the foreground, and it becomes a more important element in the treatment than interpretation of the transference.

While Winnicott's views differ significantly from the classical position, they share with it the common feature that the frame is set and maintained by the analyst. For the classical analyst, a patient must adapt to the analyst's frame, and if this cannot be done, the patient is deemed unsuitable for treatment. For Winnicott, the analyst sets the frame, based on empathic attunement with the ego needs of the patient. Presumably, if the analyst is not able to adapt the frame to the patient's needs, the analyst is unsuitable to treat the patient. In both cases, the frame is viewed as a consistent, invariable structure, established and maintained by the analyst, which supports the treatment.

More recently, analysts from the intersubjective/relational school have challenged traditional attitudes about the nature of the frame. Bass (2007) views the frame as co-created by analyst and patient in an endeavour to establish the conditions which will make the therapy process tolerable or even possible for the patient. The frame contains elements brought both by the analyst and by the patient and reflects aspects of both of their lives and their relationship. The frame is not viewed as a series of relatively inflexible rules, but rather as a set of preferences unique to each patient-analyst pair and subject to revision throughout the course of treatment with each patient. The frame changes over time as the patient, analyst, and their relationship changes. The frame is thus viewed as an evolving system of shifting arrangements. Bromberg (2007) adds a self-state perspective to this understanding of the frame. In his view, various and differing frames are employed in every treatment in accord with varying self-states of both patient and analyst.

The relational, as well as the classical and developmental views, seem united in agreement that the frame (or frames) functions to guarantee that patient and analyst can enter the intense inner dimension of a psychoanalytic treatment. The establishment of the external frame serves the internal psychic function of demarcating a realm of experience that differs from consensually validated "normal" external reality. This protected inner realm of psychic reality is timeless and non-local. It is a potential space for analytic work—a space in which the patient can regress as needed and in which unconscious dynamics can emerge.

Various features of this internal aspect of the frame have been highlighted. For some, such as Bleger (1967), a stable external frame facilitates the development of a symbiosis, representing an early state of merger with a mothering parent figure. Within a stable frame, the patient will be able to regress and bring into the treatment the most primitive, most non-differentiated aspects of the self. The frame thus delineates a potential magical realm, where the omnipotent, infantile self of the patient can emerge. To use the felicitous phrase of a patient of Francis Tustin (1986), the external frame provides an internal "rhythm of safety" for both analyst and analysand. The establishment of this type of frame allows the patient to feel secure and is a precondition for the development of dependence on a good object via internalisation of the functions of the analyst. The patient feels safe and can use the analyst as needed.

Modell (1988) amplified Bleger's ideas. He identified a type of transference engendered by the frame itself and differentiated it from that of the classical "transference neurosis". Modell calls the transference derived from the reliable, relatively constant psychoanalytic setting the "dependent/containing transference". He believes that this type of transference is continually present, that it symbolically provides the grounding for work with early deficits in the patient (e.g., those related to early deprivation), and that its presence enhances and strengthens mutative interpretations regarding the transference neurosis.

Arlow and Brenner (1990) provide a different view of the internal function of the external frame. They point out that the frame does not necessarily serve a symbiotic function, but rather anchors the treatment in the adult world of contractual relationships, as for example, through payment of the fee and holding to a regular appointment schedule.

Chausseguet-Smirgel (1992) highlights both aspects of the internal function of the frame. She describes the situation evoked by the frame as an archaic matrix of the Oedipus complex. While, on the one hand, the frame guarantees the establishment of an enclave in which the patient is able to abandon himself to narcissistic regression, on the other hand, the frame presents the patient with a reality oriented "paternal function", opposing the wish to return to prenatal existence.

The psychoanalytic frame—present to future

This overview of the literature on the frame indicates that irrespective of theoretical differences, there is widespread agreement that the establishment of a frame is necessary in order for an analytic, therapeutic process to occur. The question posed in this chapter is whether this type of frame can be provided when using internet technology to conduct analysis or analytic therapy.

Some state that this is not possible. For example, Curtis (2007) characterises internet treatment as conducted in an autistic space—a space which she views as limited to two-dimensional information and "artificial intelligence". Curtis refers to Bion's concept of an analytic setting and process as one in which a patient learns from experience "within the context of two minds in the same time and space emotionally containing each other". In her view, when using the internet, two minds are not in the same time and space, emotional containment cannot occur, and it is not possible to detect and manage the analytic process.

Clearly, according to the temporal and spatial limits of consensual, external reality, in the world of internet treatment at a distance, analyst and patient are not meeting "in the same time and space". Due to "daylight saving time", the time difference between Beijing and my office is twelve hours from March through October and thirteen hours for the remainder of the year. The United States has four time zones, but China, an even vaster mainland, has only one time zone. It is 9 am my time here in the USA and 9 or 10 pm when my patient and I meet in Beijing. But a therapist on the West coast would have to start at 6 am to make that appointment time with a patient in China. The impact of the time difference is accentuated (depending on the American therapist's location and the time of the appointment in China) when the therapist is in session in the evening while the patient is in the morning of the next day. However, extending traditional notions about what constitutes time and space to the realm of psychic reality—the world of the unconscious mind—we can say that patients and their analysts interact in a setting outside the limits of physical space and linear time, no matter where they are located geographically or in what time zone they reside. From this perspective, during the analytic hour patient and analyst are in the same time and space, and that time and space may or may not coincide with the physical location of either party.

At the boundaries of the session, this is clearly not the case. For example, it is jarring to me when at the end of a session, at nearly 10 pm in China, my patient closes the hour saying "Goodnight" or when in an unthinking morning moment I greet her with "Good morning" at the start. In these situations, we are compelled to acknowledge the obvious distance between us represented by the difference in time, which during our emergence in the unconscious realm of the analytic hour has disappeared. This and other features of my experience using the internet for psychoanalytic treatment is echoed in the experience of colleagues who have used Skype in treating patients in China (Rosen, 2010).

Sand (2007) has stated that conducting psychoanalysis in cyberspace requires the development of a "consensual hallucination". This is the nature of the unconscious realm, where analyst and patient, whether in the same geographic location or separated by thousands of miles, are in the same time and space. The objection that internet analysis, by virtue of the technology used, can only occur in autistic space is countered by various authors who have pointed out that virtual reality itself possesses qualities that are similar to the potential space of the therapeutic relationship (Fischbein, 2010; Lingiardi, 2008; Malater, 2007). Cyberspace is described as functioning as a transitional space and is easily adaptable as a play space for identity exploration and development that is free from social sanctions.

A second objection (Curtis, 2007) raised to using the internet for treatment is that sufficient emotional containment cannot be provided. In this regard, the possibility of frequent dropped calls and pixelated screens does make containment exceedingly difficult. On an internal level, a dropped call may be akin to a fragmentation of the relationship, a Bionian "catastrophe". In a conventional in-office treatment, one would rely on elements of the invariant or co-constructed frame and on the reliability, consistency, and emotional presence of the analyst to contain and control a regression or a crisis. If these elements are present, in addition to adequate levels of computer memory and speed of broadband connection, these types of disruption can be manageable. A non-internet, traditional treatment can tolerate disruptions, such as a UPS delivery to the office door in mid-session, so long as they are infrequent and the emotional impact on the patient and analyst is attended to.

Curtis's (2007) third objection to the viability of internet psychoanalysis is that it is not possible for an online analyst to detect and manage the analytic process. Tuckett (2005) describes psychoanalytic treatment as requiring three analytic capacities: (1) the capacity to sense the relevant psychoanalytic data (e.g., affects, unconscious meanings); (2) the ability to conceive what is sensed, and (3) the capacity to offer interpretations based on these, as well as to sense and to conceive the effects of these interpretations. While it is true that using the internet to provide treatment does pose challenges to both patient and analyst in sensing and managing an analytic process, certain ways of constructing the setting make it more likely that containment is possible.

Earlier I outlined several prerequisites for treatment, and if these are compromised the treatment is not viable. Some analysts have found taking additional measures to support the frame helpful. For example, the patient's camera can be placed so that the analyst has a profile view of the patient on the couch and the patient can easily turn to view the analyst when feeling insecure. Others attempt to compensate for the greater distance inherent in a two-dimensional relationship via screen by making extra efforts to solidify that relationship through tone of voice, or by asking the patient to process certain emotion-laden material in their native language, even though the material is not understood on a conscious level by the analyst.

These extra efforts highlight the many challenges posed by our countertransference when working with patients across cultures via the internet. In spite of these challenges, many individuals who provide psychoanalytic treatment to Chinese patients using the internet agree that it is possible, given the appropriate patient-analyst match, to create an analytic frame that provides a rhythm of safety and emotional containment sufficient to allow an analytic process to develop.

The future

The history of psychoanalysis has been marked by controversies over the introduction of changes to the prevailing paradigm, as psychoanalysis has changed and evolved in response to encounters with new frontiers. According to *Merriam-Webster* (2007), the word frontier can be used to denote two types of boundary. It can indicate both a line of division between different or opposed things, and it can also mean a new field for exploration and development. As was illustrated above, offering psychotherapy and psychoanalysis via the internet expands and redefines the boundary of analytic experience. Does this practice break new ground in a constructive and creative way or does it transgress a boundary that serves a useful purpose?

Some analysts believe that teleanalysis is breaking the frame and degrading psychoanalysis. They contend that cyberspace and psychoanalysis are cultures that are opposed to one another and reject the idea of psychoanalysis using the internet. Curtis writes that the internet and cyberspace contribute vitally and importantly to our theoretical discourse about the nature of analysis, but have nothing to offer psychoanalytic practice (2007, p. 135). Some opponents find that the technology itself is not adequate to encompass an analytic process. They condemn the use of the internet for psychoanalysis, largely basing their arguments on the incompatibility of an intimate personal encounter with the distance imposed by internet contact and find the use of internet technology incomprehensible. Some go so far as to view analysis using the internet as a form of heresy. The first argument made in advancing this proposition is an objection to using modern technology in psychoanalytic practice. The second concerns political considerations that fuel objections to internet treatment. I would like to counter these objections.

First, there is a historical precedent within psychoanalysis for the use of new technology. Berger (2005) points out that Freud used the technology of his day. He used the postal service in his analysis of Little Hans. Freud also introduced a new psychoanalytic application for an existing "technology" in his use of the couch. Over the decades, analysts have adapted their practice to changes brought by new inventions. For example, most contemporary analysts use the digital clock to keep time. Other examples of technological applications that have brought changes to psychoanalytic practice are the telephone, cellphone, answering machine, voicemail, even the electric light. When adapting new technology to their clinical work, analysts have needed to analyse the meanings of this. For example, Berger (2005) illustrates the way in which using digital clocks has changed our relationship to the structure of the session by fostering for analyst and patient alike a sense of exactitude we otherwise would not have.

Second, political considerations play a prominent role in the rejection of the idea of internet psychoanalysis. The use of the internet to conduct psychoanalysis is a highly charged political issue that is being debated intensely in the American and International Psychoanalytic(al) Associations. The IPA featured a panel on teleanalysis at the annual meeting in 2009 (Scharff, 2010). The International Working Group on Teleanalysis offered a two-day workshop at the pre-congress in 2011. The organisers of the 2009 panel and the speakers presented the view that psychoanalysis must make use of information technology such as the telephone and internet both in order to adapt to the current social reality of a global economy and to meet the needs and demands of those in rural areas where psychoanalysis would not otherwise be available, the needs of business executives and the like who wish an analysis but travel too frequently to commit to meeting four or five times weekly, and the desires of young adults who have grown up with the new technology. The panellists affirmed that use of information technology does not preclude attention to the analytic dyad, or depth work. Affective attunement, unconscious communication, an appreciation of resistance, and work with the transference and countertransference are all part of analysis by Skype or telephone. When transcripts of analytic hours with patients seen via the internet were presented along with non-internet sessions, the audience, which was blind as to the distinction between sessions, was not able to distinguish between them (Fishkin, April 2011, personal communication).

Opponents argued that psychoanalysis is "chasing after technology" as an alternative to in-depth person-to-person work and that telephone analysis/internet analysis is not analysis. An unstated resistance to the use of internet analysis has its root in the truism that change brings disruption to the status quo. The acceptance of the use of the internet for analysis is likely to have a large impact on training policies. But psychoanalysis has been responding to cultural developments from the beginning and this responsiveness has led to new and valued pathways of understanding.

One area currently under exploration is the impact of the use of screens for treatment on voyeuristic, exhibitionistic fantasies in the patient and/or analyst. For example, Isaacs Russell and Neumann (2011) are investigating the interaction between exhibitionistic and voyeuristic fantasies, the use of internet screens for treatment, and shared parental bed child-rearing practices. Lingiardi (2008) mentions that internet treatment may evoke intrusion anxiety in analysts. Peering through a glass screen and viewing a two-dimensional patient on a couch in the patient's residence may bring up many very early and previously unanalysed impulses.

Currently, the internet is supplanting the telephone in being used for analysis for candidates who live at some distance from their analysts, provided a certain number of hours are completed in the same physical location. For instance, the training programme of the unaffiliated International Psychoanalytic Training Institute, located in Chevy Chase, Maryland provides analytic training for candidates from more remote areas such as Panama. The candidates travel to see their analyst and join the analytic class for courses in person, while the rest of the analysis and the classes are conducted by Skype or telephone. The IPA is currently establishing a psychoanalytic training programme in China, although very few qualified analysts reside there. Chinese candidates are permitted an internet training/personal analysis after completing a specified number of hours of in-person treatment (Snyder, 2011b, personal communication). At present a consensus seems to have emerged, at least within the IPA, that internet psychoanalysis is acceptable as a form of treatment for some candidates. Internet analyses are not at this time acceptable as control cases in most training institutes. APsaA and IPA institutes in the USA currently require that for control cases, treatment must occur four times weekly in person on the couch. The meaning of "in person" in a virtual world remains to be fully thought out. To view internet video encounters as not occurring in person is problematic. Psychoanalysis using the internet challenges analysts and analytic institutions with the need to rethink current notions of the nature of time, space, and what constitutes a personal relationship.

Conclusions

Meeting via the internet will have a unique meaning and function for each analytic couple (Malater, 2007). Using the internet as a vehicle for treatment affects the way that conscious and unconscious material is received, experienced, and processed by both patient and analyst. It impacts the types of transference/countertransference, the types of defences used, and the nature of unconscious material such as dreams and associations that emerge. It affects the analyst's capacity to foster a therapeutic alliance and the nature of enactments that are likely to occur. A firm but flexible frame is essential to support analytic treatment using the internet.

Internet psychoanalysis poses questions about accepted concepts of time and space and the nature of the mind and of persons. It challenges accepted traditions, such as control case requirements that candidate-analyst and patient be located in the same geographic location. Paradoxically, a theory and therapy that has been described as subversive to cultural status quo and convention (Thompson, 2002, p. 82) is at present being used by some to oppose this innovative form of practice.

I have challenged the statement that the internet, though a valuable resource for society, has nothing to offer psychoanalysis. I believe that internet applications in psychoanalysis are making a profound, necessary, and valuable contribution to psychoanalytic thought and practice on a global level. In the next stage, empirical research needs to be conducted to validate these impressions and the clinical findings that indicate potential positive benefits for patients. We have found that, when used within clearly defined parameters, internet videoconferencing technology allows sufficient contact and engagement between patient and analyst to provide effective and ethical psychoanalytic treatment.

References

Arlow, J. A. & Brenner, C. (1990). The psychoanalytic process. *Psychoanalytic Quarterly*, *59*: 678–692.

Bass, A. (2007). When the frame doesn't fit the picture. *Psychoanalytic Dialogues*, *17*: 1–27.

Berger, N. (2005). New medium, new messages, new meanings: Communication and interaction in child treatment in an age of technology. *Journal of Infant, Child and Adolescent Psychotherapy*, *4*: 218–229.

Bleger, J. (1967). Psychoanalysis of the psychoanalytic frame. *International Journal of Psychoanalysis*, *48*: 511–519.

Bromberg, P. (2007). The analytic moment doesn't fit analytic "technique": Commentary on Tony Bass's "When the frame doesn't fit the picture". *Psychoanalytic Dialogues*, *17*: 909–921.

Buckner, L. (Ed.) (2011). *China American Psychoanalytic Alliance Handbook*. Retrieved June 25, 2011 from http://groups.yahoo.com/groups/CAPATREAT/files.

Chausseguet-Smirgel, J. (1992). Some thoughts on the psychoanalytic situation. *Journal of the American Psychoanalytic Association*, *40*: 3–25.

Curtis, A. E. (2007). The claustrum: Sequestration of cyberspace. *The Psychoanalytic Review*, *94*: 99–139.

Fischbein, S. V. (2010). Psychoanalysis and virtual reality. *International Journal of Psychoanalysis*, *91*: 985–988.

Fishkin, L. (2011). Personal communication.

Freud, S. (1913c). On beginning the treatment (further recommendations on the technique of psychoanalysis, I). *S. E.*, *12* (pp. 121–144). London: Hogarth.

Gabbard, G. O. (2001). Cyberpassion: E-rotic transference on the Internet. *Psychoanalytic Quarterly*, *70*: 719–737.

International Psychoanalytical Association (2007, March). Equivalency procedures for assessing individual applicants for IPA membership or for recognition as IPA child and adolescent analysts trained in non-IPA organisations. Retrieved June 25, 2011 from http://www.ipa.org.uk/eng/about-ipa/ipa-procedural-code.

Isaacs Russell, G. & Neumann, D. A. (2011). *Screen Enactments in Internet Analysis with Chinese Patients.* Manuscript in progress.

Lingiardi, V. (2008). Playing with unreality: transference and computer. *International Journal of Psychoanalysis, 89*: 111–126.

Malater, E. (2007). Caught in the web: Patient, therapist, e-mail and the Internet. *Psychoanalytic Review, 94*: 151–168.

McGaffin, K. (2011). Personal communication.

Merriam-Webster's Collegiate Dictionary (11th edition) (2007). Springfield, MA: Merriam-Webster.

Modell, A. H. (1988). The centrality of the psychoanalytic setting and the changing aims of treatment. *Psychoanalytic Quarterly, 57*: 577–596.

Neumann, D. A. (1985). A psychotherapeutic computer application: Modification of technological competence. *Behavioral Research Methods, Instruments & Computers, 18*: 135–140.

Rosen, C. (2010, March 5). *Can You Hear Me? Can You See Me?: Conducting a Skype Internet Analysis in Chinese.* Paper presented at Symposium 2011: Our Practice Today, Treatment and Transformation, Mount Sinai Medical Center, New York City. Retrieved March 29, 2011 from http://internationalpsychoanalysis.net/wp-content/uploads/2011/03/CaroleRosenpaper.pdf.

Sabin, J. (2010, October 12). *Health Care Organizational Ethics: Psychoanalysis in China.* Retrieved June 25, 2011 from http://healthcareorganizationalethics.blogspot.com/2010/10/psychoanalysis-in-china.html.

Sand, S. (2007). Future considerations: Interactive identities and the interactive self. *Psychoanalytic Review, 94*: 83–97.

Scharff, J. (2010). Telephone analysis. *International Journal of Psychoanalysis, 91*: 989–992.

Snyder, E. (2011a). *How Skype Video Works.* [Power Point slide presentation.] Paper presented at American Psychoanalytic Association winter conference, New York City, January 15.

Snyder, E. (2011b). Personal communication.

Thompson, M. G. (2002). The ethic of honesty: The moral dimension to psychoanalysis. *Fort Da, 8*: 72–83.

Tuckett, D. (2005). Does anything go? Towards a framework for the more transparent assessment of psychoanalytic competence. *International Journal of Psychoanalysis, 86*: 31–49.

Tustin, F. (1986). Autistic barriers in neurotic patients. New Haven, CT: Yale University Press.

Wallerstein, R. (2009). Defining psychoanalysis: A review and a commentary. *Psychoanalytic Dialogues, 19*: 675–690.

Winnicott, D. W. (1955). Metapsychological and clinical aspects of regression within the psychoanalytical set-up. *International Journal of Psychoanalysis, 36*: 16–26.

CHAPTER SEVENTEEN

Psychoanalysis using Skype

Anna Kudiyarova, PhD

I would like to discuss the usefulness of Skype for providing psychoanalytic treatment. Nowadays there is a big discussion about the question: should we officially recognise psychoanalysis conducted via Skype or not? My answer to this question is unequivocally, yes, we should. But I have only gradually come to such a conclusion. I first heard of psychoanalytic sessions on Skype from my colleagues, candidates in training under the auspices of the International Psychoanalytical Association. Being very obedient to all analytical rules, my first reaction was indignation and anger. How might anyone think that it was possible? This was a violation of the setting! But many analysts and candidates in the post-Soviet regions have no other option. Having tried it, I have found Skype to be an extraordinarily useful medium in which to practise psychoanalysis and psychoanalytic supervision. So I would like to share my experience in this field, to explain the way it is done for those who have not used Skype, and to present some clinical cases via Skype to show how closely they resemble in-person sessions. Today, I use Skype for sessions in three ways: 1) in supervision as a supervisee and as a supervisor; 2) in analytic treatment with my own analyst, and 3) in analytic treatment for my patients who live in remote cities in my country, Kazakhstan, and other countries. I will focus mainly on the treatment applications of Skype.

Many analysts might be uncomfortable working with Skype for analytic treatment just because they have not enough technological experience. So, first, I want to explain what Skype is. Skype is a Voice over Internet Protocol (VoIP) system that enables free internet calls between two computers, regardless of their locations. It is a peer-to-peer network in which voice calls pass over the internet. This internet-based audio/video service allows a user in one place to communicate with a Skype user in another place. Skype users search for other users to connect to, enabling them to search other Skype users and send them messages. Skype's encryption is inherent in the Skype protocol and is transparent to callers. Because of this integration the communication between users is considered to be private, although several security concerns exist. You can go to the website to download the free software at http://www.skype.com/download/. Some computers have a built-in camera, and if it does not, you will need to install a webcam. It is also useful to use a headset to provide maximum sound clarity. Second, I want to describe the analytic Skype session. It is a forty-five-minute encounter between analyst and analysand conducted computer-to-computer, point-to-point in real time using Skype technology, so that they talk into the computer microphone, look into a webcam and at the computer screen, and therefore see each other while talking and interacting even though they may be miles apart. If the patient uses a microphone headset, I can often hear his breath in the strengthened mode, and this gives more information about his feelings. Sometimes I have actually bent down to the computer to catch something more precisely, and, I think, unconsciously to be closer to the patient.

Now let us think about Skype in relation to psychoanalysis. If we search the internet, we find 6,580,000 results for Skype therapy, 389,000 results for Skype psychoanalysis, and many newspaper and magazine articles referring to *Skypo-analysis*, *distance analysis*, *remote analysis*, *teleanalysis*, and even *Skypic dialogue*! Personally I prefer the term *analytic Skype sessions*. Reading these articles I found that there are many supporters in favour of Skype for teaching psychoanalysis and providing supervision. I found many opponents against using Skype in psychoanalytical treatment.

I looked for scientific papers evaluating analytical Skype sessions, and did not find any. I did find a report from a discussion at the IPA Congress which proves that the subject is under discussion. The conclusion in that report was that "Psychoanalysis must adapt to the current social reality posed by the global economy and use its supporting information technology in order to consider the individual, exceptional needs of analysands in training who live in rural areas and in repressed cultures, as, for instance, Eastern Europe and China, executives who travel for work, and young adults who have grown up on technology" (Scharff, 2010). But I did find many interesting papers about analysis using the telephone, some from twenty-five years ago. They introduce many of the same questions about integrity and effectiveness as are raised by the use of Skype in psychoanalytic treatment.

Doubts about using Skype for personal analysis abound. Detractors complain that the analysand is not present. Analyst and analysand are not together in a shared room. There is no common space in Skype. A computer stands between the patient and the analyst. There are too many technical problems. There is no couch. The analyst cannot intervene via Skype if something happens to the patient. Skype will not permit the development of transference/countertransference. Skype does not allow the analytic process to grow. Soon Skype meetings will replace live meetings between analyst and analysand.

I usually turn on the internet, then open Skype. A green light with my screen name appears on the screens of everybody who is in my network. Then I wait for my patient to call me. It is like hearing a door bell, and answering the door. After establishing communication with the usual greeting, the analysand and I do a sound check, and adjust our webcam position if it has slipped. Then I turn the focus of the camera away from my face to the wall of my office, the same wall that the patient would see if lying on my couch. This is similar to the view of the analytic patient who cannot see my face because she is lying on the couch looking away. Some patients prefer to sit up in treatment, and when they are in Skype sessions, they prefer to sit in front of the screen of the computer placed on a table before them. Others, who use the analytic couch when in my office, lie down on a sofa, putting the computer on a side table so that I can see the same amount of the patient's face as I would do in my office. Just like in the live session, the patient can decide whether to remove shoes or not. The difference is that you see the patient and yourself on the same flat screen. At the end of the session, I again turn the screen towards me so that my face appears on the screen to say goodbye, as I would do when the patient stands up in my office and heads for the door. I try to make the arrangements of our Skype sessions as close to real, live sessions as possible.

Psychoanalysis has been equated with the couch. However, some psychoanalysts have found that eye contact is essential in fostering the analytic process, at least for some patients. The lifeblood of psychoanalysis is not in the number of sessions or the use of a couch, but rather in the nature of the psychoanalytic process. In traditional in-person psychoanalysis the analytic process develops in a situation without eye contact but the analysand is aware of the presence of the analyst. In Skype psychoanalysis the same holds true, except that the presence is virtual. Like traditional analysis, the essence of Skype analysis is the quality of the relationship between analyst and analysand, and the nature of the psychoanalytic process.

In a Skype session, there may be sudden interruptions. Thus, an additional rule was set up. My patients and I have agreed they are to call back if that should happen, and I wait for a call because we noticed that if we call back simultaneously, we could not establish contact, and the delay wasted our valuable minutes. The difficulty of staying connected can be frustrating and even anxiety provoking. Nevertheless technical problems can augment awareness of internal feelings, fears, and anxieties. We want to discuss reactions and association to these technical glitches to gain dynamic understanding of the impact of changes in setting.

During a Skype session, when my patient Lera was telling me that she felt that her boss was not attentive to her, suddenly the call was dropped. Lera felt sure that I myself had disconnected the call, like the boss who ignored her. Later in the session when I was listening silently, Lera thought that I had disconnected again. She was anxious about a repetition of losing my attention. Sometimes the microphone breaks or the audio disconnection is so bad that we have to cancel the session, and that brings up fears of abandonment. Once when there was a noise so loud that I could not hear Ayzhan, I apologised for the fault on the line, but Ayzhan said she did not mind the interruption because it gave her a chance to rest in silence for a moment. One time on Skype, a patient's microphone failed. If that had happened at the beginning, we might have cancelled the session. But it happened almost at the end, and we decided not to interrupt the session. So she wrote her thoughts on the Skype chat function, and I replied in my voice. Sometimes the connection is not sufficient to support the video. If the image fails, we do not interrupt the session, because the main vehicle for doing the work is the speaking voice, as it is in a telephone session or a live session. One patient had been in a bad mood all week. I realised that this could be a reaction to losing her in-person sessions. I said to her: "You are in a bad mood with me because it is my fault that we have to use Skype sessions, and you cannot lie down on my couch any more."

Usually you think of a patient using Skype from a setting at their own home or office. But for two of my patients who chose to continue with Skype that was not possible. They continued to come to my office, and my assistant let them in, even though I was not there. One of them needed the privacy from her family and the other could not afford a laptop and had to borrow one at my office. One day Sagadat, the woman who owned a laptop but needed privacy, came to my office for her session as usual but she could not call me because her laptop was broken. My assistant lent her a laptop to call me on Skype. Seeing my assistant's screen-name I declined her call more than once because I was waiting for my patient. I learned later that Sagadat had felt badly rejected by my refusals, a repeat of non-responses from significant people in her life. After a few attempts and refusals, my assistant explained the situation to me on Skype chat and I accepted the call. As I did so, my assistant handed her laptop to Sagadat with my face already on the screen. Sagadat went from feeling upset and rejected that she could not reach me to feeling elated that I had been brought to her. "Suddenly, as if by magic, you were there, smiling, waiting just for me, delivered to me on the blue plate with the gold trim, like in the Russian fairy tale."

Yes, there are technical problems, noise on the line, communication failures, and poor image quality. But are those inherent only in Skype sessions? Even in a traditional situation, there can be unpredictable noises such as a howling siren that signals fire, police, or emergency, a barking dog, or a sudden knock at the door when another patient has mistaken the time of the appointment. In my country, the electricity may go off unpredictably, and we continue by candlelight or simply sit in the growing dark, listening and talking only. On Skype, the same occurs, and the call continues, thanks to the battery on the laptop. On the other hand, it must be admitted that technical features increase anxiety when conducting the session. The live sessions do not confront me with failures of the ability to hear or see. A Skype session demands more thorough preparation and a more sensitive attitude towards the patient.

What can we not do via Skype? We cannot stop the deep regression of a patient in an acute psychotic state. This means that we do not work with such a patient on Skype. On the other hand we would not work with such a patient four to five times a week and we would not ask him to lie down in a live setting either. Maintaining the optimum frequency of analytic sessions depends on the capacities of the patient, not on whether this is a live or virtual analytic contract. I follow what I have been taught, that we do not recommend analysis on the couch for psychotic patients, and that we use face-to-face sessions with some patients who do better with that, and usually only neurotic patients should lie down. We begin a long-term treatment only if we think that the potential patient is analysable after a careful evaluation. The same is true for Skype, except that many colleagues agree that evaluation criteria for the use of Skype must be stricter than for in-person analysis. I also believe that if Skype is to be effective it must be combined with in-person sessions, and it must have been established in person before moving to Skype.

A Russian colleague compares an analyst using Skype with a mother using the telephone. A very busy working mother cannot be at home with her infant in person. The busy analyst does not stay with the patient when the patient cannot be with her. The mother cannot use the telephone to take care of her infant or toddler. The analyst cannot use Skype to intervene in an emergency. But the mother can call home from work to talk to a five-year-old who is able to respond or initiate calls and have a conversation about whatever is happening. Similarly the analyst can maintain an effective therapeutic relationship with a patient. Another metaphor I like is that of breastfeeding and bottle-feeding. Live sessions have the immediacy of breastfeeding and the introduction of Skype may feel like a switch to bottle-feeding. For any number of reasons, a working mother shifts her baby from breast to bottle but she still holds him at her breast, gently embracing him. There are technical aspects the mother must negotiate—sterilising the bottle, warming the milk, just as the Skype analyst must deal with hardware and software. Who can say that the mother feeding her baby by bottle loves her baby less than the mother who feeds her baby by the breast? And like the analyst who begins the treatment in person and then moves to Skype, with an occasional in-person series of sessions, some mothers combine both kinds of feeding.

The erotic transference flourishes on Skype, too. My patient F, laughing, said to me that she put on her make-up, powdered her face, and suddenly stopped herself before she added her perfume. F said: "I knew I did the make-up for you, because you would see me, but you could not feel how I would smell." Live sessions are full of smells—of a sweaty body of the patient who comes running in late, of a woman with an intolerably strong smell of perfume, a savoury meal, a steaming cup of coffee. Yes, the difference here is essential. And lack of smell may be the only weak point of the Skype technology. Unconscious communication flourishes on Skype too. When I was invited as a Fulbright visiting lecturer to Mississippi Valley State University, I arranged to continue sessions with some patients by Skype. A once-a-week therapy patient brought a dream about her trip to the delta of a river. She was preoccupied with the delta and kept wondering why she was so interested in that topic. Unknown to her, I had flown there by Delta Air Lines.

Skype sessions may seem less intense or less rigorous for an analyst. Some analysts might prepare only a small corner of the office that will be picked up by the webcam, and leave the rest a mess. Some analysts might dress for business only the top half of the body visible to the patient and leave the lower part of the body in casual attire. For myself, I cannot imagine that I would sit in slippers, or cross-legged at a live session, but in Skype sessions I can let myself wear tracksuit trousers. Is it my laziness, neglecting the etiquette rules, or disrespect for the patient? Yes, and no. If it is the only session at that hour, it is nice to save my time and energy. Using technology to have a session instead of visiting the analyst's office sharpens awareness of who visits whom. Is the patient reaching the therapist in her home base, or is the therapist entering the patient's space?

When I introduced the option or the need for Skype analysis, some patients felt that their homes or offices were not conducive to analysis because they were used to working in my office. It became a point of conflict for some patients. Other patients slowly got used to the idea that it was not necessary to leave the office or house to have a good analytic session, and even discovered that their own walls provided more relaxation.

My patient from another country, smiling, said: "I notice that now you always are with us in our house." At first, I could not understand what she meant. She used to have her sessions at her office computer. Then she got the internet at home and was constantly online. I am not constantly online. When I dial up onto the internet, a green light with my screen name lights up on the screen of my list of contacts. She liked seeing that I was online, and having me close to her. I did not know that it was possible to make myself invisible when I am online. In the process of discussion, we explored the transference significance of her keeping me secretly close and then she taught me how to make myself invisible even when I am online. Our patients advance our computer literacy.

Some of my readers are already full of disagreement concerning the value of sessions on Skype. Admittedly nothing will replace a live session with analyst and patient together in person. However, as we say, half a loaf is better than no bread. Considering that there are absolutely no qualified experts in wide stretches of Asia, Skype sessions may have a big future. Even in my city, where my patient S travels an hour and a half to reach my office, and almost as long to return home, it seems reasonable to use Skype for her convenience some of the time. For the patient who has to fly on business, the combination of live and Skype sessions helps keep the continuity of the analytic process.

Nevertheless there are many nuances to consider. How do we assess whether the analytical process has reached its goal? Is quality of the analytic process in analysis through Skype equal to what it could have been in person? Even the word "through" points to a certain barrier between me and my patients.

Let us ponder this by revisiting the history of psychoanalysis as a method. Free association was invented to reach the patient's unconscious. Classical psychoanalytic practice specified use of the couch, an iconic feature of classical psychoanalysis ever since. Freud admitted his need for a couch to avoid being stared at all day by his patients. Free association is still the essence of analytic interaction, but the couch, the shared room, the length and frequency of sessions are negotiable. Classical psychoanalysis was invented at a certain time (late nineteenth century) and place (Europe) for a certain type of patient (with hysterical neuroses). Psychoanalysis now inhabits a much wider world including Asia, and the twenty-first century brings with it rapid technological advances for daily living. That new technology lets more potential patients in many different regions explore the healing benefits of free association. One may say, in advance, that this method will not work for every patient, and it will work only for a specific type of patient, but for those who can use the internet, Skype sessions will be an addition to the mainstream of live sessions, when patient or analyst cannot be in the same location. If Freud the founder of psychoanalysis were living in the internet age I believe he would embrace Skype sessions because he stood up for the application of the psychoanalytic method among the wide masses.

I would like to underline that I work via Skype with the patients who have already worked with me in person in my office, and have been forced to move temporarily to Skype because of my or their travel abroad. One patient of mine prefers Skype because she resides in another country. But even in that case, she first came to my city, had one week of live sessions, and now she comes every summer for a week.

Because of the absence of any analysts in Kazakhstan, I underwent shuttle analysis, as so many Eastern European and Asian beginners have done. I flew to the United States back and forth two to three times a year for some years. It gave me the advantage of live sessions but it was exorbitantly expensive. Such training demands deep pockets. Skype sessions have the advantage of contained costs, making analysis available to a wide range of the professionals who decide to be trained in psychoanalysis, and to patients who also want to save time and money. By the way, international telephone calls are much more expensive than Skype. Skype analysis is the treatment of choice for individuals who live in communities with little or no access to analysts. Analysts are willing to consider Skype analysis for patients and candidates in large, far away countries with few resources. Three hundred members of the China America Psychoanalytic Alliance in the United States, and analysts from Canada, Norway, and Germany especially, have been attempting to export psychoanalytic psychotherapy to China via Skype. But they are less aware of the needs at home. When I made presentations to the colleges in West Virginia and Mississippi, I was surprised that nobody could tell me whether there was a psychoanalytical society. We joked that I, a Kazakh woman, first introduced psychoanalysis to remote America. If those young psychologists in the hinterland should like psychoanalytic training, they would have to either leave their city, or use Skype.

The rhythm of modern life contributes to the need to accept Skype psychoanalysis. Many patients and psychoanalysts are mobile, travelling for pleasure or business or commuting from home to office. Skype helps to overcome the obstacle of distance. Despite business trips, it is possible to continue analysis almost without interruption. For example, last year I had to leave my country, Kazakhstan for one year. I wondered what to do with my patients. Only one of my analytical patients (four times a week) made the decision to postpone her analysis for one year. Four patients, after a lot of discussion, decided to continue our meetings via Skype. Moreover, some of my psychotherapy patients have preferred Skype sessions. Looking back now, I regret that earlier in my professional life I was too rigid to work via Skype with an analysable woman who had an extrememly intensive work schedule. I lost the opportunity to work with her and to help her, but at that time the analytic rules were all-important and I wanted to be a good student. I did not have the confidence to begin Skype sessions with my patients, especially with two control case patients. I was afraid of my supervisor. I did not know if my institute would agree to accept those cases. I was uncertain if I would be able to keep the analytical process going. When technical issues appeared, I felt guilty, as if it was my fault. Later on, when I did proceed to use Skype, I was relieved to see the progress of my patients.

A clinical vignette

Balnur is a very bright woman, with an excellent academic record, an early history of separations, trust issues, and a tendency to destroy relationships, including her first marriage. Divorced, she had begun a relationship with a boyfriend but she remained suspicious and persecutory towards him. I worked with Balnur four times a week in person for nine months. I won a Fulbright fellowship in December, 2009 and planned to leave for the United States in August 2010. But I waited until after the new year to tell her of my departure. When I had to be in the United States for some months, we continued on Skype, but with only two sessions a week. We agreed that after I returned home we would resume four-times-a-week psychoanalysis in person.

Over the course of sixteen months in psychoanalysis in person and then on Skype, Balnur progressed from holding a suspicious, persecutory attitude to her boyfriend and an accompanying negative transference (which appeared surprisingly quickly) to a more positive and stable relationship with her man and with me. After many interpretations, and working through, Balnur was able to see and prevent her inner tendency to destroy relationships, and to more deeply explore her inner life—moving from the experiencing to the observing position. Balnur had difficult issues with separation in her early life, and this would be our first separation.

At first she seemed to be calm and unemotional about my going away as if my announcement had no impact on her. I knew the separation would be hard for her, and yet I did not realise how complicated and how strong her feelings would be. Even if I was anticipating anger, I was surprised at how quickly she developed a negative transference.

When I asked her to talk more about my leaving, she railed against me: "It was cruel. I felt I was deceived. You may be the only person I trusted, and now it's as if you have once again proved that I must trust nobody." Through her tears, Balnur continued: "It was very painful. I felt lonely, misunderstood, as if you temporarily sheltered me and then threw me out again. It means you actually do not need me. Really, I could not even imagine that I would need you." This gave us an opportunity to work through in the transference her conflicted early separation experiences brought up now by my going away. I said: "You have got used to needing nobody because separation is painful." Balnur replied: "Do you want me still to trust someone, to feel so upset over and over again? I am awfully angry with you. It is a pity that I am only a job for you, but not a person." I said: "It is hard to experience this, I know, but if we understand that my leaving evokes so many strong feelings, it gives you a chance to learn more about yourself." Balnur was able to express openly her negative feelings and thoughts towards me because we had built an alliance based on helping her to recognise and put her inner experiences into words.

Balnur told me she would look for work in another city, as if wanting to distance herself from me as I was distancing myself from her. In July, she asked to stop our sessions already, even though it was agreed that our summer vacation would start in August when I left for the United States. I thought this was her attempt to leave me before I could leave her. I said that she was retaliating, and she agreed: "I know how I can hurt, how I can be cruel with people." We met twice in early August to say goodbye and arrange for sessions twice a week on Skype. Instead of calling in mid-September, as planned, she did not call until October, as if she wanted to punish me by forcing me to worry about her. Having done that, she was ready to resume, and was actually glad to see me through Skype. I saw her smiling, bright-eyed face for all of three Skype sessions. Then she disappeared. When she called again, I was surprised to see that she was no longer calling me from my city in Kazakhstan. She had indeed moved to another city. I learned that she had been hospitalised because of pregnancy problems, and had give birth to a son. In November, she returned for regular Skype sessions.

Each time I asked her to change the time or day of our Skype session because of some mismatching holidays in Kazakhstan and the USA, Balnur retaliated. She changed the session time, forgot and missed a session, and once appeared on the screen for only the last five minutes of the session. I pointed out to her that she might be doing this because my request evoked some feelings. I said that she was struggling for power and control. Balnur said, "I don't want to be dependent on you, to miss you, and have to admit I miss you." Even when she did not name her feelings, I could see her face on the screen, and I felt her feelings. I constantly worked on her resistance. I felt her silence was tense and hostile. Balnur said that she didn't want to let me enter her family as she felt I did on the computer screen at her home when she had her sessions on Skype. On the other hand, she felt closer to me than when seeing me in person at my office because now I came to her. Balnur was able to tolerate her complicated conflicted feelings about me and other important people in her life and this newfound ability allowed her to stay in warm relationships with me as well as with her own mother, and with her mother-in-law. She said: "I now have three Moms."

I noticed also that as Balnur was able to express her feelings towards me in more complicated ways, I felt both pleased and proud for her and our work. She could say to me during the session: "I don't trust you now. From my point of view, you are not speaking sincerely. Your tone of voice makes me not believe you." Despite this, she continued to have a strong alliance with me. Then I thought her ability to say her negative opinions directly to me might be connected with her wish to please me like a child wanting to impress the teacher. In our culture that is not easy for people to do. Now Balnur can speak aggressively with a louder voice and an angry facial expression because I have worked on the issues with her to help her understand the transference feelings.

As we went on with the Skype sessions in the second year, I saw that Balnur began to be more trusting of her relatives and of me in the transference. Many Skype sessions were filled with warm, tender feelings even if only temporarily. She was beginning to show signs of her capacity to stay with me through my absence and work with me while I was away as well as to build stable relationship with her partner and plan to live with him. It was clear evidence of her progress in analysis with me and its impact on her life. During the last few months Balnur has begun to call her man her husband, recently showed more and more respect towards him, and acknowledged that his behaviour was in some ways more adult than hers. I thought it was evidence that she did not need to be always in full power. She consistently sees her husband in a more positive light. The more we worked through her ambivalent feelings about him, the more she experienced a warm attitude to him.

When Balnur said that she missed the city where we had both lived, where she had been physically in proximity to both her boyfriend and me, I asked if she missed our live sessions as well. Smiling nostalgically, she replied: "Yeah, it was a happy time. I often recall the smell and taste of cherries from the tree near your office." Then Balnur decided to return to her previous job in our city. She was coping well, maintaining stable relationships, and controlling her old tendency to destroy. Her decision to go back to our city was, I thought, partly connected with our work and with the thought of resuming in person when I was to return. Balnur had become appreciative. She was aware that even if it was painful and hard for her, she had experienced a profound change in herself. When she said: "You know my tendency to destroy is getting smaller," she smiled when I replied, "Because your ability to tolerate mixed feelings is getting bigger!"

Back at work in the city, but still calling me in the United States on Skype, Balnur was forced to shift her baby from breastfeeding to bottle-feeding. She said: "I feel guilty that my breast abandoned him." I replied that she may be accusing me that I forced her to have Skype sessions instead of the live ones. She nodded. Then Balnur said softly and fearfully that there was something she hadn't told me. I asked her to tell me what she was afraid of. She was afraid to tell me that she wanted to work with me as colleagues in the psychoanalytic sphere in case I should refuse to see her. I helped her to consider whether this was a new version of her mistrust of me, or increasing jealousy of me for being able to help her. Now we have started to talk about resuming our live sessions. I anticipate that it will be interesting when Balnur starts to come to my office for analytic sessions in person, as they were before.

Conclusion

To illustrate the use of Skype for maintaining analytic continuity I have presented one of my cases, which I think is analytic. Of course, it is questionable what qualifies as analytic process. There are many examples in the literature and at scientific meetings in which one well-known psychoanalyst criticises another's clinical vignette for not being analytic. Even though (or perhaps because) I am fairly new to Skype, I wanted to show how I used Skype to provide psychoanalytic treatment as a way of encouraging others to try it for themselves, and to contribute to the discussion of all the issues that arise.

There are many questions to be pondered. How can we think about the analytical third in a Skype session? When will Skype analysis be recognised officially as an accepted way of conducting a training analysis? What billing issues are to be confronted when a patient and a psychoanalyst live in different regions, states, and countries? How will insurance companies respond to teleanalysis? Likely, in the West, the spread of Skype sessions will depend on the opinion of the insurance companies. They are in a position to advance this kind of psychological help if they see it as cost-effective. In the East, where the insurance companies do not influence policy, the spread of Skype depends on word of mouth from individual patient and analyst. Hopefully, in the future, American, Latin American, European, and Asian psychoanalysts will present the arguments for and against using Skype for providing analysis and share their work in the practice and teaching of psychoanalysis. Eventually, in a large discussion, we can explore, challenge, argue against, and support the usefulness of Skype analysis in the psychoanalytic treatment and training.

References

Aronson J. (2000). *The Use of the Telephone in Psychotherapy*. Northvale, NJ: Jason Aronson.

Attala, L., Tremblay, A., Corti, G., Saint, S. & Bartoloni, A. (2010). In sight but out of mind. *Journal of Hospital Medicine*, 5: 189–192.

Bassuk, E. L. & Buckner, J. C. (1992). Out of mind—out of sight. *The American Journal of Orthopsychiatry*, 62: 330–331.

Dixon, B. (2010). Out of sight, out of mind? *The Lancet Infectious Diseases*, 10(8): 513.

Inanloo, E. (2006). Out of sight and out of mind? Part II. *Archives of Disease in Childhood*, 91(3): 273.

Kester, G. (1993). Out of sight is out of mind: The imaginary space of postindustrial culture. *Social Text*, 35: 15–32.

Leffert, M. (2003). Analysis and psychotherapy by telephone: Twenty years of clinical experience. *Journal of the American Psychoanalytic Association*, 51: 101–130.

Manosevitz, M. (2000). Telephone psychoanalysis: Talking about bodily states in the absence of visual cues. Paper presented at Symposium: Talking Cure in the 21st Century—Telephone Psychoanalysis. American Psychological Association 108th Annual Convention, Washington, DC, August.

Osnos, E. (2011). Letter from China. Meet Dr. Freud. *The New Yorker*, January 10. http://www.capachina.org/zips/Meet%20Dr.%20Freud%20-%20The%20 New%20Yorker.pdf. Last accessed March 25, 2012.

Park, J. (2011). China on the couch. Interview of Elise Snyder on PBS. January 26. http://www.pbs.org/wnet/need-to-know/culture/china-on-the-couch/6764/. Last accessed March 25, 2012.

Richards, A. (2001). Talking cure in the 21st century: Telephone psychoanalysis. *Psychoanalytic Psychology*, *18*(2): 388–391.

Scharff, J. S. (2010). Telephone analysis. *International Journal of Psychoanalysis*, *91*: 989–992.

Wan, W. (2010). Freud coming into fashion in China. *Washington Post*, October 11. http://www.capachina.org/CAPA/Washington_Post.html. Last accessed March 25, 2012.

Zalusky, S. (1998). Telephone analysis: out of sight, but not out of mind. *Journal of the American Psychoanalytic Association*, *46*(4): 1221–1242.

CHAPTER EIGHTEEN

Four women analysts reflect on their teleanalyses when candidates

Betty S. de Benaim, PhD, Yolanda G. de P. de Varela, PhD,
Lea S. de Setton, PhD and Anonymous, PhD

L ike most candidates, we would generally prefer in-person analysis, but there were no analysts in our place of residence in Panama and our family commitments did not permit relocation to a centre of psychoanalytic training. So we were grateful to have the option of teleanalysis, some of us using the telephone and some of us preferring Skype, each of us to varying degrees of satisfaction with the use of technology to have psychoanalysis. The use of technology also made it possible for us to participate in a distance learning programme of psychoanalytic education. After graduation we all brought clinical expertise and theoretical knowledge to share with other mental health professionals. Each of us will now share some thoughts on the theory and technique of teleanalysis compared to traditional in-person analysis, based on our reading and our personal experience. As we proceed, we prefer not to indicate which of us is the "I" in our individual narratives in order to protect the privacy of our patients and ourselves.

Privation and regression

In the early twentieth century, Freud recommended: "Analytic treatment should be carried through, as far as is possible, under privation—in a state of abstinence" (1919a, p. 162). Lying on the couch, the analysand is deprived of the sight of the analyst, but knows that the analyst is present nevertheless. As one patient expressed it: "It is difficult for me not to look at you while I talk, but I know you are there and listening to me." In the early twenty-first century we still follow the abstinence recommendation, most obviously when we work with teleanalysis, a contemporary adaptation of Freud's traditional analytic treatment model developed for analysands who live at a distance from analytic centres. Some detractors of teleanalysis claim that offering to continue a treatment by phone or over the internet is the opposite of abstinence, in fact it is an indulgence, a denial of separation anxiety, a failure of mourning, a distortion of the fundamental principles. I will argue that teleanalysis that stays true to Freud's original recommendations is a contemporary adaptation that preserves the integrity of the technique.

In teleanalysis conducted by telephone, analysands are in a state of privation, having no view of the analyst as they would have in traditional analysis upon entering or leaving the consulting room. Going beyond Freud's recommendation to analysts to stay out of sight, analysts using the telephone for sessions deprive the analysand of the entire physical presence of the analyst. Nevertheless, the auditory sensory experience of listening to the analyst's breathing over the phone line fills in for the lack of visual contact. The mutual attunement to breathing rhythms drives the relationship towards a re-creation of very early mother-infant experience. In my view, this enhanced sensitivity to communication by the breath is central to the effectiveness of teleanalysis.

Freud noted, in analysis conducted under the recommended privation, the occurrence of temporal regression, that is, a regression in development, in which contact with infant, child, and adolescent parts of the personality that have been split off and lost to the total personality, is renewed. Regression to an earlier state of dependence is a state of mind achieved through free association, a kind of abandonment of ego organisation that results in a more unconscious informed experience (Bollas, 1993).

The analytic situation, in which there is deprivation of the analyst's presence and the stimulation of regressive processes by free association, provides for the construction of early experience, to which we do not otherwise have access because the earliest experiences occurred before any representation was possible, and so there are no words with which to express them. The analysand cannot simply tell the story but has to live it with the analyst. It is through the early contextual transference (that part of the transference to the therapist's holding capacity that "derives from early experiences of environmental provision"), that we receive the image of the regressive experience we need to address (Scharff, 1998, p. 257). Then we can put words to it: we give the analysand a possible construction of early life. Being without memory for the events or words to capture the experience, the analysand is unable to confirm or deny the construction. Confirmation comes to us in various indirect forms, such as in associations that are analogous to the construction received. As Freud put it:

> "It appears, therefore, that the direct utterances of the patient after he has been offered a construction afford very little evidence upon the question whether we have been right or wrong. It is of all the greater interest that there are indirect forms of confirmation which are in every respect trustworthy. One of these is a form of words that is used (as though by general agreement) with very little variation by the most different people: 'I didn't ever think' (or 'I shouldn't ever have thought') 'that' (or 'of that'). This can be translated without any hesitation into: 'Yes, you're right this time—about my unconscious.'" (Freud, 1937d, p. 263)

In summary, we have no way of knowing if the analyst's constructions represent or even resemble the patient's experience, unless the patient follows them with his own associations and elaborations validating the analyst's point.

The patient in teleanalysis with webcam who connects with the analyst not in person but in computer-to-computer contact featuring a face on the computer screen positioned behind the couch and a voice coming from the speakers, experiences an added element in terms of privation. There is the tantalising presence of the analyst behind the glass of the screen, but it is only a virtual reality. I think that this particular situation pulls for regression to an early schizoid way of relating and to traumatic moments in the infant-mother dyad, where words were not sufficient to express the conflict. Let me offer two examples: Miss A and Mr. B.

Clinical example: Miss A

Miss A, who lives at a distance from her analyst with whom she has until now been in condensed analysis in person, gets ready for the first analytic session through teleanalysis. She positions the couch in front of the glass doors of the closets that ring her room. She places the computer screen behind her head, as if the analyst is sitting behind her. The session starts. She feels that something in her immediate environment is making her anxious. Why is she anxious in a familiar place at home? The patient communicates her discomfort and her anxiety by looking around uncertainly. The analyst is affected by the uncertainty and nervousness, and by her view of the analysand surrounded by glass. The analyst thinks that the analysand looks as though she is in an incubator. This is just a construction the analyst offered in response to her countertransference and to the patient's affective reaction. Knowing that she was premature at birth, the analysand immediately accepts the construction, but it is her ensuing associations which validate the construction. Her associative process takes her to the memory of a dream in which she is looking at a baby in an incubator, through the glass of the window at the hospital nursery. In the incubator lies a baby with teeth in place of eyelashes. The dream offers the opportunity to make a construction that will explain the repetition, through somatic responses, of an early maternal deprivation. The eyes became an aggressive tool to take in, as if by force or stealing, that which was denied to her. The baby was chewing her mother in an anxious attempt to hold onto some part of her, thus establishing a way of relating through curiously augmented body parts.

Clinical example: Mr. B

Mr. B was sent to boarding school in London in a traumatic way when he was eleven years old, as a punishment for a deed he actually did not commit. As a result he spent his adolescent years away from his country and family. In addition, while he was at boarding school his family was transferred from Paris to Panama. When he did return from school for visits to his family, it was not to his own country but to Panama, a foreign, disorienting place for Mr. B who had no knowledge of Spanish. Having finished high school, Mr. B was living in Panama for a year during which he felt lost and depressed. He began in-person four-times-a-week psychoanalysis, and progressed to the point where he could consider going away to college, but he was not ready to finish analysis. So we agreed that when he left for college, we would continue the treatment by Skype with webcam.

Now in teleanalysis, Mr. B offers a dream: "I am older and living in a house that is mine. I am sitting in the dining room, but instead of walls there are fish tanks that surround me, covering all the walls." Mr. B takes the calls for the sessions from a room in which he has in front of him, his fish tank, and behind him, the computer with me on video camera. The fish are his only affective links. The deprivation imposed by the analyst's physical absence together with the regression produced by the free associative process allows for the reconstruction of his schizoid defence. He expresses his desire to be part of the outside world through the mobility of the fish, but he feels imprisoned behind a glass wall through which he can only observe longingly an external world that seems out of reach and from which he is excluded because he feels insignificant and invisible. At the same time he feels surrounded by his intrusive, tantalising mother, always looking at what he does, and never at him.

The two analysands experienced early deprivation which was reconstructed in the analysis stimulated by the physical absence of the analyst and the freely associative process. The transference to the analytic context focused on the screen as a glass between the self and the object, making the object both available and at the same time, painfully unavailable. Contrary to the views of those who claim that teleanalysis is not analysis, teleanalysis demonstrates analytic process according to the principles set down by Freud, including regression to early stages of being, and offers the opportunity for constructions and interpretations of deep material.

* * *

My personal analysis in a distance learning analytic programme

I had always wanted to be a psychoanalyst but in my country, Panama, it was impossible. Then I found the International Institute of Psychoanalytic Training (IIPT) which provides distance learning in psychoanalysis for qualified mental health professionals who live remote from a training centre that includes an object relations perspective. Courses are presented in weekly telephone conference calls, supervision occurs on the telephone or by Skype, and in-person courses are organised on a modular basis requiring travel five times a year. A personal analysis four times a week with an approved analyst is required but, in the design of this institute, in-person sessions can be augmented by telephone sessions. The way the courses were organised allowed me to participate in psychoanalytic education, and the fact that sessions by telephone were accepted meant that I could find a well-trained analyst.

I was in analysis four times a week for five years using a combination of sessions in person and on the telephone. I travelled five times a year for condensed analysis—approximately two sessions per day over the space of a week, for a total of fifty in-person sessions per year. My telephone analysis took place in my office, my sessions with my analyst occurring in-between my clinical hours. The sessions were part of my working day. Sometimes it took me a few minutes to switch my attention from a patient to myself, but this difficulty was minor compared to the advantage of continuity that provided safety and stability within which I could develop the openness and basic trust required for free association.

Whether sessions took place in my office on the telephone or in my analyst's office in person, the analytic space consisted of a transitional space, located in the analytic relationship. In this co-created space, the essence of the analytic process took place, and the importance of the physical space seemed to fade. Whether in person or on the telephone, I experienced my own resistance, my transference fears and wishes. I unravelled the latent content of my dreams, and responded to the impact of interpretation.

I had a dream of being in a boat during a mild storm after which I woke up, anxious and confused. During a telephone session, I tried to analyse the dream, feeling, as I said to my analyst, that it represented something important. My analyst noted that the main affect in the dream was a fear of collapse, a fear of death. At that moment, I remembered a terrible experience from the age of five. I was with my family on a boat, when a storm suddenly tore into the boat. The ceiling of the boat flew away, the floor broke up, and water was coming in. My nanny fainted and fell on the floor. My mother and younger sisters were crying. My father and my uncle spent hours baling out the water in pails. I felt that we were all going to die. We were all terrified until we reached shore safely. Recalling this in a telephone session I felt again as if we were all going to die. My analyst sensed my feeling of dread and helped me to realise what I had been unable to face, that I was afraid of losing my father who is now elderly. Reliving this vivid experience could not have been any more immediate in person.

The major work of analysis is done in the unconscious of the patient whence the natural history of the analytic process emanates (Meltzer, 1967). I felt that, using only the audio-verbal route, it was possible to work with my unconscious and to experience an analytic process. The essence of the treatment was not the setting, but the interpsychic relationship. The continuity of telephone sessions allowed my processes of mourning to proceed uninterrupted by long absences. This continuity was essential for me to revisit the incomplete experiences of mourning the death of my child, and the early death of my mother, both of which were difficult for me. To enter these processes in-depth required continuity and space in analysis over time. I believe that interruptions in my analysis would have been frustrating and anxiety-producing, and would have blocked the work. To go into it deeply I wanted to talk to my analyst over the months, without having to leave my family.

I did not experience any important differences between the telephone sessions and those that were held in person. This may not be true for everyone, and every case should be considered individually, but for some of us it is effective, and the only way we can complete analytic training. From my own experience, I have seen the benefits of technology for promoting the growth of individuals like me and my classmates, and the development of organisations such as the International Institute for Psychoanalytic Training at the International Psychotherapy Institute where I trained and now teach. In today's world, where global communication has become so central in business, medicine, science, and social media, psychoanalytic education has to embrace technology-enhanced communication if psychoanalysis is to stay alive and make progress.

* * *

My conflicted experience of teleanalysis

I find it difficult to write about my experience with teleanalysis because of my conflicting feelings about it. Teleanalysis is a life-changing opportunity for which I am grateful but it poses difficulties. I agreed to telephone analysis because there were no analysts in my region. The ease of telephone analysis, free from the burden of commuting time to my analyst's office, was an advantage when juggling the daunting tasks associated with an analytic training programme, work, home, and family. But being unable to go and see my analyst whenever I felt I needed him to be there in person was a serious drawback. I want to discuss my concern with the temporal and spatial aspects of the arrangements, and problems with constancy and containment.

The advantage of mobility afforded by telephone analysis meant that I did not have a clean physical and temporal separation between analysis and work. I felt that I did not have a reliably private setting in which to be truly focused on my analysis. The analytic container was punctured by the potential for interruptions from both sides, including knocks on the door, phones ringing, dogs barking, and deliveries being made.

My analyst operated from several locations. Although I met him for in-person sessions at one office, I spoke to him on the telephone at both his offices, and had never seen him in one of them. This fluidity in location prevented me from imagining myself in the office with him. Added to that, the difference in time zones between us meant that I was not always in the same location for each session either. On occasions when the phone number I believed my analyst would be at was incorrect, I felt frantic about trying to find him as the time for my session trickled away. This difficulty in connecting led to feelings of not being held in mind.

On several occasions my analyst's phone was actually not working and he was not aware of the problem, which meant that I could not reach him. At other times there were problems with static in the line, poor reception, and dropped calls which required hanging up and re-dialling. These technical interferences in the line interrupted time, thought, and a sense of connection. It felt unsafe to have my analyst so far away and so silent, hidden from my emotions. Particularly at moments of regression I could not be sure that he was aware of my sense of danger or the level of difficulty I was experiencing. It was not possible to jump on a plane and travel in the middle of a painful period where I needed the physical holding of my analyst's presence and the visual constancy of his office.

In conclusion, I would much prefer analysis in person, but I did feel that analytic process occurred despite technical interferences and compromises in the setting for the analysis. The experience fundamentally changed me despite the limitations of teleanalysis.

* * *

Experiencing teleanalysis as the patient and now as the analyst

When I wanted to begin my personal analysis, I chose an analyst I trusted. I knew her from her association with a North American institute that I respected, and I thought that she would be sympathetic to my need for telephone sessions. I am trilingual, and I had lived in the United States as a child, and so for me it was not a problem to have my analysis in English. In fact, I felt quite at home. We began with a block of in-person sessions to establish the relationship and foster the development of early analytic process. We agreed to continue analysis by telephone four times a week and to meet for a series of in-person sessions several times a year.

This was the only possibility I had for analysis, since I live in Panama, a country where there were no analysts at that time. I felt that using the telephone to augment in-person analysis would give me an opportunity to have analysis with a reputable analyst, and so I decided to take it. The analyst gave me a regular time four times a week, and I provided myself a physical and emotional space from which to make the call. I chose a sofa that was near the phone in my home, and it became my analytic couch four times a week. The time was early in the morning, and it became my personal hour while others were still asleep. When the house was silent, and no one was there to interfere, I awoke from my sleep and went into a space where I worked on my dreams, thoughts, and feelings. I got used to using the phone and relating to the voice of the analyst through the phone. My mind awoke to analysis, and I moved easily into sharing my dreams and everything that came to my mind.

Telephone analysis allowed me to have the continuity I needed. It allowed me to work over time at an unhurried pace and to transcend the geographical barrier. Miles of ocean and land between us, and a time difference of one hour for half the year, were not allowed to be obstacles to my communication with my analyst or to my thinking and developing. The analytic field was established through the power of communicating. Words carrying images and feelings were carried at an immediate velocity through thousands of miles. I felt the proximity of my analyst. Sometimes when there were long silences, I had to check, and ask, "Are you there?" When I felt afraid of losing contact, the sound of the voice became the powerful evidence of our communication being open.

When sometimes I travelled, as I must do for training and to stay in touch with my family, I could continue my analysis by phone from a different location, provided I could find a private and quiet space to allow the process. The change in the time zone was a difficulty but many times it was possible to overcome that. These modifications in the time and place of the setting for my analysis affected the process and had to be analysed. Other times, when it became too complicated, my analyst and I decided that the conditions were interfering with the maintenance of our communication, and we interrupted the process until I returned home. This loss made me aware of the importance of the original setting, in my home, at the same time, in the same sofa, with the same phone. The change in the setting had an impact on me and on the analysis, and emphasised the importance of maintaining the same setting during the phone analysis.

During the in-person sessions early in my analysis, I opened up some issues that were very difficult for me, and I feel that to do so by phone would have been harder for me. I returned to these issues many times during the series of in-person sessions. Once these issues were opened up I felt contained and understood, and then phone analysis felt like a safe place to continue to work on them. Even so, on the phone, as in person, I experienced resistance. When I was five minutes late, I could not blame it on traffic or not getting a cab. I just had to walk from one room to the other! My internal struggles were expressed in these five minutes of lateness and worked through on the phone.

I would have preferred in-person analysis, and that is what I prefer for my analysands, now that I am an analyst myself. But the phone analysis worked very well for me, and without it I could not have become an analyst, which my country needed. On the phone, I could work on my issues, integrate my split feelings, and experience resistance, transference, and working through. From my own experience, I believe that phone analysis is possible if you can combine it with in-person analysis. But I think this is a personal decision. It was very important for me to have the opportunity of telephone analysis, and that may not be a key issue for other people.

Midway through my analysis, the International Psychoanalytical Association brought analytic training to Panama. This meant that I now also had the experience of condensed analysis, a requirement of the new analytic training programme. The blocks of intense condensed sessions (two sessions a day, separated in time, over ten days) gave me the opportunity to work in-depth on difficult issues. I was glad of the in-person sessions to confront my sadness about the sudden ill health of my previously spry elderly mother and my feelings about all that she had meant to me. I would have found it very difficult to leave those in-person sessions if I had to wait for months before I could return to analytic work. Instead I continued the process on the phone, working and deepening my understanding. I spoke about her vitality and her intrusiveness, my feelings of loss and guilt, and I examined my contributions to the quality of our relationship. Having phone analysis allowed me to continue to prepare for her death, to be able to share deep emotions with her, and to take extra care of her, cry together, and say goodbye before it would be too late.

Then it was time to return for routinely scheduled condensed analysis. I continued talking about my mother, who had become even more ill, and resolving more of my anxieties about losing her. Towards the end of that period of condensed analysis, I received the news that my mother was dying. I had to interrupt my precious in-person sessions to come home to Panama. By a strange coincidence, my analyst had to interrupt the condensed analysis on the same day! That same day, unknown to either of us, my analyst's mother was dying on another continent. Like me, my analyst had to fly to her country of origin to attend her mother's funeral. My phantasy is that in some way our unconscious minds were connected by shared resonance with maternal preoccupation, and in an uncanny coincidence, we both lost our mothers on the same day.

During my analysis by phone, I felt held and contained by my analyst's voice. At certain moments when there was static on the line or a long silence, we both felt the need to assure ourselves that the other was on the line, and if not, to repair our interrupted contact. I felt that the phone line was like the umbilical cord that connects the baby with the mother, and that it was equally vital for keeping our communication alive. This situation makes me think of the importance of the voice of the mother and the significant others, from the beginning of our lives in pregnancy, and ever after. During my analysis by phone, my analyst's voice and my voice became the main vehicles of communication that kept alive my analysis. I became very sensitive to sounds during our sessions, the sound of breathing, the tone of voice, the rhythm of the breathing and speech, words and silence. The sense of hearing acquired a special sensitivity that gave me information about the existence of the other through the line.

Even though neither one of us could see the body of the other, we could feel its physical presence. For example, when the analyst coughed or sneezed, my phantasies went to her health. I wondered if she was getting sick. I worried that I might be making her sick, and the fear of losing her came to mind, a real worry because I still needed my analysis, and a significant transference from my concern about my mother, and possibly also a physical expression of my analyst's countertransference, augmented by stress concerning her own mother's health. Body language was not seen but heard through these different physical manifestations—alterations in the tone of voice, quality of silences, heaviness and rhythm of the breathing, coughing, and sneezing.

Phone analysis allowed me to feel intense emotion, elaborate my dreams, associate, and experience transference and countertransference. I was able to think, work through my issues, and integrate my self. So, when one of my patients asks for a telephone session, I am willing to accept the request, analyse the dynamic meaning of the change in format, and explore its impact, as the following example shows.

Clinical example: Maria

A thirty-five-year-old woman I will call Maria consulted me because she was very depressed, crying all day, and unable to get out of bed since the death of her mother who had died on the operating table after a visit to Maria. An only child, Maria was raised by her mother after her father divorced when she was two years old. He did not call or visit, possibly because her mother was angry and kept him away. The only memory that Maria has of him from childhood is of his voice on the telephone when she was used as an intermediary by her mother to ask for money. Maria's mother was of the lower class and had to work long hours to support her child, with the help of Maria's grandmother as babysitter. Maria's mother wanted Maria to get good grades and marry well, which she did. She graduated as a physician to please her mother but really she would have preferred acting. When a medical director made a negative comment about a patient of hers, she just quit medicine.

Maria married Carlos, who has a profession and a financially rewarding position. At the beginning they had a good relationship. She helped him with his job, and he was fascinated with her. After their daughter, now age six, was born, he became a good father, but he was always busy with work. The daughter began sleeping in the marital bed. The couple's sexual life was poor, the couple had infertility problems, and Carlos had an extramarital affair, which was devastating to Maria.

Maria regards Carlos as a very good person, but one with a black cloud over him. When he comes home, he is in a sour mood and complains about everything she has done around the house. Nothing is good enough for him. She feels very lonely, and misses her mother who had become her best friend and who functioned as a buffer between Carlos and María. Yet when Carlos was unfaithful, Maria stayed with him rather than return to live with her mother because she experienced her as too strict and controlling.

After a year of psychotherapy, Maria became pregnant. After the delivery, Maria began analysis on the couch three times a week. Maria has progressed in many ways. Her mood has improved. She takes care of her two children, and she has a part-time job. She does not allow Carlos to devalue her, and she is becoming more independent. Yet it has been difficult for her to come to all her analytic sessions. She misses for reasons that are not compelling, and about once a month or every other month, she prefers to have a telephone session because it will be more convenient for her.

For two weeks before the session I will present, Maria had been holidaying at the beach. On her return she called to request a telephone session instead of her usual in-person session. It is always difficult for Maria to resume sessions after a separation, related to the loss of her father when she was two and the re-traumatisation of losing her mother in adulthood. Maria frequently prefers to have the first session after a break by phone.

Maria: I came back from the beach. I have such mixed feelings about going there. It is so much work to prepare for it that the first thing I have to do when we arrive is take a rest. It is a whole enterprise and I don't enjoy it. I get tired. The first day we all slept in one bed, my husband and I and the two children, and I awoke with a stiff back. It is very difficult to sleep with all the children in the bed. And I said to myself, this year I will not take pills for the pain. But I felt a lot of stiffness in my back and I had to have some. On the other hand, Carlos was feeling very tense since he had to travel to Japan. We didn't have sex for two weeks. I made an effort to be with him, but we are all in the same bed! We seem to be doing everything we can not to have sex. Putting the children into our bed ….

Yesterday Carlos had a family therapy session with his brothers, and I drove my sister-in-law to her session with her psychologist. I had helped my second sister-in-law prepare a budget for my third sister-in-law who manages the family finances, so she gets the right amount of money she needs. And I visited my father-in-law, who is sick and is quite disconnected. So I entertained him. My sister-in-law called me to thank me for my help. And Carlos also thanked me for helping his sisters and keeping his father company. I told him that the problem was he overloaded me but he said that I was overloading myself. So I told him, you think everything is about work. I need some pleasure too. And you do not take care of me.

Analyst: I feel you tell me little stories about other people and other therapies, and avoid telling me about you. What about your sexual pleasure?
Maria: We have had so many complications that we can't have sex and I can't feel the sexual pleasure. I have other pleasures.
Analyst: I feel that what goes on with me is similar to what goes on with Carlos. You bring in to your bed the two children and you bring into our session your sisters-in-law and your father-in-law.
Maria: Analysis is difficult for me. I like it but it is difficult. Sometimes I feel afraid, that I am getting stronger and I am feeling I want to separate from Carlos, I feel so distant from him. That is terrible. I need love, care, and attention. I need to feel that I am the centre of someone's life. I have never been the centre of Carlos's life. When my mother was alive she filled in for the emptiness. Now I really feel it. I am busy with many things: my children fulfil me, and I do my work. What freaks me out is that Carlos doesn't notice the emotional emptiness.
Analyst: He doesn't notice your feelings and that makes you feel …
Maria: Angry and sad. I have told him. When we fight, I speak out and tell him how I feel. After that, we have like a peace period. We are content with each other but this lasts a very short time. I want him to be with me and think about me. This has been my desire for such a long time, hasn't it?
Analyst: You have wanted to be the centre of the life of a man for a very long time—to be the centre of your father's life, and now of your husband's life—and you feel it can't happen.

Maria: Yes, this is so true. I always wanted to be the centre of my father's life, but he never paid attention to me. I remember when my mother made me call him for the alimony, and how it was a constant fight all the time—me calling, him not coming with the money, me calling him again, insisting. That happened since I was a small girl. It hurt me that he never called me to find out about me, wonder how I felt, ask if I needed something. He never took me out, to a park, to have an ice cream, to the movies. Nothing. I was very angry at him. Yes, he totally disconnected from my mother, but why from me? Wasn't I his daughter? Not even a phone call. Sometimes I think that my mother was very angry at him and didn't allow him to get closer to me. She kept him at a distance. She was tough. I don't blame him for having separated from her. Now I understand.

My mother filled all the space when I was a child. She provided me with everything. She worked very hard. She was out of the house for many hours. She was strict—she wanted me to do things, be a good student, marry well, get a profession. I did all those things. But when Carlos and I had problems, she was my friend. She took me out, helped me with my child, and we used to go to the movies a lot. She didn't have money when I was a kid, so we used to go to movies where we paid fifty cents and saw two movies. She made me laugh. She was strict and controlling but was also lots of fun. And when I had problems with Carlos, she was like a buffer: she made it easier to be with him; she took me away from my suffering; and she was always with me. Now that she is dead, I am alone with Carlos. It has been very difficult, because he doesn't want to be with me, have fun, go out, anything. I understand that he is very stressed out at work, but that is not a good enough excuse for being irritable all the time.

Analyst: So when you had problems with Carlos, you escaped into your mother's company and relationship. Without her, you feel the emptiness of no closeness and intimacy with Carlos, and you miss being close to a man, but it is an old way of relating to men in your life. You find yourself with another man who cannot get close to you.

Maria: It is so true. My first boyfriend was that way too: he used to drive me crazy, wanting to be with me, and then going out with other women. He ignored me like my father. I stopped that relationship but it took me a long time.

Discussion

Maria's mother had high expectations of Maria and directed her choices when she was young. After Maria was married, her mother became her best friend, spending time with her daughter that she had not had when Maria was a girl. Maria was grateful, and yet resistant to her mother's attempts to control her. Maria now works her body hard for long hours in voluntary exercise, a way of staying close to her mother whose circumstances compelled her to long days of physical labour and perhaps a hope of transforming drudgery into physical resilience. When she lost her mother suddenly, Maria became deeply depressed. It occurs to me that Maria's preference for the telephone after a separation may relate to having lost her mother. Separation may activate a fear that she or I will die when driving home after being together in person at my office which is in a medical building. Since I at least would prefer to have the session in person, I think she sets up the distance of the telephone contact in order to experience me as another man she cannot get close to.

Maria passively accepts her husband's wish to have the children in the bed with them. In agreeing to this, Maria is showing her own resistance to intimacy. The children are the glue that keeps her and her husband together and they are also a buffer, just as Maria's mother was a buffer between Maria and her husband. From another perspective Maria seems to be repairing her broken internal couple, represented by the two children in the bed. In the material there is a profusion of the numbers two and three—two children, three sisters-in-law, three in the marriage when the latest affair is counted in, and three triads of Maria, mother, and Carlos; Maria, mother, and me; and Maria, father, and me.

After she had been in psychoanalysis for some months, in an unusually assertive move, Maria travelled to visit her father. She was quite upset to see him installed in his new life with his wife and children, and will never go to visit him again. Nor will she lie on my couch any more. I find this a curious coincidence of refusals that points to an activation of the paternal transference. Refusing the couch, Maria does not claim her own space in my office, and remains ambivalent about analysis, although she ensures her place in my calendar by always paying promptly and without question for the many sessions that she misses for reasons that seem unimportant, or asks for a phone session. I find myself not believing her excuses for not show-ing up in person, much as she and her mother did not believe her father's excuses for not show-ing up with the money.

When Maria requests a phone session at short notice, I agree to her request, rather than miss another session. My own analysis was partly on the telephone and so I am quite comfortable with that medium and convinced of its usefulness, but I always preferred the in-person sessions for myself, as I do for Maria. This comfort on my part led me to go along with the request. I now see that I felt obliged to please her, as she felt she had to please her mother. I am being given to feel controlled by her, as she was controlled by her mother and is controlled by her husband. In addition, Maria often requests a shift in the schedule to a time later in the day, which I see as an attempt to reconnect with her mother whom she saw at the end of her work day. I see the phone session as an enactment of her history with her father as well. As a child, Maria longed to see her father but all she got was his voice on the telephone. She is replaying her story of talking to her father on the telephone, this time trying to find it an adequate substitute. Perhaps Maria wants me to miss her and long for her full commitment so that I will understand her painful longing for her father from deep inside my own experience. I am being experienced in the light of the paternal transference on the phone, the maternal transference in person, the two parents kept split, just as they were in real life.

Conclusion

Analysis by telephone is an adaptation of psychoanalysis that we should embrace in our mod-ern times, to allow us to overcome geographical distances in order to work on our minds. The field that is established in an analysis could be conceived of as a virtual space. Is it not true that all analyses are created in an artificial space and time, made up by the analyst and the analysand? Psychoanalysis is a mental process that could be said to be located in an office but it does not reside only there. The analytic space becomes a mental space that transcends the physical spaces in which it occurs. It is intangible and does not need a room to be able to be. This is a big advantage for the mind.

As analysts, we are working with the mind and in the mind. So why locate our work in a room or an office? Space and time are not restricted to specific, concrete places. They exist universally and especially in our minds. Telephone analysis is different from in-person analysis because of its heightened reliance on voice for the communication of emotion and unconscious fantasy, and yet it is the same in that it involves conscious and unconscious communication between two minds. A telephone session feels as if it were in person in that, like in-person analysis, telephone analysis is the product of two people in a relationship, creating an analytical space, a field, and a powerful, reparative unconscious interaction.

References

Bollas, C. (1993). An interview with Christopher Bollas. *Psychoanalytic Dialogues*, 3: 401–430.
Freud, S. (1919a). Lines of advance in psycho-analytic therapy. *S. E.*, *17* (pp. 157–168). London: Hogarth.
Freud, S. (1937d). Constructions in analysis. *S. E.*, *23* (pp. 255–269). London: Hogarth.
Scharff, J. S. & Scharff, D. E. (1998). Geography of transference and countertransference. In: *Object Relations Individual Therapy* (pp. 241–281). Northvale, NJ: Jason Aronson.

CHAPTER NINETEEN

A male analyst reflects on his teleanalysis when a candidate

Geoffrey C. Anderson, PhD

I was long interested in pursuing analytic training. However. I live in the Midwest, far from any analytic training institute, and there my personal and professional commitments mean that moving near a traditional institute is out of the question. When the opportunity arose to pursue training in a distance-learning model institute with which I was already familiar, I was ready to begin. But I would need a personal analysis. Once again my geographical location was an obstacle. There was no local analyst. In order to complete the personal analysis component of the training, I was going to have to do a distance analysis. The institute was open to candidates working by telephone provided an adequate portion of the analysis would be conducted in person. The institute required a level of in-person analysis sufficient to establish an analytic relationship of integrity and to provide the foundation for an authentic analytic process to develop. I had received a long-term psychodynamic psychotherapy in person with a local therapist who had some analytic training. She and I had explored many of my defences and Oedipal conflicts but not my pre-Oedipal issues with object relatedness. For instance, I was aware that there were family-of-origin issues still to be addressed, particularly my relationships with my parents in the past, in the here-and-now, and in their symbolic meaning to me. My psychotherapy had been limited in that the therapist had not been able to interpret the transference fully and the treatment lacked sufficient intensity. I hoped that an analysis would confront these issues. But where would I find an analyst?

I had to find someone who was a qualified analyst and who would be willing to work with me by telephone. I also wanted someone with whom I could have regular work in person. This narrowed the options to working with someone who was easy to get to by air or preferably someone within reasonable driving distance. I was located a three hour drive from a city which had formerly had a traditional analytic institute until a few years ago. By searching the website of the American Psychoanalytic Association I found several training analysts still residing in that city. I sent out an email to all of the analysts I could identify by this means and received two responses. One was from a psychologist who informed me that there might be difficulties with this because of cross-state licensing issues. The other email was from a lay analyst who would be interested in working with me in this format and was intrigued by the distance-learning model. She would be willing to have a telephone interview to gather more information. I was both excited and anxious about this telephone interview. What would it be like to talk to some-one I had never met about my earlier treatment and my desire to be an analyst?

I was nervous about being turned down because that would mean having to work with someone at a much greater distance. We spoke by telephone and had a good conversation about the training requirements of the distance-learning institute, my previous psychotherapy train-ing and experience, and a sketch of what I had worked on in my prior psychotherapy. It was a good conversation, and so, as we spoke, my initial anxiety about the interview gave way to feeling more relaxed and comfortable with the process. I began to get a sense of the competence and professionalism of the analyst, whose way of working was in sharp contrast to that of my previous therapist, and she got a preliminary sense of me as a potential analysand. At the end of our phone interview we agreed to meet for two in-person evaluation sessions on a Saturday with a couple of hours between them.

I could have entered into analysis with a personal analyst on the faculty of the distance-learning institute, easily accessible by air, but I preferred not to. The institute had made the deci-sion to let candidates choose their own personal analyst as long as that analyst was qualified in a manner equivalent to that required of a training analyst approved by the American Psycho-analytic Association or the International Psychoanalytical Association. I was glad to have that option because I wanted an analyst who was not part of my evaluation process, for conscious and unconscious reasons. The conscious motivation for my preference was to be free of the transference as much as possible in my learning experience as an analytic candidate, and from the complications of dual relationships like those I had experienced in our small community with my previous therapist, who I felt had not handled that situation well. One of the uncon-scious motivations that I am now aware of was to avoid the activation of an internalised over-anxious and hovering critical-mother imago. For all these reasons, I hoped that the evaluation would lead to a commitment for analysis.

On the appointed date I travelled to the analyst's home city and met with her in person for the first time. I felt an immediate comfort with her quiet and contained style. We discussed in greater detail what I had worked on during my psychotherapy. As the first hour drew to a close, it felt as though very little time had passed, and I looked forward to the second session. After spending a few hours exploring the city, I returned for the second in-person session in which I continued to share my personal history with the analyst. It was both relieving and anxiety-producing to speak so openly of my past and the issues that had brought me to therapy. As the session wound down we began to discuss the possibility of an analysis conducted by telephone with regular in-person sessions following the model of the consultation. The ana-lyst said that, based on my openness during the two evaluation sessions, she was willing to begin. She remarked on my willingness to share painful material with her and my capacity to bear the pain without being overly defended. We agreed that we would begin four-times-a-week analysis conducted over the telephone and that once a month I would travel to her office for two in-person sessions separated by an hour or more in-between. We also agreed on the arrangements for the telephone analysis. I would lie on the couch in my office and call her at the designated time. I would use a headset in order to facilitate communication without having to hold the phone in my hand. Given the travel distance and our schedule I would be able to drive down, have the sessions, and return to my home on the same day. So the decision was made. Her willingness to work with me in this unusual frame allowed me the opportunity to learn in an environment uncomplicated by a dual relationship in the training institute. I have come to appreciate the wisdom of my choice and I value it more and more as I continue my growth as an analyst.

As my analytic training progressed alongside my analysis, I began to learn more about the analytic process and to see how it was occurring in my own analysis. Communicating consciously and unconsciously on the telephone, I was able to free associate and to be made aware of my defences through the analyst's interventions. I shared dreams and we analysed them together. I discovered that I could not hide myself in recounting the events of my life in four-times-a-week analysis as I could do in once-a-week or twice weekly psychotherapy. I quickly ran out of life events to share and was forced to experience the unconscious productions of my mind more directly. I had sometimes experienced the transference powerfully in my psychotherapy but I did not feel immersed in it and I did not feel safe enough to speak of it directly. I did not detect it in my free associations in psychotherapy as clearly as I did in the analysis. Increasing the frequency of sessions to four times a week gave more time for the transference to intensify and be made clear to me. The analyst's evident ability to contain and reflect on the transference was helpful in exploring the deep roots of my reactions and in the resolution of many of my anxieties. I say this here not to state the obvious concerning analytic process but to convey that I experienced a deep and satisfactory analytic experience over the telephone.

For the most part the experience on the telephone was one of feeling contained and being able to sustain the analytic process. I free-associated and my analyst listened. She asked questions, made observations and occasionally gave an interpretation. Awareness of being on the telephone was present but not usually intrusive in my mind. I experienced an ongoing analytic process that built from day to day and week to week. The rhythm of the analysis was maintained, as it would be in person, in contrast to what I have heard of the experience of condensed shuttle analysis in which the candidate has multiple sessions over a defined period of time, and no contact with the analyst between times. I had the normal arrangement of four sessions a week at the appointed time and I experienced the process developing from the beginning of the week to the last session of the week. I also had the experience of the rhythm of breaks in the analysis for the analyst's away times. I found this to be most helpful to me in understanding my own analysands' experiences of my absences during my training.

In the first months of analysis, there was the usual process of a beginning, for me to know the analyst and for her to know me. We learned the way we would work together as we began to build up the hours of the analysis. In the beginning, I was anxious each time I called, wondering if my analyst would be there to answer the phone. One of the ways I would occupy myself in my anxiety in the early phase of the analysis was to focus on the telephone as a medium. I would listen to the quality of the phone line connection. I would concentrate on the type of sounds on the line and the noise of the interference, which could be different from day to day. I also had to deal with the paranoid fantasies that someone might be listening in to my conversations with my analyst. The rational side of my mind would chime in, saying, "If they are they must be terribly bored listening to my free associations every day." These reactions were in marked contrast to what it was like to go to the analyst's office for the in-person sessions. There I would distract myself by looking around the office from her couch. I would pay attention to the smells and textures and the objects in the room that I could see. Both reactions made use of my experience of the environment of the analysis in a defensive fashion. I was protecting myself from feelings of attachment to and dependency on the analyst. The way in which these were different in person and on the telephone continued as a theme for exploration throughout the analysis. In some ways it felt like two different analyses and in other ways it was definitely a unified experience of one analysis.

A number of things became apparent to me as the analysis progressed solidly into the opening phase. I realised that my analyst could not see me, and so I could hide my behaviour from her. I could get away with things. Early on I decided that I did not want this to happen. If I became aware of a physical response such as a posture or rhythmic motion I must describe it to her so that she could make use of the information in our work. I also needed to describe my reactions to the use of the telephone to my analyst as they occurred. Of course this did not address the behaviours that were beyond my awareness but that the analyst might have observed in person.

If there were a silence on the line I would ask if she was still there. Initially we investigated the anxieties these silences evoked both in the use of the telephone as a medium for analysis as well as in my associations. After a time they became an expected part of the frame of our work. Either of us might check in if the silence seemed too quiet. Usually we found that the connection was still present but there were a handful of times where the line was dead and we had to re-call. Each of these incidents was analysed for the specific experience of abandonment and loss that had been stirred up in me. After several months of work I invested in a stereo headset, which I modified to work with my telephone so that I could hear the analyst in both ears. This greatly enhanced the experience of hearing the analyst's breathing, movements, and other ambient sounds that increased my awareness of her presence through the phone. This seemed to reduce the experience of the distance between us and allowed me to create a fuller mental experience of her presence.

One particularly striking experience on the telephone happened on a day on which there were construction noises outside the analyst's office. I was aware of the noises as an intrusion in much the same way that I would have been if I were present in the office. About halfway through our session someone began to pound on the analyst's door. The pounding persisted until the analyst excused herself to address the situation. I was in essence left in limbo on my headset unable to hear anything after the analyst had stepped outside her consulting room. I experienced anxiety, flashes of the analyst being attacked and murdered, and fears that I would be left in limbo forever. In the moment I was aware that my images were fantastical and unlikely but the emotional experience was quite powerful. I spoke to the analyst about the fantasies when she returned to the phone. She apologised for the intrusion but did not discuss what actually happened at her door. So I was usefully left with my fantasies to explore. In retrospect I can see the very deep roots of the fantasy lie in projective identifications with my mother in relation to her deeply paranoid and violent father. At the time I was able to analyse the aggression in my rage at being left by the analyst and in my Oedipal fears of an angry father bursting in on the mother and child in intimate connection. I do believe that the impact of the experience was more powerful as a result of it occurring during a telephone session and my lack of contextual input, which would have allowed me to construct different kinds of defences against the fantasy. This scene highlights the way in which the telephone as a medium for the analysis created a much more powerful and less defended internal experience of fantasy.

I was to become very aware of the analyst as a mental construct throughout the course of the analysis. When on the telephone I was much more aware of the process of creating the analyst since I was not experiencing her in an actual physical manner. I was noticing a kind of visual image of the analyst floating at the edge of my awareness. When in her office I was aware of her physical presence in person, and of the mental construct of her that I was bringing with me from the telephone analysis. I was then able to surrender this need in the physical presence of the analyst, and then there was no visual image of the analyst in my mind, until I returned to the use of the telephone. This made me wonder whether the experience of the analyst in the physical dimension might be used to defend against knowing how much the analyst is a mental creation of the analysand in the transference. I am sure that I would have been more blissfully unaware of the process of projection occurring if I were in a traditional in-person only analysis. As it happened I was always noticing, often on the edge of awareness, that I was creating an image of the analyst. By the end of the month, between in-person sessions I was aware of being uncertain of what my analyst actually looked like. I was also beginning to become aware of the pieces of my mother, my wife and my previous therapist I was grafting on to my analyst. Whenever I had this in central consciousness it could become a direct part of the work in a productive way. I certainly found this to be a very powerful part of the analysis.

I was also quite aware as time passed of the ways in which I began to relate to my analyst in in-person sessions more as a unique person in her own right. My initial anxiety about the sense of intimacy of her office and the physical proximity of being in the room with her began to lessen. I began to become aware of aspects of the analyst as a person that were part of her presence as an analyst. She was gentle and compassionate and had a great capacity to contain my anxieties and help me digest them. This was in such stark contrast to my experiences with my mother growing up that at first I was not sure it was real. As the experiences began to accumulate I began to be able to understand that this was truly a part of her character as well as her professional stance, and it had a profound impact on me. One aspect of the dual nature of the analysis was the manner in which this experience of the analyst as a person, in person, was parallel to the experience of the analyst as a mental construct, on the phone. On the phone the analyst as a person was less accessible to me until towards the end of the treatment when the two experiences began to come together. I was aware of this split in my experience more clearly as the analysis progressed and it became a topic of exploration in the analysis.

My analysis progressed quite well. As the various defences, conflicts, and anxieties were analysed, I became aware of a kind of growth I had never experienced before. It was a growth of my self and character as I let go of archaic ways of dealing with object relatedness. One of the most profound changes was a dropping away of fears and anxieties about how I was being judged by others. As a result of this I was able to allow myself to show my intellect and capacities in my training programme and other aspects of my relationship to the institute. I took on more responsibilities in my work as a faculty member in the psychotherapy programmes. I wrote more freely. I began to be more self-reflective in my work as an analyst and psychotherapist. I was able to make better and freer use of the supervision experiences, and I lost my anxiety about presenting my work in public. As the analysis moved into the termination phase and my dependency on the analyst began to decrease, I noticed an interesting change in the two modes of analysis. I began to experience the phone and in-person sessions as much less distinct from each other. As the transference lessened and I was more comfortable experiencing the analyst as a whole person, I brought the mental construct and the actually experienced analyst together. This synthesis marked the final work of the analysis and was mostly complete at termination.

Following the termination of the analysis I have experienced the continuation of the analytic process within myself. I have a well-developed capacity for self-analysis. I can become aware of when I feel something is blocked in unconscious processes and I continue to be curious about the unconscious in others and myself. My experience is of having had a successful and complete analysis. This would seem to be confirmed by the fact that I successfully completed training and graduated as an analyst. I have worked with many well-respected analysts internationally and received positive feedback on my skills and abilities. I have assumed advanced leadership positions within my institute and co-led study programmes in distance analysis. Certainly this one experience does not provide sufficient evidence of the capacity of telephone analysis to be a viable medium for effective therapeutic work or candidate analysis, but it is an illustration of the potential of working in this way for future work with both patient and candidate. Further study should be undertaken to confirm my experience as being the norm and not an exception. I am grateful to have had the opportunity to experience analysis in this way, as it would not have been possible for me to undergo the analysis otherwise.

CHAPTER TWENTY

Technology-assisted supervision and consultation

Janine Wanlass, PhD

A distressed supervisee leaves me a phone message. "I think we'd better talk before my next session with L (patient). I'm annoyed and pretty rattled." An experienced clinician, the supervisee knows when he is overwhelmed and muddled by his countertransference response. I return his phone call, and we agree to speak briefly by telephone later that day. This is a decision of necessity and convenience. I have no open clinical hours. He needs my assistance before his next scheduled supervision. I believe that even a brief consultation will help, and we can discuss these clinical issues in more detail when we meet in person.

Any practising clinician has either sent and/or received a similar message. Generally, we see such action as clinically prudent and ethically responsible—a clinician who is seeking consultation when mired in a difficult case. Unless it is patterned behaviour by the supervisee, we do not focus on the method of supervisory contact. Thinking about the use of the phone is pre-empted by the clinical dilemma that prompted the call. In fact, such contact amounts to a form of technology-assisted supervision and consultation (TASC). We are using a mechanical device such as a telephone, computer, or videoconferencing equipment to conduct a supervisory encounter over a geographic distance.

In reality, distance supervision of psychoanalysis and psychoanalytic psychotherapy has existed since the beginning of talk therapy, when Freud often responded to clinical concerns by letter. For many years, we have used audio and video recording technology to enhance supervision of students in graduate training, allowing us to see and hear the actual session material rather than relying on the trainee's self-report (Clark, 2010). Although the use of technology or distance communication in supervision is not new, rapid technological advances are changing the face of supervision in concert with similar shifts in the provision of counselling services. Systematic research, thoughtful consideration, and meaningful discussion of these changes and their effects on the supervisory process have not kept pace with the technology, as evidenced by the relative scarcity of available literature on the topic (Groman, 2010; Manosevitz, 2007). Professional licensing boards and ethics committees of professional mental health associations are struggling to quickly and effectively frame guidelines and regulations for distance mental health practices (Coursol, Lewis & Seymour, 2010; McAdams & Wyatt, 2010).

This chapter addresses four primary aspects of TASC. First, it outlines significant ethical concerns. Second, commonalities with and adaptations from traditional supervisory processes are described. Third, drawing from my supervisory experiences over the telephone and Skype within the United States and abroad, some unique challenges in applying TASC are portrayed. Lastly, the relative benefits and weaknesses of TASC are discussed with recommendations for further thought and research. Although supervisory services utilising technology often incorporate a variety of formats including email, text messaging, bug-in-the-ear, and videoconferencing, this chapter will focus exclusively on telephone and Skype use.

Ethical considerations

Much of the ethical debate and reported concerns regarding TASC are drawn from the parallel discussion of distance counselling. Under the Health Insurance Portability and Accountability Act of 1996 (HIPAA), distance counselling is not prohibited, but adequate privacy and security standards must be met (Baker & Bufka, 2011; Barnett & Scheetz, 2003). These standards would also apply to distance supervisory practices. The American Counseling Association (ACA), the National Board of Certified Counselors (NBCC), and the American Mental Health Counselors Association (AMHCA) have developed specific ethical guidelines about technology-assisted distance counselling (Kaplan, 2006; McAdams & Wyatt, 2010; Trepal, Haberstroh, Duffey & Evans, 2007). No doubt other professional organisations will incorporate similar changes as ethical codes for each mental health discipline are revised. State licensing and regulatory boards for mental health practice are beginning to weigh in on issues of technology. According to research by McAdams and Wyatt (2010), some state licensing boards have forbidden distance counselling and supervision completely, some have established additional certification requirements for distance counsellors and supervisors, and still others are considering what, if any, regulations to establish.

Part of the question is one of jurisdiction. Who has regulatory authority over distance counselling and TASC? Given that the supervisee and supervisor are in different geographic locations, where does the supervisory encounter take place? Certainly, the supervisor is required to be licensed to practise and supervise in her home state, but is she also required to meet licensing and supervision standards for the state in which the supervisee resides? What about providing consultation to clinical practitioners in foreign countries with vastly different licensing standards? For example, I supervise a graduate student in Mongolia, where mental health practice is in its infancy and only psychiatrists are licensed. Although granted permission by my local licensing board to proceed, what ethics and standards guide such a decision? Should Skype supervision count as face-to-face?

In discussing this issue with my state licensing board for professional counsellors, we devised a solution that met both the spirit and the language of the law. We puzzled over the definition of face-to-face, because it was clear that when the law was passed, face-to-face meant in person. We agreed that the student would be supervised in person by a licensed psychiatrist in Mongolia and receive additional support and supervision from me via Skype. Both forms of supervisory contact seemed ethically necessary, as the Mongolian psychiatrist would have legal authority and greater expertise about relevant cultural issues in local clinical practice, but I had more experience with psychotherapy interventions, professional ethical guidelines, and masters programme training requirements. In addition, my existing mentoring relationship with the student was an important factor in providing containment for her anxiety as she adjusted to clinical practice in a foreign country.

Most writers on this topic of jurisdiction conclude that the supervisor should enquire about standards and restrictions to providing supervision in both jurisdictions—where the supervisor practises and where the supervisee resides (Kaplan, 2006; McAdams & Wyatt, 2010). This is particularly critical when the supervisee is unlicensed or accruing hours for clinical licensing at the level of independent practice, but it also seems relevant when providing clinical consultation to seasoned, licensed mental health practitioners. Supervisors should be aware that some guidelines are discipline specific. For example, professional counsellors, psychiatrists, social workers, nurses, and psychologists may have different requirements regarding TASC.

Jurisdiction is not the only ethical issue facing distance supervisors. Other relevant concerns include the supervisory pair's familiarity and comfort with technology (Vaccaro & Lambie, 2007). For example, younger practitioners tend to be much more adept with Skype than older, "technophobic" practitioners who may require more training to achieve a level of technological proficiency and comfort. Managing confidential information across phone or internet presents some unique challenges (Barnett & Scheetz, 2003; Olson, Russell & White, 2001; Vaccaro & Lambie, 2007). For telephone supervision, I prefer a landline rather than a cellphone, because cellphone communications are less secure. I have supervisees encrypt any clinical notes sent by email, which prohibits access without a password. I encourage supervisees to minimise conveying identifying patient information, such as names, initials, or places of work. If they are working in an agency, educational institution, hospital, or business setting, we discuss who has access to their email account. For example, instructional services administrators typically can override personal passwords to enter an email account, which could compromise a patient's privacy (Kanz, 2001).

Supervision should be conducted in a private space, such as a clinical office, where the discussion cannot be overheard (Coursol, Lewis & Seymour, 2010). Research on distance counselling and supervision supports the use of a specific informed consent for TASC, outlining these confidentiality risks and safeguards (Baker & Bufka, 2011; Barnett & Scheetz, 2003; Kanz, 2001; Kaplan, 2006; Olson, Russell & White, 2001; Trepal, Haberstroh, Duffey & Evans, 2007; Vaccaro & Lambie, 2007). In their informed consent for patients, clinicians seeking TASC could include an explanation of their use of distance supervision and the confidentiality risks it poses (Coursol, Lewis & Seymour, 2010). While the confidentiality concerns are not insignificant, in some instances distance supervision may offer greater confidentiality, such as in rural areas where a local supervisor may be acquainted with the patient being discussed. I see a number of local clinicians in treatment, and I am much more comfortable seeking consultation on such cases from a distance supervisor, who will likely have no professional contact with my patients.

The question of managing clinical crises presents some complexity for distance supervisors (Janoff & Schoenholtz-Read, 1999; Kanz, 2001). The supervisory pair should discuss in advance what to do when a crisis occurs. Does the supervisee have a direct means of contacting the supervisor? For example, I supervise an experienced clinician in China by Skype, but she has a phone number to contact me should an emergency arise or should some difficulty occur connecting over the internet. I must confess that this plan emerged when her internet server crashed, and she did not know how to reach me by phone. Neither of us anticipated this possibility, and so we were caught unprepared. Backup means of communication should be arranged when setting the frame for clinical supervision. Additionally, supervisory pairs need to discuss available community resources and methods of hospitalising unstable patients. The supervisory pair can identify and contact a senior local clinician who can serve in a supervisory role should the supervisee require more assistance. Although such arrangements would be typical in any supervision, with TASC the supervisor must rely on the supervisee to identify local resources.

One of the more interesting and challenging ethical dilemmas I encounter as a distance supervisor occurs when consulting in cultures less familiar to me. For instance, I knew very little about Mongolia or Mongolian mental health treatment prior to my graduate student's sudden relocation to this region. With the assistance of my student, I quickly educated myself to help her provide culturally sensitive mental health practice. I could not think of a better alternative than the arrangement we constructed, but I certainly questioned my ability to be an effective supervisor in this context. Fortunately, I was familiar with using translators for teaching and psychotherapy, as I had used translators in China and supervised student placements where translators were required. This helped me understand and problem-solve practical issues she encountered with translation, plus consider the effect of a translator on the therapeutic process itself. Together, we had to think through applications of Western ideas of therapy, such as how to establish a therapeutic frame or explain confidentiality in a setting where routine office visits and HIPAA do not exist.

In China, mental health practitioners often consult clinicians in Western countries, particularly regarding psychoanalytic psychotherapy, which is less known there (Fishkin, Fishkin, Leli, Katz & Synder, 2011). Receiving consultation from me on his couple work, a supervisee expressed distress about the short-term nature of his excursions into couple therapy. Sensing that he was blaming himself for what might be a cultural difference in practice, I asked about the typical length of couple therapy in his community. He informed me that couple work is usually brief in nature, and I was able to discuss with him the conclusions he was drawing about his own competency based on a cultural norm. We were able to consider how a particular couple's dynamics aided by this cultural norm were transmitted through projective identification, leaving him feeling responsible for the couple's eventual divorce. Additionally, my experiences in China have impressed upon me the psychological significance of government policies on family emotional life, such as the "one child rule" or the legacy of the Cultural Revolution. To be an ethical, competent distance supervisor, I must ask and learn about these matters, rather than make assumptions based on Western ideas about Chinese culture. Although cultural issues exist in any supervisory pair, they are magnified when the participants come from vastly different, geographically distant cultures. The supervisor must rely in part on the supervisee to educate the supervisor regarding social issues and common practices, which has an effect on the supervisory dynamic. The power differential is significantly lessened, as in some ways the supervisor becomes the student of the supervisee.

Comparisons to traditional supervisory practices

Technology-assisted supervision and consultation (TASC) shares more commonalities than differences with traditional supervision. Central to its effectiveness is the supervisory relationship, which helps contain the supervisee's anxiety and vulnerability, acts at times as a parallel process to the patient/psychotherapist encounter, and provides a protected, generative psychological space for thinking (Coursol, Lewis & Seymour, 2010; Manosevitz, 2006). Jacobs, David, and Meyer (1995) describe the initial phase of traditional psychoanalytic supervision, where each party listens to the other's tone, content, non-verbal cues, expressed needs, areas of heightened focus, and overall manner. It is a time of getting settled in the supervisory encounter, evaluating the match between supervisor and supervisee, and finding a way of working together.

In TASC, the initial phase may be in person or at a distance. Starting with an in-person format is preferable, particularly when the future communication will be by telephone, as it allows both supervisor and supervisee to establish a concrete mental picture of each other to carry across time and space (Manosevitz, 2006). Although I do not consciously try to imagine my supervisee when speaking by telephone, my mind naturally drifts to an image of her, which helps solidify a sense of connection. As the initial in-person contact ends, the supervisory pair must adjust to the loss experienced with the shift to a distance modality. It is important to anticipate and process this shift, as it represents a change in the supervisory frame. In one such instance, I remarked on a sort of wistful, longing I felt between us. My supervisee commented, "Well, I knew it would be different now that we're not meeting in person. It's just what's possible." Although this was a factual representation of the change, it sidestepped the direct affective expression of loss, something this supervisee defended against consciously but transmitted over the telephone in her tone of voice.

Sometimes the supervisory relationship begins through distance technology. When this is by telephone, my initial point of identification is the supervisee's voice. My mind creates a fantasy image, again not consciously constructed. I am often startled when I eventually meet the supervisee face-to-face, because my fantasy image and her actual features do not match. It is similar to seeing a movie version of a book you have read, where the actor may or may not resemble the character you have imagined. Although the loss of visual cues makes non-verbal communication more difficult to detect, I find I pay more attention to the subtle changes in vocal tone, pitch, and volume. I listen for shifts in position or breathing, as the supervisee moves about in his chair or emits a sigh. I make my own non-verbal communications explicit, telling the supervisee in words what I might otherwise convey in a facial expression or bodily stance. I rely on the supervisee to do the same, and I ask for a description when I suspect something may be happening that I cannot see. For instance, a phone supervisee was describing an intense countertransference response. I thought she might be crying, but I was unsure. When I asked, she responded that she was, but she had not wanted me to know. We then spoke about her need for me to see her as competent, and her wish to cover up signs of vulnerability.

When using Skype, the interaction with supervisees is quite similar to that in person, because I have a face-to-face connection and am able to detect most non-verbal cues. What is different, however, is that I see a slice of my supervisees' external world. We are no longer just in my office; rather, they are bringing their home or office into the supervisory space. I learn something of them through their choice of art and furniture or a child's sudden, unexpected entry into the supervisory encounter. As a supervisor, I need to be sensitive to the increased vulnerability this creates for my supervisees, as I see more of their personal life than would typically be known. I also need to be cognisant of potential distractions and their clinical meaning. For example, in one instance of Skype supervision I was inordinately preoccupied with a sunset I could see through the supervisee's window, prompting thoughts about our different time zones. As I struggled to make a connection between my "distraction" and the clinical material, the supervisee associated from the time reference to a sense of temporal discontinuity that he had experienced in the patient's self-narrative. Most of my moments of distraction do not have such blatant clinical relevance, but I attend to them as I would during an in-person supervisory session.

Much as in traditional supervisory arrangements, a frame for the supervisory work is established and maintained (Coursol, Lewis & Seymour, 2010; Groman, 2010). Typically, the supervisory pair selects a regular time for meeting, establishes a means of contact, decides how clinical material will be transmitted, and agrees on a fee and method of payment such as wire transfer or cheque sent by mail. The pair establishes that the supervisee will send process notes by password protected email, will telephone the supervisor at the appointed hour, and will pay the bill as agreed. In setting a fee for supervisees from other regions, either inside the United States or abroad, I ask the supervisee about fee schedules in his geographic area. Where possible, I attempt to take this into consideration when setting a fee. For instance, most clinicians in China make significantly less than those in the United States, and so I often reduce my consultation fee. I do explore fully the supervisee's need for this fee reduction, and I avoid entering into a masochistic fee arrangement that I will later resent.

In addition to the practical aspects of the supervisory frame, it also involves a mindset about the clinical work. In this arena, I see no differences between TASC and traditional supervision. Each involves meeting the supervisee at her developmental level, identifying areas of clinical strength and challenge, working from a particular theoretical orientation, agreeing on supervisory goals and areas of focus (some that are evident at the outset, some that emerge over time), and joining together for the well-being of both supervisee and the patients she serves. Since I operate from an object relations framework, TASC involves examining our supervisory relationship and process in addition to the clinician/patient relationships being discussed. Once when I was travelling for an extended period, I supervised some of my regularly in-person supervisees by Skype. One supervisee saw little difference between Skype and in person, noting that I seemed "in the room" with her either way. Quite familiar with Skype, she comfortably discussed the week's clinical events with her patients. Another supervisee felt Skype was "too close, too intrusive", as she could hear the rhythm of my breathing through the microphone and felt the intensity of my gaze. She expressed a level of panic much more intense than in my office, perhaps resulting from a combination of my being away and the "in-your-face" experience amplified by the technology. Much as in traditional supervision, I think my absence and the change in frame simply amplified existing aspects of these supervisory relationships, bringing them into the room for consideration.

As in the example of preoccupation with a sunset backdrop mentioned earlier, parallel process moments occur in TASC just as they do in traditional supervision. One supervisee was describing his struggle with a patient who constantly attacked the frame by missing sessions, showing up late, rearranging session times, and ignoring phone calls in a manner that created worry and frustration for the clinician. At the same time, the clinician was wrestling with his own set of ordinary life challenges, such as sick children, a change in jobs, and weeks disrupted by holidays. In an atypical manner, the supervisee made requests for changes in supervision meeting times, called late to cancel, bounced a cheque, and forgot a scheduled Skype session. I felt irritated and confused, wondering about the meaning of the supervisee's sudden shift in behaviour. As we processed these events in supervision, he was able to consider what was playing out in both supervisory and counselling arenas and linked his behaviour with his patient's actions. In each instance, the attacks on the frame followed a limit-setting experience, where both supervisee and patient had been unable to verbally express their anger and disappointment.

As displayed in these supervisory examples, the content and process of TASC mirrors that of traditional in-person supervision, requiring a similar skill set and working relationship to be effective. The supervisory match (both in general and for a particular case), the supervisee's level of defensiveness, the working through of transference responses, and the creation of a psychological space for thinking all contribute to the relative helpfulness of the supervisory encounter. But what challenges are unique to TASC and how can those be addressed?

* * *

Unique challenges and potential contraindications

Just as some patients are not appropriate for distance counselling, some supervisees cannot manage TASC. Those with a history of maternal deprivation seem particularly vulnerable to struggles with containment under the TASC arrangement, especially if they began their supervisory experience in-person. For some, the telephone feels too distant, either replaying the absent parent or creating a sense of being dropped. Similar to an absent maternal gaze, the lack of visual contact may produce an untenable sense of disorientation or rejection. One supervisee described feeling "unanchored" without the visual connection. Another supervisee remarked that it brought to mind her futile attempts to get her mother's attention while on the telephone. In the first instance, the supervisee's difficulties with the phone could be discussed in supervision and the work went forward. She used her personal therapy to pursue the origins of her "unanchored" feeling. In the second instance, however, the affective flooding proved unmanageable for the supervisee, and she switched to a supervisor in her local area. Certainly, one might argue that it was not the telephone per se that made the situation unworkable, but the level of vulnerability proved too traumatic for the supervisee to continue. Since I try to draw a clear boundary between therapy and supervision, I did not pursue the specific origins of the supervisee's personal associations and traumatic regression as I might in a therapist/

patient dyad. As practitioners of TASC, we have to acknowledge that this style of supervision will not work for everyone, particularly when there are other available in-person alternatives. Providing adequate containment is a challenge in many supervisory pairings, particularly with new clinicians treating more severe patient populations, but the difficulties are magnified in distance work.

The telephone and Skype each produce their own form of challenge for the supervisory dyad. With the telephone, the main problem is the loss of visual information. In reviewing the literature, I find that this is the primary source of opposition to distance supervision (Barnett & Scheetz, 2003; Kanz, 2001; Olson, Russell & White, 2001). For TASC to be effective, the supervisory dyad must acknowledge this loss of visual content and decide how it will be addressed (Groman, 2010). For example, each participant may have to train herself to put into words what she might otherwise display. Although this has been compared to counseling with visually impaired patients, it is not the same process. Unlike sighted persons, visually impaired individuals have developed compensatory sensory processes and are accustomed to the lack of visual cues. When I use the telephone for supervision, I have to consciously remind myself to describe my nonverbal responses and ask about the supervisee's bodily cues. As when conducting psychoanalysis where I am in a state of reverie outside the analysand's visual field, sometimes I like the private space where I can react outside the supervisee's gaze, as it provides more space for thinking. Periodically, the lack of visual contact frees me up to imagine how the supervisee might respond, such as a moment where I envision an eye roll through the phone line. So, the telephone creates both a loss and a potential space.

Additionally, silence has a different impact when delivered by phone (Groman, 2010). In person, I can usually detect whether the silence is a reflective space, an expression of the supervisee's anxiety, a moment of disorientation, or a hostile missive. Over the telephone, I have far fewer cues to establish context. There are moments of silence where I wonder if I am still telephonically connected to my supervisee, leading me to speak prematurely or check the power on my phone. Similarly, sometimes my supervisee will remark, "Are you still there?," a statement I do not hear during in-person consults. Although there are dynamic meanings to be processed and understood regarding these feared disconnects, there are also times when the technology itself actually does present mechanical problems that have dynamic repercussions. For instance, I once had difficulty hearing a supervisee when the volume on her phone suddenly dropped, but this technical failure carried dynamic meaning, conveying to me her feelings of not being heard in other ways.

While Skype offers visual cues, visual images may be distorted depending on the quality of the camera, the position of the supervisor or supervisee operating the equipment, and the strength and continuity of the internet connection itself. For example, supervisor or supervisee may position the face too close to the camera. Problems with the internet connection may create a delay in the transmission so that voice and image are not in sync or the image may break up, freeze, or disappear completely. Unlike the telephone, complete drops or disruptions of Skype connections are not uncommon, particularly during times of high internet use or in geographic areas with poor internet accessibility. Given these possibilities, I find it helpful to discuss in advance how the supervisory pair will manage such events. For instance, at what point do we switch to phone if the connection is unsustainable? If we experience frequent drops, should we use voice only Skype instead, without the visual image? Additionally, the immediate impact of the disruptive event is important to process. For example, the supervisee may "lose his place" in describing the counseling interaction we were discussing, finding it difficult to reconnect to the affect he felt in the first telling.

When using Skype, I have noticed I typically hold more tension in my body during the supervisory hour than during my in-person sessions. Perhaps this results from my underlying concerns about the sustainability of the connection, having to attend to the computer screen as well as the session, a self-consciousness created by seeing my image on the screen, or a heightened attentiveness to compensate for the distance. This tension may be unique to me, as I am only moderately comfortable with my technological skills. Although infrequent in my experience, technology challenges and interruptions on Skype can consume a significant portion of the supervisory hour, leaving the supervisor feeling anxious, frustrated, and inadequate in solving the problem. Sometimes these difficulties are repetitive and severe, necessitating a change in equipment or location.

* * *

The future of TASC

A strong argument for TASC is its expansion of accessibility (Fishkin, Fishkin, Leli, Katz & Synder, 2011; Olson, Russell & White, 2001). More clinicians can obtain supervision and consultation, particularly in geographic areas where such expertise is lacking or complicated by dual relationships. Additionally, clinicians can contact geographically distant experts in very specialized areas of mental health practice, potentially improving their standard of care with patients (McAdams & Wyatt, 2010). Making consultation more readily available likely increases a clinician's willingness to seek help and support with difficult clinical cases. We know that seeking consultation is a protective factor in reducing clinical errors and ethical misconduct. A less compelling yet still salient benefit of TASC is convenience. Some clinicians using TASC within their local areas comment on time and money saved from reduced transportation demands. The clinician no longer sacrifices two hours of driving time to obtain supervision. She can schedule a Skype supervision session in between two regularly scheduled patients, making more effective use of her time.

But TASC is not without drawbacks. Distance supervision does not replace the in-person experience. Perhaps it is comparable to the difference between visiting a place in person versus seeing it in a film. Each covers the geographic area, but in different ways. Our attachment to in-person supervision is more than just nostalgia or tradition. There is something almost unquantifiable about the value of sitting with a supervisee in person and experiencing the clinical material together, in the same physical space. Additionally, lack of equivalence and reciprocity in state licensure requirements makes TASC difficult to practice and regulate within the United States. For the clinical supervisor, carefully checking all applicable state licensure laws and/or asking licensing boards for permission to practice across state boundaries is cumbersome. For regulatory boards, overseeing practice in one region is challenging, but expanding investigations across state boundaries creates significant added expense and responsibility.

One thing seems clear. TASC is not going to disappear (Anthony, Nagel & Goss, 2010). As technological developments continue, it will likely become a form of "traditional" supervision. Given the inevitability of this shift, why not think about it together as a clinical community? More research is needed to evaluate the overall clinical effectiveness of distance supervision, the impact of technology on aspects of the supervisory process, and the ethical complications and dilemmas associated with TASC. Drawing from that research, we need more clinical writing about the distance supervisory experience to establish some consensus on practical, ethical guidelines for the implementation of TASC.

References

Anthony, K., Nagel, D. M. & Goss, S. (Eds). (2010). *The Use of Technology In Mental Health.* Springfield: Charles C. Thomas.

Baker, D. C. & Bufka, L. F. (2011). Preparing for the telehealth world: Navigating legal, regulatory, reimbursement, and ethical issues in the electronic age. *Professional Psychology: Research and Practice, 42*(6): 405–411.

Barnett, J. E. & Scheetz, K. (2003). Technological advances and telehealth: Ethics, law, and the practice of psychotherapy. *Psychotherapy: Theory, Research, Practice, Training, 40*(1/2): 86–93.

Clark, G. (2010). Traditional uses of technology in counseling trainee supervision. In: Anthony, K., Nagel, D. M. & Goss, S. (Eds.), *The Use of Technology in Mental Health* (pp. 256–268). Springfield: Charles C. Thomas.

Coursol, D. H., Lewis, J. & Seymour, J. W. (2010). The use of videoconferencing to enrich counselor training and supervision. In: Anthony, K., Nagel, D. M. & Goss, S. (Eds.), *The Use of Technology in Mental Health* (pp. 280–288). Springfield: Charles C. Thomas.

Fishkin, R., Fishkin, L., Leli, U., Katz, B. & Synder, E. (2011). Psychodynamic treatment, training, and supervision using internet-based technologies. *Journal of the American Academy of Psychoanalysis and Dynamic Psychiatry, 39*(1): 155–168.

Groman, M. (2010). The use of telephone to enrich counselor training and supervision. In: Anthony, K., Nagel, D. M. & Goss, S. (Eds.), *The Use of Technology in Mental Health* (pp. 269–279). Springfield: Charles C. Thomas.

Jacobs, D., David, P. & Meyer, D. J. (1995). *The Supervisory Encounter: A Guide for Teachers of Psychodynamic Psychotherapy and Psychoanalysis.* New Haven: Yale University Press.

Janoff, D. S. & Schoenholtz-Read, J. (1999). Group supervision meets technology: A model for computer-mediated group training at a distance. *The International Journal of Group Psychotherapy, 49*(2): 255–272.

Kanz, J. E. (2001). Clinical-supervision.com: Issues in the provision of online supervision. *Professional Psychology: Research and Practice, 32*(4): 415–420.

Kaplan, D. (2006). Ethical use of technology in counseling. *Counseling Today* [online]. [Accessed May 26, 2012]. Available from: http://ct.counseling.org/2006/12/ct-online-ethics-update-4/

Manosevitz, M. (2006). Supervision by telephone: An innovation in psychoanalytic training—A roundtable discussion. *Psychoanalytic Psychology, 23*: 579–582.

McAdams, C. R. & Wyatt, K. L. (2010). The regulation of technology-assisted distance counseling and supervision in the United States: An analysis of current extent, trends, and implications. *Counselor Education and Supervision, 49*: 179–192.

Olson, M. M., Russell, C. S. & White, M. B. (2001). Technological implications for clinical supervision and practice. *The Clinical Supervisor*, *20*(2): 201–215.

Trepal, H., Haberstroh, S., Duffey, T. & Evans, M. (2007). Considerations and strategies for teaching online counseling skills: Establishing relationships in cyberspace. *Counselor Education and Supervision*, *46*: 266–279.

Vaccaro, N. & Lambie, G. W. (2007). Computer-based counselor-in-training supervision: Ethical and practical implications for counselor educators and supervisors. *Counselor Education and Supervision*, *47*: 46–57.

CHAPTER TWENTY ONE

Teletherapy and teleanalysis in training psychotherapists and psychoanalysts

Jill Savege Scharff, MD

P sychotherapists in the United States routinely use the telephone as the most usual, practical, and efficient way to screen requests for treatment, arrange appointments, and make referrals. Through tone of voice, manner, and ease of communication this telephone communication conveys an impression of both therapist and potential patient (Zalusky, 2000). The experience of each other during the telephone call includes all the elements—resistance, defensive functioning, alliance, and transference and countertransference—that will colour the subsequent therapeutic relationship, or end it before it begins. However, psychoanalysts who do use the telephone to initiate the therapeutic contact have mainly discouraged its use between sessions and eschewed telecommunication as a legitimate setting for the conduct of psychoanalysis. In Chapter Six I gave a detailed account of those analysts who pioneered the use of the telephone, the videophone, and the headset and showed how, even without visual cues, erotic, negative and paranoid transference could ripen, might be intensified, or be hidden from view, as it is in in-person sessions, and could be interpreted effectively (Aronson, 2000a, 2000b; Leffert, 2003; Lindon, 2000; Saul, 1951; Zalusky, 2005). A number of chapters have described how it is possible for the therapist to add visual input from a webcam in sessions that occur using Skype rather than the telephone. With or without visual input, each participant creates and sustains a mental representation of the other in fantasy, and in this way, a new type of analytic process develops (Zalusky, 2003a, 2003b). Nevertheless, until now, even supporters of teletherapy have tended to view it overcautiously as second best, a therapeutic compromise, a trauma, or merely better than nothing, a view that diminishes its value (Benson, Rowntree & Singer, 2001; Lindon, 2000; Sachs, 2003; Zalusky, 1998).

In the current environment where people must travel and relocate for work and are familiar with telecommuting, patients are asking their therapists to offer treatment on the telephone or internet. In their study of teletherapy, Richards and Goldberg (2001) found that of 120 psychologists surveyed, 83 per cent had done telephone therapy in the past two years. It is more difficult to find figures on the practice of telephone analysis. In a survey sent electronically to 140 analysts from seven Latin American institutes, only sixty could be delivered and thirty-two responded. Fifty per cent of the responders thought it not possible to do psychoanalysis by telephone while 34 per cent thought that it is possible (Estrada, 2009). The fact that the sample size was so small means that these results concerning the perception of effectiveness of telephone analysis are not significant and indicate merely a trend. The fact that so many email addresses were not valid indicates how much more the analytic community needs to develop in the area of technology. The American Psychoanalytic Association (APsaA, 2011) reported that of 859 respondents to the 2011 Psychoanalytic Professional Activities Benchmarking Study, 28 per cent use the phone and 9 per cent use Skype for psychotherapy, 9 per cent treat analytic cases over the telephone, and 4 per cent use Skype (the brand name of a voice over internet service) for psychoanalysis. What is needed now is more complete study and review of narrative reports and clinical workshops on treatment on the telephone and internet (Benson, Rowntree & Singer, 2011; Hanly, 2009, personal communication).

Psychoanalytic psychotherapy using the telephone is not the same as it is in traditional settings in that the patient is not in the same room as the therapist, and the pair of them communicates only with sound. Yet teletherapy and traditional therapy are more alike than different. Admittedly the therapist cannot see the body and therefore cannot read the body language of her patient but their minds still interact and, unseen, so do their bodies in response to what they hear. I use an analogy to capture the similarity and differences in traditional and technology assisted treatment. Teletherapy seems to me to be like a CD book while in-person therapy is more like a DVD movie. Both are fully engaging. Both have value. Listening to a book, or to a patient on the telephone, the mind's eye sees the scene and fleshes out the characters. When we watch a movie, or observe the body language of a patient, the visual enhancement of the characters in the movie or the patient in in-person therapy makes it seem more real. Nevertheless, at a movie or a therapy session, we are dealing with internal characters in time and space, and a narrative beyond what is in front of us, a narrative that includes us. Each modality is valuable, each tells a story, presents a conflict, loss, or dilemma, introduces and develops characters, and engages the reader or viewer or therapist or analyst in an imaginative, and hopefully transformative, experience. In teletherapy and in traditional therapy, the transformation comes not from what happens but from how we are engaged in the dynamics and how we convey our understanding of what is happening and what is evoked.

Since 2003, teletherapy has included the possibility of visual transmission as well as voice, using a web camera with Voice over Internet Protocol (VoIP) (a free service often referred to by one of its trade names, Skype, but here I prefer to use the generic term). Computer to computer, VoIP delivers a startlingly clear voice directly via a headset to both ears, which means that the voice is totally vivid and feels close by, with even less space between the parties than in the conventional office setting. But suddenly the call may be dropped or distorted, and there is disagreement about the degree of security Skype promises, and so videoteleconference service purchased from a company with a medical-grade platform is more secure but more expensive and less often used in private practice. I explained the security risks and technical problems in Chapter Eight. It is a good idea to tell prospective patients about these options and the security risks involved so that they can give informed consent for what is still an experimental methodology.

The teletherapist using the telephone or VoIP without webcam listens without seeing the patient, but he is not actually reduced to working with a single channel of perception because auditory input recruits other senses. Lacan (2006) claims that we have "but one medium: the patient's speech" (p. 347) but that dictum overlooks the affective tonality and rhythm of the voice. Brainsky (2003) acknowledges the importance of tone, timbre, and verbal content, but then diminishes the value of vocal communication by seeing voice as split-off idealised and persecutory part objects (p. 23). Of course the use of the telephone relies upon speech and analytic listening as the primary mode of exchange but more is conveyed than mere verbal expression. Our imagination senses the emotional atmosphere and ranges freely among all the senses, as it does in traditional in-person treatment. The idea that we have access to only one medium, speech, hardly does justice to the unconscious transference/countertransference dialectic between two resonating personalities. It has been my experience that deep unconscious communication and affective attunement support in-depth work on the telephone as they do in traditional treatment despite the absence of literal physical presence. Here are four clinical examples drawn from teleanalysis on the phone or VoIP but without webcam in order to show that unconscious communication, affective attunement, and countertransference imagery do occur when sessions are conducted remotely, even without visual input.

Clinical example 1

Ms. A had previous in-person psychotherapy in her home town with a local woman psychotherapist who framed interpretations in terms of the Oedipus complex. In treatment with her, Ms. A had revisited childhood memories, stabilised her mood, worked on her adult development, and had received considerable benefit at that time, but a feeling of daily dread persisted. Ms. A felt that she needed an object relations approach to recover from that persistent anxiety. Having no trained therapist locally, she travelled to meet me and establish a way of working in person before continuing in telephone therapy.

Ms. A had been talking about loneliness, neglect, and abuse during her childhood. One day she told me she had felt so miserable and desolate as a young child that she wished she would die. She fell silent. I had a sensation of her dropping out of contact. On an earlier occasion she had talked of a balcony overlooking a patio where she used to play, and this image came to me. I said, "I see you all alone on a balcony, desolate, looking over the edge, longing to be held and imagining dropping." She cried with relief, and told me that in her silence she had been remembering looking over the edge to the ground below where her relatives might be upset to find her shattered if she had jumped, as she often wanted to. But they never noticed her misery. She said that for the first time, someone was there with her on the balcony. She often referred back to this moment of the treatment. She said that when my comment connected with her memory of her suicidal fantasy, she felt both understood and held safe. She said later, "It was the coincidence of your voice and my thinking that meant so much to me." Some months later, she said, "I have gone away from that balcony, and it is not a dangerous place any more."

From that time on, although Ms. A still felt anxious on occasions, she no longer suffered from a daily sense of dread. We therapists are taught that non-verbal cues provide the harmonics of language and human interaction, and that working on the telephone we will have lost our way of establishing a treatment relationship and of receiving communication and feedback after interpretations. Once we let go of the ideal setting of traditional treatment, we are free to appreciate what is possible in terms of unconscious communication via the transmission of sound alone. This example shows that non-verbal communication and effective intervention can occur without vision and bodily presence. Ms. A said later that she had experienced a transformative moment.

Clinical example 2

Mr. B, talking to me on the telephone, had been telling what he could remember of a traumatic rape as a boy at the mercy of a pederast with long nails. I felt the full impact of what he had been through and the horror of recalling it. Upset by what he remembered and could not remember, his body reacted to the stress of this process by producing what he described as a rash on his ankles. His mind reacted with a dream in which he saw what he described as "many small cuts" on his leg. This might have meant that he felt injured or had been literally scratched by the nails. But the image that came into my mind was of an injury more like a graze with scratches going vertically and horizontally. I had a frightened, helpless feeling, my mind's eye looking at the broken skin. What I saw there did not fit the words he had used to describe the rash on his actual leg or the cuts in the dream.

The image filled me with dread, and it persisted. I struggled to contain it. If I shared it, I might interrupt the flow of Mr. B's associations, and worse, I might be leading the flow of associations, like an attorney leading a witness. But his associations were stuck. Since Mr. B was unable to proceed, I decided to speak. I said that the image had entered my mind as a graze or more specifically a fabric burn. Did he have any idea why I might have that image? He was shocked and immediately tearful but then found his words to tell me that he realised that these were marks from the ropes with which he was tied up to prevent his escape, and an additional source of trauma that he had forgotten until then.

The transmitted image gave rise to strong emotion in both of us. Mirkin (2011) also reported that intense affects are experienced and worked with in teletherapy. The man's words had obscured the source of the marks, but his unconscious had conveyed it to my unconscious in eidetic form. I cannot explain how that happens, but I offer it as an example of unconscious communication received on the telephone.

Clinical example 3

Ms. C, a psychotherapist who began psychoanalysis in person, changed to telephone sessions when her analyst transferred to a different centre. At first she experienced grief over this arrangement. She missed the physical space, the ritual of the waiting room, and the visual contact with her analyst. Later she realised that enjoying those visual aspects had not left as much room for her imagination. Explaining further why she came to prefer their telephone sessions, she wrote, "I had the freedom to look inward at the objects that flickered across the screen of my mind. I needed all those phases: the initial holding, the grief over losing it, and the increased enjoyment of psychic space that allowed me, especially during the termination phase, to internalise my analytic mother" (Kwintner, 2009, personal communication).

Clinical example 4

Mr. D's six-month termination process after a four-year treatment in person had to be conducted on the telephone. On the second last day of his treatment, Mr. D, speaking from his home, said, "I like it here, and I've spent years lying on the couch looking at the leaves and the squirrels. It's been a more personal relationship than if you were one of those analysts with an office in a building."

From the imagery and the tone of his communication, it seems as if he is still in the office with me. The leaves and the squirrels are objects that he had cathected during the four years of in-person treatment at my home office prior to his move. He had taken the image of me in the office with him to his telephone sessions in his new location months later.

In the last telephone session, Mr. D experienced me as a woman who would be seeing someone else in his time slot: "I will be losing my place to someone else. I'm worried about starting anything that will end forever, that can't continue with you. Is there a need for closure? I'm worried I won't do it, and I will feel cut off and abandoned. What do I do?"

I felt his anxiety, and for a moment I worried whether he was ready to terminate, but I also noticed that he showed strength in being able to contemplate his reaction to loss. I asked, "How do you draw this to a conclusion? How do you protect yourself from feeling upset by me, a woman with other interests no longer devoted to you?"

"I dunno," he said. "I know you have other interests. 'Us' finishing is not an attack on me. It is time for that to happen. I'm scared it is not time, that I will backslide, that I won't know what to do without you. It's such a strange, unique relationship, a business relationship, a doctor/patient relationship, and other elements. I've never had anything like that. I'm trying to prepare for how I'll feel and how I'll think."

In the termination session, Mr. D conveys gratitude for and loss of the transference object, does not deny affective upset and estrangement, resists and accepts the move to working on his issues alone, and prepares to move forward. It seems to me that the termination sessions proceeded much as they might have done in person. Although his treatment may be described as virtual, his experience was not. It is emotionally real, different from in person but valuable in its own right.

Once we have embarked on teletherapy by telephone or VoIP we should subject our work to process and review by consulting with a group of colleagues who are studying the effectiveness of treatment by telephone and on the internet, and who are working together to develop an appropriate ethical stance. We should also maintain dialogue with psychoanalytically oriented psychotherapists who reject the teletherapy option because breaking with tradition could meet with disapproval and loss of affiliation with colleagues. The threat of this anxious and guilty sensation is what creates the commonly held view (despite a lack of research data) that in-person sessions are better, a view held mainly by those who have not tried to do analysis by telephone or internet.

Institutional and personal resistance to teleanalysis

Our willingness to accept an innovation like teletherapy is affected by the reactions of our colleagues and our professional associations. There are many reasons to shy away. I want to go into these in some detail, not only because they affect what we can offer our patients, but because institutional forces and decisions affect what we can offer colleagues who want to train as psychotherapists or psychoanalysts but live far away from a training centre.

Some training institutions teach that teletherapy is wrong because it is omnipotent for any therapist to assume that only one person can help the patient. Certainly freedom of choice of referral is essential. But surely continuity of care is an equally compelling value. Why waste years of building trust, sharing history, making links, developing hypotheses, developing an effective therapeutic relationship, and establishing the transference/countertransference dialectic? Why should the patient have to start again, when technology is available to support the continuation of treatment to its conclusion? Private practice therapists are free to make their own decisions within their understanding of an ethical analytic stance, but they naturally want to respect the positions taken by working parties of the major professional associations. Teletherapy has been an experimental and controversial method but there are signs that further study may lead to more acceptance.

In the institutional context, some of us do not want to act without full authority. We may be unwilling to face sanction by disapproving colleagues, and afraid of losing income, causing others to lose income, or being accused of resisting the emotions of absence and reunion after separation (Zalusky, 2000). Feeling accused of colluding with dependency rather than analysing the fear of separation, we feel shame and guilt. Holding on to the reality that those who experimented with telephone treatment were indeed criticised, we bind ourselves to the past as a resistance against uncovering the current truth about what is possible. Many of us are actually doing teletherapy but keep quiet about it for fear of disapproval. Of those who try it, many are more ill at ease at first than their patients (Leffert, 2003). Having had no experience of the telephone for treatment purposes, Hanly (2009) reluctantly accepted the need for continuing his patient's analysis on the telephone because he was worried that it would be a distancing tool, and felt afraid that the patient might feel abandoned by the lack of his presence and return to a state of anxiety (see Chapter Twelve). His experience reassured him, and his account of it shows, that analysis can be done effectively on the telephone. Similarly reluctant, Ellman, persuaded by the persistence of his patient, agreed to teleanalysis and was surprised to find it effective (Ellman, personal communication). Teleanalysis allows us to "put the welfare of the patient above the demand for procedural conformity" (Sachs, 2003, p. 28).

Therapists who feel anxious about engaging in teletherapy can learn from patients who are at ease with technology. We can also take comfort in changing attitudes towards "telehealth care". For instance, in the United States in July 2009, the House of Representatives approved the Labor, Health and Human Services Appropriations Bill for Fiscal Year (FY) 2010 in which

$15 million is allocated to the Office for the Advancement of Telehealth in the Department of Health Resources and Services. This funding is to support programmes that work with and support communities in their efforts to develop cost-effective uses of telehealth technologies to bring health services to isolated populations and health-related education to the practitioners who serve them.

Even those who accept the validity of telediagnosis and teleconsultation for a medical problem, or who conduct psychotherapy by telephone, cannot imagine the telephone with all its limits on vision and atmosphere supporting a full analytic experience. Some of us who do want to reach out to those in remote circumstances cannot get over the objections to the telephone or VoIP and we insist that patients travel to see us, but this imposes financial and emotional hardship on them and their families, and if the patients happen to be mental health professionals then the burden also falls on the patients that they themselves must leave in order to come to see us. Of course, not all therapists and analysts are suited to working on the phone or the internet, and we should all be free to select how best we can practise with integrity. Yet even those who do not choose to practise in this way could welcome and authorise teletherapy and teleanalysis as valid implementation of our psychoanalytic methods. In my view, even full analytic training can occur when residential courses are supplemented by personal analysis, supervision, and seminars over the telephone or the internet.

Teleanalysis in psychoanalytic training

Clinical psychology and psychotherapy have been taught in well-respected distance learning programmes for years, but psychoanalytic training programmes have been more reluctant to embrace communications technology even though the need for psychoanalysis to adapt to the changing needs of the global economy has been addressed in discussion at psychoanalytic meetings for at least ten years. Still the establishment has insisted on in-person sessions. So, psychoanalytic training centres pioneered the experimental use of analysis offered in modules of immersion (either the analyst travelling to the analysand's location or vice versa or both) instead of the usual three to five times a week rhythm of traditional sessions. There were many variations of rhythm: one week per month, one weekend every two weeks, three months per year, or a variable schedule set to meet the analysand's and analyst's schedules. The analysand travelled to meet the analyst, a plan that also introduced the analysand to the resources of the analytic centre, and the analyst travelled to the analysand's location, or some combination of those arrangements. Training analysts were pleasantly surprised to find that an analytic process could take place even under these conditions.

There were, however, drawbacks. The candidates experienced hardships in terms of expense and time away from family. The time away from practice at a time of higher expenditure for analysis and for travel to analysis created financial strains. The absences also imposed a strain on the people with whom the analysand was learning to do analysis under supervision. At the personal level, there was the toll on the analysand of opening up to a regressive process and having to bear the disruptive effect of affects stirred and not easily contained during the break (Hutto, 1998). Equally problematic was the tendency to shut down until the next opportunity for analysis came around, the unconscious having a tendency to close up when the analyst is away (Fink, 2007). Hutto (1998) pointed to the risk of repeating a cycle of disruption and loss that would hinder the development of intrapsychic representations especially in patients with severe early trauma. Some analysands in concentrated analysis longed for intermittent telephone contact but this was frowned upon as a break in the frame, and so they accepted pain and deprivation. Nevertheless, the general agreement is that shuttle/condensed/concentrated/interrupted analysis is better than no analysis; the analyst so trained can meet standards of competence as an analyst; and the next generation gains the benefit of in-person analysis and a vital local centre for psychoanalysis.

Telephone analysis as the main frame of treatment would surely have been more convenient for the pioneer analysands in shuttle/condensed analysis, the frequency of their sessions more consistent, but it was not an option for them at that time. If telephone analysis were to become an option in some circumstances, these graduate analysts, having invested so much in the ordeal of their training, might idealise condensed/shuttle analysis and reject the innovation of telephone analysis as a soft option. I propose that remote analysis by telephone or VoIP in the training of analysts who live outside training centres can be as effective as in-person analysis and is more affordable, and therefore more effective in bringing psychoanalysis to outlying areas.

In a report to the American Psychoanalytic Association (APsaA) concerning telephone analysis in relation to training standards, Benson, Rowntree, and Singer (2001) recommended that telephone analysis not be used as an alternative to in-person analysis. However, they did allow that, in extraordinary circumstances, continuation by telephone might be justified, but first, "… in almost every situation, the in-person analysis should be established or well under way" and "… waivers should (usually) not be granted unless the portion of the analysis conducted via telephone is temporary and could be expected to be a minority of the total training analysis" (p. 2). They recommended that any possibility of teleanalysis be considered in consultation with a non-reporting colleague, and then by the education committee of the institute, which must ensure that the proposed teleanalysis is the only way to preserve the depth and intensity of the training analysis, and that it will not jeopardise liability coverage or break licensing laws. With these assurances in place, the education committee could then ask for a waiver from APsaA where the request would be considered in the context of the candidate's progress in training, and if the waiver were granted, the impact of teleanalysis on that candidate's training would be continually evaluated through assessment of performance. Benson, Rowntree, and Singer (2001) had substantial questions about whether an analysis conducted in such a way would constitute acceptable training, but they did recommend further study. "We took a cautious step toward permitting some use of the telephone, but we didn't feel we could go further without more data … and our small working group did not continue to study it or gather data" (Benson, 2010, personal communication).

Benson, Rowntree, and Singer responsibly raised the licensing issue. States vary in their requirements. Professional associations all recommend that teleanalysts be licensed in their mental health professions in the state where they work and be held to the licensing requirements listed by the state in which the patient lives, but the rules and the exceptions vary state to state. In any case, there are only two states, Vermont and New York, which license psychoanalysts specifically. There is no case law as yet to indicate the level of exposure a non-compliant analyst might face, although a case is pending in California. Because disputes may arise over licensing requirements that vary among states, the American Telemedicine Association is lobbying for a federal licence for all health professionals.

According to the International Psychoanalytical Association (Task Force Report, 2009) teleanalysis may be approved in psychoanalytic training in exceptional circumstances where there is no alternative, provided that an analytic process is already established in person, and that the analyst and candidate are convinced of its value and necessity, acknowledge the experimental nature of the undertaking, and agree to review its efficacy from time to time with consultants who will explore whether candidates analysed in this way can meet the standards of functional equivalence. "There are questions about the IPA policy concerning remote analysis which need to be discussed and settled" before teleanalysis can be approved for candidates in training (Charles Hanly, personal communication).

In the American Psychoanalytic Association, there is renewed awareness of the need to study teleanalysis (Procci, 2011), and some candidates who live far from an analytic training centre have successfully applied for a waiver to have their analysis partly on the telephone or VoIP (Zeitner, 2011, personal communication). In the International Psychoanalytical Association, an analytic candidate whose analysis was partly on the telephone was approved for graduation on an individual basis (Aryan, 2011, personal communication). Remote analysis for training of psychoanalysts under the direction of the International Psychoanalytical Association is still in evolution (Sachs, 2009).

When psychoanalysis is not available locally, potential analysands in rural areas or repressed cultures, such as Eastern Europe, remote parts of Latin America, or China, who are looking for access to psychoanalytic insight have options—emigration, shuttle condensed analysis (when the analyst visits the analysand's local area or vice versa at regular intervals for twice-a-day sessions), and interrupted condensed analysis (when the analysand visits the analyst's location for a few months at a time), or telephone analysis. Of these, teleanalysis is the least disruptive to families and, in the case of candidates, to their patients and their analysands. Teleanalysis provides more continuity than shuttle or condensed analysis, and more sustained yet modulated intensity. When shuttle or condensed analysis offers two sessions a day, the dedication to intensity may be highly effective in jump-starting the analytic process, but may provoke regression. For some candidates, therefore, it may increase resistance. Shuttle/condensed analysis becomes an exciting object, a very full feed, after which there is deprivation. This let-down can be modified somewhat by maintaining continuity on the telephone, but even so, such telephone sessions may become relatively decathected until the telephone sessions are re-established as valuable in and of themselves.

Distance learning of psychotherapy and psychoanalysis

If we can show that teletherapy and teleanalysis are effective adaptations of traditional in-person psychotherapy and psychoanalysis, the question arises as to whether these can also be effective in the training of psychotherapists and psychoanalysts.

Training example

For psychotherapists who live remote from a training centre, an experimental distance learning institute with an advanced psychotherapy training programme was developed with a modular curriculum in which in-person immersion training courses five times a year alternate with weekly telephone, VoIP, or videoconference seminars (www.theipi.org). These weekly seminars augment the in-person training courses and so provide for a continuous learning process, which is essential (Doarn, 2008). Once participants get used to the virtual classroom format, they are able to interact in real time to discuss the concepts or clinical material being presented, and they develop a group process that resonates with and illuminates the ideas and problems under study. From the immersion courses they are known to the faculty and therefore also known personally to their assigned supervisors. At first, supervisors were anxious about whether they could hear their supervisees clearly, but using a headset helped with that. They were worried that they would not feel in touch with the supervisee and the material, but found that written process notes helped with that. Sachs (2003) also recommends the use of written process notes in telephone supervision, especially when supervising those for whom English is a foreign language. So participants email process notes to which they associate in the supervision session. Some of them choose to switch to VoIP to have face-to-face virtual contact but others prefer to continue on the telephone. Great care is taken to protect the confidentiality of the patients by having the supervisees remove identifying information and password protect their process notes, and by requiring supervisors and supervisees to erase them immediately after the session. As in in-person supervision, when the supervisee reports the session, a process of imaginative reconstruction is triggered in the sensitive supervisor. Similarly, unconscious group dynamic responses occur in relation to the clinical material under discussion in case conference teleseminars, and these can be recognised and analysed by the group as a parallel process, the study of which can illuminate the dynamics of the therapist-patient pair.

How is supervision possible without visual clues? In supervision and seminars on the phone or VoIP, as in teletherapy and teleanalysis, one finds that when one route of communication is blocked by working on the telephone, other routes compensate because of cross-modal channels of communication (Anderson, Scharff, Scharff & Symington, 2009). Unconscious communication can occur on auditory, visual, and sensory routes. Language is embodied in the resonating sensorimotor system. A purely auditory communication on the telephone provokes a visual image in the listener. In studies of monkey behaviour, it is seen that when a monkey sees *or merely hears* an action taken by another monkey, mirror neurons fire in the observing *or listening* monkey brain (Galese, 2003). Unlike the monkey, the analysand has words with which to convey actions and memories of behaviours. By a similar action of the mirror neurons in humans, when these words are heard within the analytic pair in teleanalysis, images form in the analyst's mind, as he or she imagines the emotions of the analysand, and vice versa. This neural mechanism is the basis of the empathic response, of intersubjectivity, and of intense transference/countertransference experiences in the therapy pair, and elaborated in the supervisory pair, which deepens understanding by learning from within shared experience.

Training example continued

Some participants at this distance learning institution have chosen to specialise in psychotherapy: from some participants in this psychotherapy learning matrix a desire for full analytic training emerged. Holding the philosophy that each branch of psychoanalytically oriented psychotherapy informs and learns from the other, analytically trained faculty members provided an experimental institute for distance psychoanalytic education (www.theipi.org/programs/psychoanalytic-training) (not affiliated to the IPA or to APsaA). Analytic candidates see their three training cases four times a week in person, but are in supervision weekly via telephone or VoIP. They meet with a personal analyst qualified to treat a candidate in person during the immersion courses, and they supplement their treatment with four-times-a-week analytic sessions on the telephone or internet. This allows psychotherapists who long to work as analysts but live far from an analytic training centre to have the in-depth training they want. Openness to this development allows the analyst and the analytic teacher to work remotely, and to experience a level of intensity of analytic process that prepares that candidate to function effectively as an autonomous analyst of others.

Without such a programme of personal analysis, supervision, and seminars by telephone or VoIP and in-person courses and workshops, candidates living remote from analytic centres could not have psychoanalysis to enrich their lives and could not have psychoanalytic training to bring psychoanalysis to their countries or remote communities. "We must change our way of looking at the use of the telephone if we are to provide truly patient-friendly analytic treatment and trainee-friendly analytic training" (Richards, 2003, p. 32).

Conclusion

Institutions of training in psychotherapy and psychoanalysis are now confronted with the need to reconsider attitudes about the telephone and its newer cousin, computer technology. Some analysts believe that psychoanalysis, a professional art based on the harmonics of unconscious communication, cannot possibly transcend the limits of distance, and therefore neither can the education of psychotherapists and psychoanalysts. But surely we need to stay attuned to sociocultural changes and broaden the reach of technology, do clinical research into indications and contraindications for teleanalysis, and stay open to transformation, as occurs with every living language and culture (Aryan, de Berenstein, Carlino, Grinfeld & Lutenberg, 2009).

Articles in the literature, research, and presentations at workshops of the American and the International Psychoanalytic(al) Associations show that some centres are willing to experiment with teleanalysis as a supplementary form of psychoanalysis. What is needed now is a more complete study and review of narrative reports from teleanalyses (Benson, Rowntree & Singer, 2011) and for psychoanalysts from the three regions of the IPA to pool their clinical experiences in workshops (Hanly, 2009, personal communication).

Fully aware of the objections to the use of technology in psychoanalytically oriented treatment and training, and sensitive to the challenges that it poses, I maintain that psychotherapy and psychoanalysis by telephone, VoIP, and VTC is indicated at the clinical level in exceptional circumstances to augment continuity, at the educational level to bring psychoanalytic education to people in disadvantaged areas, and at the societal level to help spread psychoanalytically oriented thinking for the benefit of our colleagues, friends, children, and families.

References

Anderson, G., Scharff, D., Scharff, J. & Symington, N. (2009). Panel on Telephone Analysis. International Psychoanalytical Association Congress, Chicago, August.

APsaA (2011). Psychoanalytic Professional Activities Benchmarking Study. *The American Psychoanalytic Association*, September.

Aronson, J. K. (2000a). *The Use of the Telephone in Psychotherapy*. Northvale, NJ: Jason Aronson.

Aronson, J. K. (2000b). Use of the telephone as a transitional space. In: J. Aronson (Ed.), *The Use of the Telephone in Psychotherapy* (pp. 129–149). Northvale, NJ: Jason Aronson.

Aryan, A. (2011). Personal communication.

Aryan, A., Berenstein, S. P. de, Carlino, R., Grinfeld, P. & Lutenberg, J. (2009). Psicoanálisis por Teléfono. Panel on Telephone Analysis. International Psychoanalytical Association Congress, Chicago, August.

Benson, R. M. (2010). Personal communication.

Benson, R. M., Rowntree, E. B. & Singer, M. H. (2001). Final report of ad hoc committee on training analysis via telephone. Unpublished report to the Board on Professional Standards of the American Psychoanalytic Association.

Brainsky, S. (2003). Adapting to, or idealizing technology? *Insight, 12*(1): 22–24.

Doarn, C. R. (2008). Interview: Telethinking with Jonathan Linkous. *Telemedicine and e-Health, 14*(10): 1019–1023.

Ellman, S. (2009). Personal communication.

Estrada, T. (2009). Telecommunications against the contemporary psychoanalysis. Telecoms incorporation or resistance in the analytical practice. http://www.ayudapsicologica.com.mx/archivos/Contemporary%20Psychoanalysis%20versus%20telecom%20technology%20F.pdf. (Accessed November 2009.)

Fink, B. (2007). Phone analysis. In: *Fundamentals of Psychoanalytic Technique* (pp. 189–205). New York: W. W. Norton.

Galese, V. (2003). The roots of empathy: The shared manifold hypothesis and the neural basis of intersubjectivity. *Psychopathology, 36*: 171–180.

Hanly, C. (2009). Personal communication.

Hutto, B. (1998). A self-report: Contrasting concentrated and standard psychoanalysis. *International Journal of Psychoanalysis, 79*: 171–173.

Kwintner, M. (2009). Personal communication.

Lacan, J. (2006). *Ecrits: The First Complete Edition in English*. B. Fink (Trans.). New York: W. W. Norton.

Leffert, M. (2003). Analysis and psychotherapy by telephone. *Journal of the American Psychoanalytic Association, 51*(1): 101–130.

Lindon, J. (2000). Psychoanalysis by telephone. In: J. Aronson (Ed.), *The Use of the Telephone in Psychotherapy* (pp. 3–13). Northvale NJ: Jason Aronson.

Mirkin, M. (2011). Compromised treatment or an interesting opportunity? *Psychoanalytic Quarterly, 80*(3): 643–670.

Procci, W. (2011). APsaA: Online treatment—is it part of our future? *Email communication*, September 26, 2011.

Richards, A. K. (2003). Fruitful uses of telephone analysis. *Insight, 12*(1): 30–32.

Richards and Goldberg (2001). A survey of Division 39 members re telephone therapy. Presented at American Psychological Association panel: Telephone Therapy—Advantages and Disadvantages, August 2000, Washington, DC.

Sachs, D. (2003). Telephone analysis—sometimes the best choice? *Insight*, *12*(1): 28–29.

Sachs, D. (2009). Faraway, so close. Shuttle analysis. Panel, International Psychoanalytical Association Congress, Chicago, July.

Saul, L. J. (1951). A note on the telephone as a technical aid. *Psychoanalytic Quarterly*, *20*: 287–290.

Zalusky, S. (1998). Telephone analysis: out of sight but not out of mind. *Journal of the American Psychoanalytic Association*, *46*: 1221–1242.

Zalusky, S. (2000). Telephone analysis. In: J. Aronson (Ed.), *The Use of the Telephone in Psychotherapy* (pp. 15–43). Northvale, NJ: Jason Aronson.

Zalusky, S. (2003a). Dialogue: Telephone analysis. *Insight*, *12*(1): 13–16.

Zalusky, S. (2003b). Adaptation or idealization of theory. *Insight*, *12*(2): 34.

Zalusky, S. (2005). Telephone, psychotherapy and the 21st century. In: M. Stadter & D. Scharff (Eds.), *Dimensions of Psychotherapy, Dimensions of Experience: Time, Space, Number, and State of Mind* (pp. 107–114). London: Routledge.

Zeitner, R. (2011). Personal communication.

Telemental health resources

Angela Carter Martin, DNP, APRN

These online resources are offered for you to check out as you explore the pros and cons of teletherapy. In providing this list, the authors and editor of this book do not express an opinion about the value of any of these sites.

General information on ethics, legal, and practice issues associated
with the use of telemental health

http://www.hrsa.gov/telehealth/

http://www.zurinstitute.com/telehealthresources.html
Offers CE, HIPAA compliance package. This website also offers plenty of detail for therapists seeking information about a variety of telemental health issues.

http://www.mdcbh.org/images/startupmemo10272010.pdfhttp://www.tmhguide.org/site/epage/93990_871.htm
Telemental Health Guide (organisation).

http://www.tmhguide.org/sitemap/

http://www.hrsa.gov/ruralhealth/about/telehealth/
The Office for Advancement of Telehealth.
http://www.telementalhealth.info/index.html

http://www.apapracticecentral.org/update/2010/08–31/telehealth-resources.aspx

www.telementalhealthcomparisons.com
An informational website that compares different telemental health options by behavioural health innovation.

http://telehealth.org/bibliography
Sponsored by the Telemental Health Institute. Offers CE, certificate education, and individual courses about telemental health.

Reimbursement

http://www.americantelemed.org/files/public/policy/Private_Payer_Report.pdf

http://www.americantelemed.org/files/public/membergroups/businessfinance/reimburse-ment/BF_MedicarePaymentofTelemedicine.pdf
Information about Medicare reimbursement.

Licensing

http://www.zurinstitute.com/telehealthlaws.html

http://www.ctel.org/
Center for Telehealth & e-Health Law.

http://www.ctel.org/expertise/physican-licensure/

http://www.ama-assn.org/ama/pub/about-ama/our-people/member-groups-sections/young-physicians-section/advocacy-resources/physician-licensure-an-update-trends.page
AMA website.

https://mail.google.com/mail/?hl=en&shva=1#inbox/134274d1b1201c35
Newsletter discussing suicide prevention in telemental health.

http://www.zurinstitute.com/telehealthresources.html
Offers CE, HIPAA compliance package for $69.00.

http://www.hrsa.gov/ruralhealth/about/telehealth/
The Office for Advancement of Telehealth.

http://www.americantelemed.org/files/public/policy/Medicare_Payment_Of_Services.pdf
Information about Medicare reimbursement.

http://www.mdcbh.org/images/startupmemo10272010.pdfhttp://www.tmhguide.org/site/epage/93990_871.htm
Telemental health guide (organisation).

http://www.zurinstitute.com/telehealthlaws.html

http://www.americantelemed.org/files/public/policy/Private_Payer_Report.pdf

http://www.ctel.org/
Center for Telehealth & e-Health Law.

http://www.ctel.org/expertise/physican-licensure/

http://www.ama-assn.org/ama/pub/about-ama/our-people/member-groups-sections/
young-physicians-section/advocacy-resources/physician-licensure-an-update-trends.page
AMA website.

https://mail.google.com/mail/?hl=en&shva=1#inbox/134274d1b1201c35
Newsletter discussing suicide prevention in telemental health.

Some companies providing platforms for telemental health

Breakthrough: www.breakthrough.com

California LiveVisit: www.californialivevisit.com

CMS Telehealth: www.cmstelehealth.com

COPE Today: www.copetoday.com

E Mental Health Center: www.e-mhc.com

MDLiveCare Health Services Inc.: www.mdlivecare.com

MyTherapyNet with Kathleene Derrig-Palumbo and Foojan Zeine: www.mytherapynet.com/

Nefsis: www.nefsis.com

Panic Anxiety Stress Society (PASS): www.PASSN.com

Secure Telehealth: www.securetelehealth.com

Tandberg: www.tandberg.com

TherapyHosting.com: www.therapyhosting.com

Voyager National Telepsychiatry Network (Using Skype): www.telepsychiatry.com